For my Young Adult son who gave me the reason to live,
deal with disaster, then to triumph.

This is for you.

If you can meet with Triumph and Disaster
And treat those two impostors just the same;
...
Then yours is the Earth and everything that's in it,
And—which is more—you'll be a Man, my son!

—Rudyard Kipling

YOUNG ADULT EDITION

MY RUDE AWAKENING

An Englishman's Journey - Book One

EDWARD CHARLES FEATHERSTONE

My Rude Awakening YOUNG ADULT: A Combat Pilot's Memoir of Purpose, Peril, and Adventure (An Englishman's Journey (Young Adult) Book 1)
Copyright © 2023 by Edward Charles Featherstone, H2Z Foundation Press

For more about this author, please visit https://myrudeawakening.com/

This is a work of creative nonfiction, a genre of writing that uses creative literary styles and techniques while maintaining factually accurate essence and narrative. While some names, characters, businesses, places, events, locales, and incidents have been changed or created, the author has strived to limit creative tinkering so as not to alter the canvas of the profound truth of the story.

All rights reserved. No part of this publication may be reproduced, distributed, or transmitted in any form or by any means, including photocopying, recording, or other electronic or mechanical methods, without the prior written permission of the publisher, except in the case of brief quotations embodied in critical reviews and certain other non-commercial uses permitted by copyright law. Please do not participate in or encourage piracy of copyrighted materials in violation of the author's rights.

No part of this book may be used for the training of artificial systems, including systems based on artificial intelligence (AI), without the copyright owner's prior permission. This prohibition shall be in force even on platforms and systems that claim to have such rights based on an implied contract for hosting the book.

For permission requests, visit https://anenglishmansjourney.com/

Editing by The Pro Book Editor
Interior Design by IAPS.rocks
Cover Design by Spiffing Publishing

eBook ISBN: 978-1-917111-11-9
paperback ISBN: 978-1-917111-10-2
hardcover ISBN: 978-1-917111-12-6
audiobook ISBN: 978-1-917111-13-3

1. First category—BIOGRAPHY & AUTOBIOGRAPHY / Personal Memoirs
2. Second category—BIOGRAPHY & AUTOBIOGRAPHY / Adventurers & Explorers
3. Third category—YOUNG ADULT [AUTO]FICTION / Coming of Age

First Edition

CLICK OR SCAN TO SONGS

I often hear people say how important music is to them, as if they are unique in this regard. But of course, it is fair to say that music plays an important role in most people's lives.

So, falling into the same trap, I will say, "Music is especially important to me."

I remember listening to specific songs at times in my life, and many of them are still my favourites today. There are others I like to avoid because of an incident or a period they'll remind me of, that I would sooner forget. And I am sure like most, when I hear one of "those" songs, the memories come flooding back. The songs referred to in these pages will certainly add depth of understanding to the emotions behind the words of my story, even though they are tracks you may not have heard before. You could discover the reason your parents enjoyed them so, and who knows, you may come to appreciate them also. My young adult son's favourite song is a rock ballad we used to play in my Air Force days when we were psyching ourselves up for a test or going into combat. Yes, you may discover that music can be a big deal in important moments in your life.

To make this possible I have included an innovative CLICK OR SCAN TO SONGS feature that allows you to immerse more fully in my life story by listening to songs as they come up.

In print versions, a 'song junctions' within the pages will offer the choice of QR codes for different streaming platforms so readers can listen to each song on their digital device.

In eBooks, these junctions will display clickable links for each of the three music platform options.

"My Rude Awakening" Complete Playlist

YouTube   Spotify   Apple

DEAR READER

What can only be described as very unusual circumstances is what led to me writing my autobiography in the style of the autofiction genre, using a pseudonym and some creative licence. The author has strived to limit creative tinkering so as not to alter the canvas of the profound truth of the story. Whilst this is a true account of the important aspects, the purpose of using this approach was for the following reasons.

Many names and some locations have been changed to remove the need for military and other clearances and permissions. I am not worried about my own identity being exposed, but doing so would expose all others. The mostly thinly veiled name changes protect those people involved. For those who want to be identified, they can easily reveal themselves and own their characters. For those who would prefer to distance themselves from the manuscript, they can as easily choose not to pierce the thin veil that protects them. The name I have chosen contains both my and my family's names.

I have altered aspects of the Royal Air Force (RAF) and British Army, being careful not to disclose classified information. To give my memoir more of a novel-like style for your enjoyment, I elected to use the Creative Nonfiction genre, and this allowed me to use creative licence on some locations and song choices. So whilst I used old photographs for reference, do I really remember some of the detail from when I was in my twenties, that you will read in the pages of my manuscript? Of course not, is the short answer. Unquestionably though, whilst Charlotte and me were very close, the love story is autofiction.

In my adulthood, I went from having an Air Force military career to building a start-up digital electronics business into a global technology corporation that became a publicly listed company—a company the public could buy shares in. The beginning of my life story, however, was filled with lots of fun between playing polo and game-bird shooting and many amazing little adventures.

From an early age, I did many extreme things, or perhaps it was the level I took it to that made them extreme. Whilst I would never shy away from doing almost anything no matter how dangerous, I was by no means reckless. Quite the opposite, in fact. I took a measured approach to everything I did, and after calculating the risk, I then set forth…fearlessly. There were numerous near misses, but unquestionably, I cheated death on at least two occasions. The first occurs in this book, the second instance is in the sequel. Both had me hospitalised in critical care and could have—should have—ended my life. One of those experiences left me on life support for a while and forever changed me. I may have twice escaped death, but I did not evade the resultant post-traumatic stress disorder (PTSD).

PTSD is a psychological condition that has you re-living your traumatic events through recuring flashbacks and nightmares. Very often you are not even aware you are in the throes of PTSD. *I wasn't.* And at the cost of being English, I would never let anyone know there was anything wrong with me. This is never a good idea. One should always speak up and get help if something is wrong.

Then, years later, finding myself alone in a world of never-ending COVID confinement, I was at a desperate all-time low. I hated the thought of therapy, thinking it exposing and showing weakness.

As I spoke with an old girlfriend, a Doctor of Psychology and Urology, she recognised my condition and came to my rescue. With the help of our history and her expertise, she quickly worked it out…and then began to work it out of me.

"There are tried-and-tested methods to treat your condition," she insisted. "We must speak about the traumas that have struck so deep they caused your psychological disorder, your PTSD, and if necessary, we can include medication." I did not like the idea of taking any prescribed drugs, fearing I could become dependent on them. My doctor friend agreed. So whilst in Covid lockdown, we began a series of online therapy sessions.

I found it difficult to open up about things I had worked so hard at hiding, so my doctor added another dimension. In my own time, she wanted me to write about the traumatic events that had caused my PTSD. There was a problem though. I am dyslexic and I soon discovered that writing about my distresses to unburden myself was easier said than done. Emotions on top of my dyslexia threatened to capsize my therapeutic efforts. The doctor was not going to let me off that easily. "Who cares?" she said. "Get it out of you. Rid yourself of this burden, your closely guarded secrets. Only you and I will read it, so be brutally honest and be open. Then pen all the wonderful things that have happened in your life, your autobiography," she insisted.

Famous last words are what those turned out to be. One thing led to the next, as they say, and with a comprehensive knowledge of my subject matter, my life, coupled with my attitude that if something is worth doing, it is worth doing properly, I began my endeavour.

Sitting quietly alone, I delved into my past, and knowing I was never going to publish it anyway, I had no problem writing from the heart. Before I knew it, these unusual circumstances and the solitude of never-ending Covid confinement turned out to be the perfect birthplace for my creative non-fiction memoir.

For two years it tore me apart, often bringing me to tears as the jigsaw pieces that created the picture of my life were taken apart and then slowly put back together again. But this time, all the pieces I had so carefully hidden were retrieved and put in their rightful places to present the complete picture of my being. And as far as the therapy was concerned…well, it worked.

What started in mid-2020 was finished by late 2022, and with both COVID and my PTSD receding into the background, I could live again. I was more than happy to shelve my therapy, but only in the figurative sense because it was not yet a book.

Then as the New Year 2023 dawned, I thought I should edit it and leave it as a legacy for my children.

That was when I met my editor, Debra L. Hartmann. Once she had agreed to take me on, saying, "Your life story is extraordinary, and I see something in your writing style," I sent her my first manuscript.

"Now leave it to me," she said.

Six weeks later, she returned my memoir, but instead of having edited it, she sent me 289 action points.

"I thought you were going to edit it," I protested.

"I have. This is step one—Developmental Editing," she replied.

I realised then that she had other ideas for me, and my literary journey was far from over. Debra wanted me to expand numerous of the existing chapters and write some new ones, on top of addressing the countless action notes.

Instead of balking at the task, I embraced it as Debra began to show me her own special talents and her even more special psychology. She knew I was still holding back and demanded more. "I want to know about the other aspects of your life that you have only touched on," she persisted. And slowly but surely, she had me reveal more and more until, eventually, I had a tell-all, multipart chronicle of my being. That was fine. I still wasn't sure I should publish it though. Then because of her skill, those sands began to shift.

"You have to publish this," she said emphatically. "It's one of the most authentic, honest, and extraordinary tales about the privileged life of a British heir that I've ever read. Think about all the people this could help." (See H2Z.org)

This was where the second part of my literary journey began, which lasted well over a year. Deciding to make this something more than just part of my therapy, I began the long process of revising the words on the pages to develop my story alongside the necessary changes that make this a creative story in the autofiction genre.

I wrote this book and its sequel for my very young adult son, and for other young adults like him, in the hope that it will teach some important life lessons and serve as inspiration during those important growing-up years.

I grew up being taught that I could have anything if I just wanted it badly enough. That sounds simpler than it is. You see, when you want something really badly, you normally need to make many sacrifices, long hours of learning, training, practising, or whatever else it may take for you to achieve your goals. That journey and how far you are willing to push yourself will determine how badly you want to achieve your objective. Because of my dyslexia, I had to make an extra effort. Only through *badly* wanting to write my creative autobiography for my children was I able to achieve my endeavour.

I hope you enjoy this very grown up Young Adult book.

It is fair to say I have lived my life in accordance with a quote from the father of modern-day novels:

> *The proper function of man is to live, not to exist. I shall not waste my days in trying to prolong them. I shall use my time.*
>
> —Jack London (1876–1916)

BEING BRITISH

IN WRITING MY autobiographical memoirs, my American editor asked me what did I think being English meant and what the difference could be compared to our American counterparts?

I was aware most Americans were descendants of British settlers who first arrived from the UK in the seventeenth and eighteenth centuries. These settlers played a significant role in shaping American society and institutions, so it is unsurprising that many American families have a strong connection to their British heritage and family history. The difference is that British families are literally closer to their heritage than their counterparts across the Atlantic. Many British families can trace their origins back centuries and are able to visit cemeteries and see tombstones of relatives from the 1800s or even the 1700s. Who says cemeteries don't have a place in our society?

The early pioneering spirit of our American brothers and sisters, which resulted in them becoming detached from their mother country, could be a fundamental reason for our differences. Americans established a democracy while the British have had and continue to have a monarchy, and the reverence of each is very different between the two countries. While politicians are typically all too eager to talk about themselves and make promises meant to get them elected, a monarch sits regally in example of service to their country and its people and their speeches have nothing to do with being re-elected.

Perhaps it is also this significant cultural difference between British and Americans that is behind why we are very conservative and keep our emotions deep inside, seldom, if ever exposing our vulnerabilities to anyone. The Jocelyn Dashwood quote, "No hugging, dear. I'm British. We only show affection to dogs and horses," which could include emotions, sums us up well.

What then made a particularly conservative Englishman literally open the book of his life, confounding the one or two people who knew what he was doing? Surely it was something immense? Perhaps cheating death twice? I don't mean the "one more yard to the left and I wouldn't be here" variety, but the real deal. The ones that take you within inches of death and leave you on life support and give you two of your three episodes of post-traumatic stress disorder. And is it that once you *luckily* find yourself again, all you previously held near and dear in the sanctuary of your unspoken private life is relegated to the "don't sweat the small stuff" bin?

A LETTER TO MY MOTHER

Dear Mum,

Of all the things I have undertaken or attempted in my life, writing an autobiography undoubtedly takes the cake. That I should even consider authoring a creative multipart chronicle as someone with dyslexia could be nothing short of ridiculous. But, then, your method of helping me overcome my dyslexia and advance my knowledge of English grammar could also be considered *ridiculous*.

Those boyhood hours spent with you, reading William Shakespeare as you helped me decipher his writing and the true meanings of some of his cryptic messages, will always remain with me. I remember how you would teach me to read between the lines and pick out certain words that were the crux of the message. How you drew my attention to what was *not said* as much as what *was said*. I remember, even in our daily conversations, you would first consider my sentence structure, word choice, and morphology before you would consider whatever I was either asking or saying. I was often frustrated when I had to repeat my question because I did not get an immediate response from you but rather a lesson in English language. Those lessons must have rubbed off on me.

The months of COVID lockdown and a lady—*there is always a woman*—are what encouraged me to finally take this *ridiculous* step. Yes, many people said I should write an autobiography because my life has indeed been extraordinary, but whilst I may have agreed, did I really mean it? Methinks not.

My having completed this though, is entirely thanks to you. I realised early on that you have been my guiding force in authoring these books, as I often mentally checked with you. What adjective would you use, or is my sentence structure correct? In that spirit, I have now spent many hours with you over the past two years and found great solace in your inspiration and influence as day by day, paragraph by paragraph, I have accomplished this endeavour.

You often said that nothing I did would ever surprise you. I may have done that now.

In words from Shakespeare's *Hamlet*, "Though this be madness, yet there is method in't."

RIP, Mum

Love,

Charles

CHAPTER 1
THE BEGINNING

"NOT GOOD, IS it, Fran?" my father said, reading a thin booklet with the Grayston House School coat of arms on the front cover. My dad didn't get very involved in my early years, but reading my school report was one thing he did do. "He is already six, and his first Year 2 report says it all. There are just no signs of improvement," my father pointed out in a gentle tone.

"Arthur, I hate the idea of him going to boarding school at such a young age, and does it have to be West Buckland, in bloody Devon? That's over three hours away. I can't understand why I have not been able to help him. A lot of use reading English literature has been to me." My mother sounded unusually exasperated.

"Frances, we don't want to make another mistake. It would be wonderful if he could stay at Grayston as a weekly or semi-monthly boarder, but they will only take him in the year he turns ten. Charles going to West Buckland is the right decision. They are known for having a very good remedial department. Let them nip Charles's problem in the bud, and then he can come back to Grayston. You cannot take responsibility for not being able to help him. Things have changed, Fran. They teach differently nowadays. Let Hamilton drive you and Charles to Devon in the Bentley. It will give you some quiet time together."

It was a conversation I had not enjoyed overhearing. All my friends were reading well. I just couldn't. Even at that age, it made me nervous.

Boarding school couldn't be that bad, but over three hours away does not sound good. How often will I get to come home? I thought worryingly.

My mum and I arrived at the imposing, castle-like West Buckland

School in Devon, in the South West of England, two days into the second term.

While we were dropping my clothes at the boarding house, Mr. Argyle, my new housemaster, said, "Sorry, not much choice of bed and clothes locker. You will just have to make do with what is left," not sounding very apologetic at all.

There were five steel double bunks around the perimeter of the dormitory. Of the ten beds, all had been taken except for the least favoured bottom bed in the corner of the room.

"There are two lockers beside each other. Take those," Mr. Argyle pointed out.

My mother opened my suitcase and was about to start unpacking my clothes into the doorless spaces when Mr. Argyle intervened.

"Don't worry about that, Mrs. Featherstone. Charles will do it later." It was an instruction rather than a suggestion.

I didn't give it any thought. There were bigger things on my mind right then, like having to say goodbye to my mother.

We then went over to the administrative section, where my mother stopped to read the foundation stone of the school to me.

In humble hope that the Great Architect of the Universe, the Maker of Heaven and Earth, the Giver of all Good, will bless and prosper the work this day commenced, and that the School to be raised will prove, under the Divine blessing, an institution for the promotion of God's glory in the extension of sound and practical education, in the diffusion of useful knowledge, upon the imperishable foundation of Divine truth.

Laid by Earl Fortescue KG October 4th, 1860

The cold and gloomy winter morning, the cold grey buildings, this cold room, and these cold, cold words sent a shiver down my spine.

Once we had finished the formalities, it was time to say goodbye. I struggled to hold back the tears, not wanting to let go of my mother's hand.

"I'll see you in a month, Sunbeam. I love you." She turned away, not wanting me to see the tears streaming down her cheeks. She knew that I had to be strong, just moments away from meeting strangers who would hopefully become my new friends.

"I can take you up to Miss Meagan, your new teacher," said a Mrs. Hyslop, evidently one of the other Year 2 teachers. I followed her to the classroom, then Mrs. Hyslop tapped lightly on the door, opened it, and announced, "This is Edward Charles Featherstone."

Miss Meagan looked nice, but the feelings could not have been mutual. She gave me a disdainful look and said, "You can go and sit on that chair in the corner, young man."

Am I being punished for arriving late? Bewildered and sad, I took my seat as instructed. A few of the boys turned around to snicker and giggle. *I hate this place,* was my irrepressible first impression.

After a while, I heard the bell ring and correctly guessed it was for first break.

"You can stay right where you are, young man," Miss Meagan told me sternly as she walked out of the door.

I looked around the room, finding it much like any other. First-term school projects on the wall. A sign that said Words of the Week, which made me cringe as I noticed how difficult they were. I thought about the sandwiches in my school bag, not because I was hungry—I wasn't—but because I would normally never waste my mother's lovely sandwiches. I was doing everything within my power to hold back the tears. This was the worst day of my life, and there was nothing I could do about it. I was so scared that I would never be able to read, that I was stupid. I hated being there, but it could have been my only chance. I hoped my dad was right, that they could "nip it in the bud."

What if they can't?

When the bell rang again, signifying the end of break, the first person to walk through the door was Miss Meagan. She came straight over to me and took both my hands as she went down on her haunches to be at my level. "I'm so sorry, Edward, or is it Charles I should call you? I thought you had been sent over from Mrs. Hyslop's class because of bad behaviour. I'm so sorry."

The most unusual introduction to Miss Meagan's class was probably the best thing that happened to me in Year 2 at West Buckland. For the rest of the year, she seemed to be continually trying to make it up to me. She soon became my favourite teacher, and perhaps I was her favourite student too.

The worst part about my Year 2 was quietly crying into my pillow, sometimes nights in a row, because of how homesick I was. I counted the days until I would be going home, and as it got closer to my once-a-month weekend pass out, midterm, or holiday, I began to feel better. My bunk bed, "the worst in the dormitory," turned out to be the best in the dormitory. Partly concealed by the lockers it gave me my own secret place where I could slip into a world of daydreams and fantasising about all the things I could do.

The best news in my Year 2 was being diagnosed as dyslexic. Hardly good news but far better than the alternative. Confirming what my difficulty was, was comforting and meant I'd be getting the right kind of help.

When my mother told me, I immediately asked, "Mummy, does that mean I'm not stupid?"

"You are the furthest thing from stupid," was my mother's vehement reply. "You just have an unusual condition the school will now work on. You are cleverer than a bag of monkeys, Sunbeam."

I didn't exactly buy the message of her endearing expression, but there were two other reasons that had me half believing her. First, I was the best at maths. I saw the patterns in everything to do with arithmetic. The second reason was chess. I may have only been six, but I was already a keen chess player and had made it into the West Buckland under-ten chess team.

It took the better part of two years before I learnt to manage being away from home. I even got to quite like West Buckland, especially the sports. And yes, I became fiercely independent. Was that a good thing? Maybe not.

Then in my third year, just before my ninth birthday, I came home for my monthly weekend pass, and it was one I will never forget. My mum and dad sat me down to speak to me, and I instinctively knew it was to give me the bad news that I would not be going back to Grayston House School. I was still struggling with my reading and spelling, but thankfully, I was improving slowly. Even so, I pretty well knew it was not sufficient for me to move closer to home and be a weekly boarder.

"Sunbeam," my mother began, "you have been doing really well at West Buckland, and I want you to promise your dad and I that you will continue making the same effort."

I knew what was coming and so was only half concentrating as I thought more about running across the field to see the horses.

"And if you do, you can go back to Grayston House after the holidays."

What did I just hear? I looked at my mum, then my dad, back to my mum. *Can I do it?* was my overwhelming thought. Never had so few words meant so much.

My mother clasped both my hands and said very quietly, "I am going to help you sort it out, Sunbeam."

Unbeknown to me, my mother had applied herself wholeheartedly to my severe case of dyslexia, something that in those days had become well known but little was known about how to treat it. That wasn't going to stop my mother, though. She believed she knew best how to deal with it. Once her mind had been made up, my father was no match for her determination.

"I love you, Mummy," was all I could say.

That was the start of her applying her purpose of helping me to read. On the nights I was at home, she had me read aloud with her, but she soon realised that I was often guessing the next words instead of reading them.

"See, Sunbeam, you're far too clever for your own good," she remarked.

Then she quickly devised strategies to help me. The first was to have me read Shakespeare because she knew I would not be able to guess the next words of his unusual turn of phrase. I particularly loved *Hamlet* and even named my first puppy Osric, after one of the characters.

My mother's other ingenious ploy was in how we read the Hardy Boys books together. This American collection of adventure stories featuring two teenage boys solving mysteries was so exciting to a young boy with a vivid imagination. First, my mother would read to me, which I adored.

"Joe squeezed Frank's arm, beckoning him to be quiet. They could hear the footsteps coming towards them in the darkness as—"

Where she stopped, I had to take over, which eventually I did without complaining, eager to find out what happened next. Not even my dyslexia was going to get in the way of me satisfying my curiosity. When the excitement had passed and the story got a bit more mundane again, my mother would take over until the next exciting part.

I loved the Hardy Boys, and in the end, thanks to my mum, I quite liked Shakespeare too. Reading snippets of Shakespeare seemed to exercise my brain and prevent me from running ahead, which was one of the symptoms of my condition.

It was while I was still in junior school at Grayston House that I finally got on top of my dyslexia, even if it was not something that would ever be cured. What my mother had done for me was far more than just help me "overcome" dyslexia. She had helped me restore my pride, my confidence, removing a dark cloud that had hung over me through my early school years. Unquestionably, the hours my mother spent helping me were the greatest gift I have ever received.

Excited to be home, I bounded up the stairs three or four at a time, followed by Osric matching my stride, my two legs competing with his four. Our love had been born the moment I was given this cute six-week-old English springer spaniel ball of fluff. He'd grabbed my heart the moment he licked my face and I smelt his puppy breath. As an only child, home only on weekends from boarding school, I cherished his constant companionship.

I was anxious to change out of my school clothes and head out into the woods to have some fun with Osric. I daydreamed about the day he would be my gundog and decided to do some training that day.

"Sunbeam, read your poem…aloud. I want to hear you," my mother called out to me, interrupting my daydream and my escape.

Ah. That bloody poem? I turned to face the framed verses hanging on my bedroom wall and started to read them out loud, which was not difficult because I knew them off by heart. " 'If—' by Rudyard Kipling," I announced. "If you can keep your head when all about you are losing theirs…"

I loosened the restricting necktie and yanked it over my head, kicking my shoes into the wardrobe at the same time.

"If you can wait and not be tired by waiting, or being lied about…"

I shuffled out of my navy-blue blazer and slid it onto a hanger. Boarding school discipline had taught me to take care of my things myself. Had I not,

I would have incurred my mother's wrath. I threw my shirt and trousers over the chair for laundry and, without missing a beat, began dressing for my afternoon in the woods.

"If you can meet with Triumph and Disaster and treat those two impostors just the same…"

I'd already knotted the laces of my boots by the time I got to the salient concluding line. "And—which is more—you'll be a Man, my son!"

I knew it wouldn't end there, so I waited for her questions, itching to get outside with Osric.

"What does Rudyard Kipling mean with the words, 'If you can dream—and not make dreams your master'?"

This one was easy. "It's fine to dream, but don't let the dreams affect your judgement," I blurted out, anxiously waiting to dash through the kitchen towards the back door. "Can we go now, Mummy?"

"No, not so fast."

"Muuuum!"

"What about, 'If you can trust yourself when all men doubt you, but make allowance for their doubting too'?"

"I must trust myself…and understand that not everyone will agree with me or even like me," I responded.

"And? And?"

"Umm… Well, other people might not see things the same way as I do, and that's okay. And if my choice is wrong, I'll still learn from it. May I go now?"

"One last question, Sunbeam. Why should you treat both triumph and disaster the same, and what is an impostor, and why does he call them that?"

I had to think about that one, a more recent difficult question of my mother's.

"Well," I began a little hesitantly. "An impostor is someone or something that comes in disguise to deceive you. And you should not overreact to triumph as it could soon lead to a downfall or a disaster."

"Good show," my mother replied, voicing her approval.

This poem epitomised a large part of my upbringing. My mother tirelessly instilled in me that the key to achieving and succeeding in all my life's pursuits was to believe in myself. I don't know what it was that caused me to be so fiercely competitive and committed in all the things I did, but I imagine Rudyard Kipling's "If—" undoubtedly played a part.

"Don't be late for dinner, and don't either of you get too muddy and wet," Mother warned as we were already bounding out of the door.

I was now ten years old, and Osric was almost two, in the early stages of becoming my first gundog.

Clearly, there would be a lot of mud. We lived in Berkshire, England, about an hour southwest of London, and the high annual rainfall meant the ground was often muddy. It was especially muddy around our parts, probably because we were in an area of thick green foliage, dense woods, and sun-blocking tree canopies. I didn't mind though, not in the least. As far as I was concerned, there was no better place to live. It was central to all my favourite places of interest. A short half-hour drive to my all-boys boarding school, Grayston House, a trip I had been making every two weeks since having left West Buckland School in Devon three months earlier. I was much happier being closer to home and quite comfortable with the thought that I would probably be doing this trip for another seven years, given that my school went all the way through to A-levels. Many of my school friends, who were also boarders, lived nearby. I was at school from Monday morning, when either my mum or dad would drive me, and it felt like no sooner had I got there that I would be getting picked up for the weekend at home, either every Friday or at least every second Friday afternoon, depending on sporting commitments.

Don't get me wrong, I loved everything about home—my family, my granddad, Osric, and especially the cooking—but when I was at school, I was surrounded by my friends. The general camaraderie, the special bonds with best friends, and the sport, which I couldn't get enough of, was all-consuming. I loved that we were all equal at school. We wore the same clothes, we did the same things, we lived in the same boarding house, and very little attention was paid to life outside of school. Outside of school, I was "Charles, you know, Arthur and Frances Featherstone's boy," or "only child," or, sometimes, "They have Rockwell Manor." I had once heard some boys speaking about me behind my back when one of them said, "That's what you call being born with a silver spoon in your mouth." That was bad enough, but when one of the other boys added, "What do you mean a silver spoon? More like a golden spoon if you ask me," followed by their jeers and laughter.

It made me cringe. In hindsight, it only strengthened my resolve to do something about it, even though right then I had no idea what.

I had great difficulty with this, just wanting to be me. The more I was reminded of who my parents were, where I came from, and what we had, the more determined I became to be recognised for who I was.

My home was central to my other favourite places. It was forty minutes from the Royal Berkshire Shooting School, a leading clay-pigeon shooting establishment that I knew well, having gone there many times when my father wanted to brush up on his shooting before the game-bird shooting season started. But it was when my own shooting instructions started there that I fell in love with the place.

Then there was Guards Polo Club, just twenty minutes from our home, where my family had been members for decades. Even though I was only just getting started and my mum had been in a constant tug of war with my father about the dangers of the game, I knew polo would become my most significant sporting pastime. This had been the case with my father and both my grandfathers, so I guess my eagerness was inevitable. This drove my enthusiasm for playing polo and game-bird shooting, to be fair, which was another sport that was passed on to me.

I smiled, remembering when I shared my thoughts with my mum about our home being so central. With a glint in her eye, she had suggested that what was central for us could be considered in the middle of nowhere for others.

Best of all though, Rockwell Manor was alongside the most wonderful Berkshire forest. *How central is that?*

As we reached the woods, my excitement mounted, as did Osric's, with him wanting to dash off. *Let's see how his whistle commands are coming on,* I thought. I blew four consecutive bursts to steady him, as opposed to a long, firm whistle to have him stop or sit. *Bloody hell, he's getting it,* I thought excitedly. "Ohhh, good boy, Osric. Clever boy!" I said as I patted him and gave him his reward.

My favourite activity as a youth was game-bird shooting. Wing shooting, as it is also known, is taking your shotgun to pheasant, partridge, ducks, or grouse whilst they are in flight.

On occasions when our family hosted formal, "driven game" shoots, our gamekeeper, as appointed "shoot captain," would oversee the day's proceedings. One of his tasks was hiring "beaters" to walk through the woods and fields and drive the birds towards a line of eager "guns," while the "pickers-up," with their retriever dogs, would ensure all the dead quarry were collected.

I loved being part of all the activities but wouldn't be permitted to join the men in the gun lineup until after I turned sixteen. Unquestionably, informal "rough shooting" with my gundog would become my favourite game-bird shooting format, venturing out on my own or with a friend. I dreamt of going into the woods on long adventures and shooting the quarry Osric "flushed out," which we would take home for our chef to prepare for our dinner. I confided all my secrets to this special creature, and he always understood, though he never answered back.

After about two and a half years and with guidance from my father, Osric would hunt and flush within shot range, be steady to flushed game birds, and also retrieve our quarry.

I was part of a large family, including uncles, aunts, and lots of cousins, including on my father's side of the family, but my immediate circle was quite intimate. It consisted of my mother, father, my maternal grandfather, and me.

My dad was a mixture of a London Sloane businessman and a country gentleman. For a middle-aged man, he was in good shape. Daily horse riding and playing competitive polo had kept his medium build in good trim. He had strong features, a mop of thick brown hair, and piercing "Featherstone" blue eyes, and he was evidently a good-looking man, not that a son could judge the looks of a parent. Jovial, smart, and quick-witted, he was fun to be around. He had been quite hands-off in my younger school-going years, leaving that side of parenting to my mum, but as I got older, he became more involved.

"Fran, you can look after the education and growing-up stuff, and I can concentrate on the important things like shooting, polo, and business," he would cheekily say to my mother.

He was typically British. There were few displays of affection, except to horses and dogs, and he was old-fashioned and traditional in his approach.

A curious aspect was that he often attracted the attention of younger women. I wouldn't have noticed if I hadn't seen him getting the occasional pinch from my mother, as if it were his fault that he had attracted this attention.

"What?" he would ask innocently.

"You know very well what," my mother would reply lightheartedly.

Perhaps there was some blame at my father's door after all.

From an early age, I developed an interest in business, always fascinated when my father and grandfather spoke about their businesses or investments. My family had shown me that having good business acumen was a surefire way of becoming fully independent, which chimed with my longing for self-recognition in my teenage years.

After I moved up to senior school, my father began coaching me in financial matters, explaining aspects of his investment portfolio. Over the school holidays, when we had more time, and with the *Financial Times* at hand, we would go through the stock prices, earnings per share, explanations around price-to-earnings ratios (P/E ratios), and so forth, pertaining to the shares in his portfolio. We would discuss how prices had moved and why he felt they'd done well or badly, and he'd ask my opinion. This became another area of common interest, continuing unabated when I later started my university studies and went into the Air Force. I loved learning about all of this, and my dad described me as a sponge for this information. My one day becoming a businessman seemed to be the right natural progression. Undoubtedly, the time spent with my dad later helped me invest in my first business enterprise.

My mother was a gifted sportswoman, and you could describe her medium-height physique as, well, sporty. She had short, dark blonde hair that was always neatly cut, and she was a sensible and practical woman, straightforward and honest with no sugar-coating. As sensible as she was, so was her wardrobe. Elegant casual. Trousers or a slacks suit, normally a silk scarf and a polo shirt with flat JP Tod's shoes. Not one for wearing dresses or skirts, she was a formidable county hockey player, then later a scratch golfer and captain of her club's ladies golf team, as well as an accomplished horsewoman.

I had once asked what horse-riding discipline most interested her and was quite tickled by her response. "Transport," she had replied. "That's how I got to school." She had then gone on to explain that in her day it was not uncommon. They didn't worry about saddles and were quite happy to ride bareback with just a simple bridle, and they would then leave their ponies grazing in a field adjacent to the school until they were ready to go home again. She was also quite academic, having studied English Literature at university and later learning computer programming.

Regardless of her sporting and academic achievements, my mother's primary focus was always on me and my character development.

A great sadness in her life was around her own mother. In the throes of a life-threatening double-breech birth of twins, my dying grandmother's last words, now engraved on an urn containing her ashes, had been:

> "If my life is a whole, it is half spoken for.
>
> The years that I have been with you have
> made worthwhile all the years before.
>
> In my womb are two whole lives. Part of them are me.
>
> Edward, I don't have to tell you who comes first."
>
> For Alexander and Frances

In the absence of modern-day medicine, luck was often what one most relied on. A lot was lost that sad day in the absence of luck. A wife to my grandfather. A mother to a pair of newborn twins, my mum and Uncle Alexander.

As a result, her father, Edward Francis George Apsley, had employed a governess to make sure his children were well cared for and at least had a substitute mother. One of my grandfather's requirements had been that the governess should also be a teacher. My mother's first and only governess was Mrs. Kearns, who not only played her part in bringing up my mother and uncle but later, when she was no longer required in the child-minding department, became the Rockwell Manor house manager. Put differently, one might say she became a permanent fixture in the Apsley household until her retirement after my parents got married.

Mrs. Kearns was a widowed English teacher and fit into the Apsley household perfectly. My mother always addressed her as Mrs. Kearns, and so did I. Mrs. Kearns had been very strict with my mother and uncle, and I was brought up with this same strict discipline. I don't remember much about her, as she retired before I started going to school. Of course, much of my mother's personality stemmed from her upbringing. But she was more than that. My mother was a woman of great dignity, moral standing and integrity. She taught me that respect is earned and sympathy should not be sought in any way. This was her character, some of her genetic inheritance.

As I was an only child, you may have expected my mother to be over protective of me, or even mollycoddle me. She did nothing of the sort. In contrast, she often told me I should keep a "stiff upper lip" and would frequently say, "Chin up, Sunbeam," if I was feeling down about something. Never would she entertain any self-pity. Even so, she was always gentle, always kind, and mothered me in the most positive way imaginable. Nothing was ever too much for her. Such was her commitment to me, as I got older, I began to feel she was very likely overcompensating for not having had a mother herself.

Sometimes she could be quite humorous in the way she reprimanded me, especially for little things. As an example, once when I was in the washing closet and she called out for me, it went something like this.

"I'm on the loo, Mum," I shouted back.

There was no immediate response, but when I emerged, my mother explained there was no need for me to announce to the world—a bit of an exaggeration—that I was "on the loo." She went on to say playfully, "It's fine to just say you are busy, Sunbeam. We will understand. Unless you would prefer to go into detail and tell us exactly *what* you are doing on the loo, hopefully sparing us the details as to whether it involved any splashes."

It was a private conversation, as outside of that it would be "rude" and "unbecoming of a young gentleman" to speak like that.

"Rude"—a word I was all too familiar with in our household. My mother, especially, was determined that I "should not be rude" and would be quick to scold, "That's rude!" or "don't be rude" if she deemed my behaviour so. She was a stickler for doing everything in her power to make sure I grew up to be a gentleman.

She was also a stickler for good manners, and it went without saying that I should stand when someone got up from the table, open doors for my elders and especially for ladies, and always say please and thank you. She never stopped reminding me I should be grateful for our privileged way of life and never think of myself as more deserving than someone else.

I will never forget my mother's reminder when I once forgot to thank a waitress in a restaurant and how I felt afterwards.

Very quietly, she said, "Sunbeam, you must always respect someone whose job it is to serve you and be sure to treat them as your equal because in some ways they are 'more than your equal.' "

Just those words made me feel very self-conscious, even if I wasn't too sure what she was getting at.

She continued, "Consider for a moment your circumstances. Your good fortune that allows you to be here, to be served. Then think about what *her* circumstances could be. She may have little choice but to do this job. Perhaps it is to provide for her young child left at home, whom she dearly wishes she could be with now. And then another child, you, doesn't have the decency to at least be polite. Imagine this Sunbeam, because you would be surprised how close that could be to the truth."

I never again made the mistake of forgetting to say please and thank you, especially to anyone serving me.

Perhaps the most important thing she ever taught me was that I could have anything I wanted and that my privilege was not the reason I'd get it. It happened over something quite innocuous that I had said I wanted to achieve. In a very measured tone, she said, "Sunbeam, you can have anything you want. Anything in the world. There is only one requirement. You must want it badly enough."

Surely it couldn't be that simple, just to want it.

My sceptical expression had my mother repeating those words as if to implant them into my brain. "Anything you want, Sunbeam, anything. You just have to want it badly enough."

As I got older, so I came to trust these words more and more. Right or wrong, I now believe anything I didn't or don't achieve is simply because I haven't wanted it badly enough.

CHAPTER 2

GRANDDAD

I HAD ONE GRANDPARENT. Edward Francis George Apsley, my mum's dad. I never knew my grandparents on my father's side of the family. Sadly, they were both casualties of the Second World War. I carry names of each of my grandfathers—Edward from Edward Francis George Apsley and Charles from Robert Charles Featherstone. It was not difficult to imagine how my parents met, as both my grandfathers had been keen polo players and often played against each other. Polo was a popular game in rural England, especially among landowners. Both grandfathers also enjoyed game-bird shooting.

Born in 1889, Granddad was the proverbial English gentleman. Standing appreciably over six feet tall with broad shoulders, he had a strong jawline, a thick mop of brown hair, and vibrant blue eyes. His open face often wore a broad smile, the mischievous glint in his eye foretelling his wicked sense of humour, but at times he could have quite a stoic and no-nonsense character. Although I was quite young when he died, I will always remember him as an impeccably dressed man. Monday to Sunday, no matter where he went, he wore a suit as his standard dress. If he was playing polo or cricket or was horse riding, he would change from his suit into his sporting attire and then back into his suit again. I later discovered they were all tailor-made by Chester Barrie—white-collared shirts, tie and family crest tiepin, and cufflinked sleeves. His shoes were Church's, and his hats were made by Lock & Co., who have occupied their premises on St. James's Street in London since 1676, arguably making them one of the oldest shops in the world. This wasn't an attempt to be ostentatious in any way. He was a very private man and kept a low profile, but he liked quality and tradition. He lived by a set of values that he held dear.

There are many wonderful stories about my grandfather, but one that really stands out for me says so much about who he was and the principles he lived by. Excelling in business, he built a successful portfolio of farms, abattoirs, and butcheries, and several large cooperatives, places where farmers could meet to buy and sell produce, probably the forerunners to supermarkets we see today. Behind one of his cooperatives was my grandfather's head office. My mother told me the story of how, one evening when he was about to lock up, two men came into his office, brandishing guns. They demanded he open the safe, threatening to shoot him if he didn't obey. My grandfather calmly refused. The men continued their threats to shoot him if he didn't comply with their demands.

His response was, "Well then, you'll just have to shoot me, because I will not give in to criminals."

They carried out their threat and shot him. He dropped to the floor, and his assailants fled in fright, leaving him for dead. The impact of the shot left him dazed for a few minutes before he recovered his senses. Seriously injured, he assessed the situation and concluded that things couldn't be too bad if he was still conscious and breathing. Given there was a lot of blood, my grandfather decided the best course of action was to patch up the wound as best he could, put on a clean shirt, donned his coat, and then drove himself to hospital.

On the way, he realised he would be going past the police station. Despite being in great pain, he thought it expedient to stop and report the incident. He pulled up and gingerly got out of his car, clutching his coat around him. The duty sergeant watched my grandfather's slow approach, later admitting that he had remarked to his colleagues, "Old man Apsley is certainly getting old." Bent over and shuffling, he made his way into the police station and announced that he'd come to report an attempted robbery and shooting. Even though the staff sergeant had thought old Mr. Apsley was perhaps getting a bit senile, he had not wanted to be disrespectful to someone of my grandfather's standing in the community, so he remarked politely, "Well, at least they missed, sir."

"No," replied my grandfather. "They shot me." He opened his coat, revealing a blood-soaked shirt, as the dressing was soddened with blood from the wound.

Shocked, the sergeant rushed my father to the hospital, where the bullet was removed, having missed his heart by less than an inch.

The next morning, after a night in hospital, he recounted the story to his family. They soon asked the obvious question, which was, why on earth had he risked his life to save the contents of his safe, regardless of how much was in there?

His reply left everyone speechless. "Oh, there was nothing in the safe except my lucky penny. The banking had been done for the day. I wasn't protecting my money. I was protecting my principles."

Hearing this story when I was older had me realise my grandfather was almost certainly subtly reminding his family of the importance of standing by one's principles.

My grandfather's courage was a testament to him being willing to give his life, standing by what he believed in. He certainly left a lasting impression on me, which has persisted all through my life. He often had a different take on things compared to those around him. For example, I once overheard a conversation about someone having made a lot of money.

"Over ten million," the voice had remarked.

I told my grandfather about it and asked, "How much is a lot of money, Granddad, and how much do we have?"

He did not immediately reply, giving it some thought first, but then said, "You will hear a lot of talk like that, my boy. It is unimportant." He then continued with his real message. "A person's wealth should only be measured by what he has given away, nothing else. Because everything else is just egotistical, self-serving, and irrelevant, as it affects just one person or family."

He wasn't finished there.

"There is no reason to ever be proud of how much you have compared to how little another person has."

I hadn't then understood all the words he had chosen, but his expression and emphatic tone made it clear. Words I now fully understand and will never forget.

Another of his lessons that I have never forgotten was when he once said, "You will one day be in business, and you will discover that very often commerce is about creating different focus points, promoting the positives, minimising or even brushing over the negatives. *Marketing* is what they call it. I have another word for it."

"What, Granddad?" I asked enthusiastically.

Because of the way he brought his mouth to my ear, I knew what he was about to tell me was important.

"Bullshit, that's what I call it," he whispered.

My giggle made my tummy wobble. I knew my granddad was being naughty using a word like that with me. And I also knew my mother would object very strongly. But I guess it's just like that. *Grandfathers can get away with almost anything.*

He smiled and carried on, "It's fine. It's how this modern world works, but always remember this. When you put your head on your pillow before you go to sleep, no matter how you have presented to the world, this is the time to be brutally honest with yourself. Top businessmen never bullshit themselves."

No giggling this time. Granddad was being deadly serious and brutally honest.

Coming home from school usually had me jumping out the back door of my mum's car in excitement, and as always, Osric was the first to greet me. After a quick, impassioned hello and licks aplenty, I most often dropped my school bag outside the front door and excitedly sprinted off to see my granddad who lived in Winston Cottage, 120 yards from the main house. Set amongst some old, established trees on the eastern side of the property, it had two access paths. One was a smooth brown concrete lane, almost dead straight, between two rows of low hedges, my mother's attempt at concealment. It had been put in as an afterthought to accommodate a catering trolley for Granddad's meals when he got a little older and did not feel like going up to the main house. It was only my grandfather, Fabrizio—our chef—and me who used this narrow runway. Everyone else used what I considered the scenic route. It was a combination of stepping stones and old timber railway sleepers, meandering through the treed garden, brush, and indigenous flowerbeds leading down to the front door. Twice the distance to get to the same destination. An inconceivable waste of time to my young mind.

Winston Cottage was a grand garden suite constructed in the same Georgian Palladian style as Rockwell Manor, even though it had only been built sometime after the Second World War. Built for my grandfather when he handed the keys of the main house to my parents, it was undoubtedly my favourite place, alongside the stable block—two areas where I spent many happy hours during my adolescence and beyond. It had large, high ceilings with a reception room and a master suite with ensuite bathroom going out to a large patio, where Granddad loved to sit and look down the rolling lawns and across into the forest. I was always amazed at the deer and the myriad other small game that would come out of the thicket and nibble on the edge of the lawn. It got its name from Sir Winston Churchill, past prime minister of the United Kingdom, a man well known to my grandfather. Theirs was a friendship that Granddad significantly underplayed, preferring to say they were "well acquainted." He told me many wonderful stories about Winston Churchill, some of which have become folklore. The one Granddad knew I found hilarious was from whilst Churchill was a member of Parliament, before becoming Prime Minister. He had gone back to the House of Commons after a boozy lunch. A female member of the house said accusingly, "You are drunk, sir, neither honourable nor gentlemanly," a play on his formal title of The Right Honourable Sir Winston Churchill and his rank as a gentleman.

Churchill replied, "And you, My Right Honourable Lady, are ugly. Tomorrow, I'll be sober."

Granddad had lots of, let's say, *peculiarities*. One of them I discovered in unusual circumstances. It was after school while we were playing a game of chess, something he began coaching me in from the age of four, when our butler arrived for what seemed no particular reason.

"How are they feeling?" Granddad asked Hamilton.

"Perfect, sir. I think they're done," Hamilton replied.

"Good show. Well, let's swap. I have another pair that needs the same treatment. The tan ones," Granddad said.

I listened to this exchange without any idea what they were speaking about, unlike Hamilton, who understood perfectly as he walked over to my grandfather's shoe cabinet.

"These ones, sir?" Hamilton asked, showing my grandfather a pair of Church's shoes, the only brand he wore.

Granddad nodded.

Hamilton took off the black shoes he was wearing and put them into the shoe cabinet. "Not sure what Mrs. Featherstone will say about my black jacket and grey pinstripe trousers with tan shoes, sir," he said, making a valid point as he put on the new pair of shoes.

I still had no idea what was going on! *Is Granddad sharing his shoes with Hamilton?*

Once Hamilton had left the room, Granddad smiled at my enquiring expression. He explained that he did not enjoy "walking in" his new shoes and simply gave them to Hamilton to do it for him. An unusual quirk indeed.

It didn't stop me from looking suspiciously at the sizes of our other staff's feet, comparing them to my father's, and wondering if he had adopted this approach.

I began drinking when I was about nine or ten years old. So as not to give the wrong impression, let me start at the beginning.

It had first taken place on an occasion when my grandfather chose to have dinner in his cottage and I had joined him. Fabrizio, our then thirty-seven-year-old chef, had come down with his catering trolley to serve us. And as always, there was ice cream in the cold compartment for our simple but favourite dessert. Having finished dinner, Granddad and I sat chatting while Fabrizio busied himself preparing our treat. First, he made a chocolate sauce by melting a slab of Lindt milk chocolate before adding chopped hazelnuts with a dollop of fresh cream in a small saucepan, which he placed over his gas plate on the server. While the chocolate was slowly melting, he swiftly prepared two crepes that he served into our bowls, along with a generous scoop of vanilla ice cream. Then, when the chocolate sauce was ready, he poured it over the bowls, me almost drooling as the chocolate and hazelnut sauce hardened on the ice cream.

Granddad sent me over to his liquor cabinet alongside a very old glass cabinet, which had in it the urn containing the ashes of my mother's mother, and had me retrieve the squat black bottle. He then poured some of The King's Ginger liqueur over the top of both our desserts. It pooled over the crepe, and there was a teaspoon or two left in the bottom of my bowl.

From then on while sharing this special treat together, he'd simply say, "Son, go and get *our* bottle," and I knew what was coming…the best part. He always left room for cheese and a cracker, and on this occasion, he prepared two, one for each of us. He carefully cut segments of Camembert cheese and placed them on French-buttered sourdough crackers, and then, using the rounded end of the cheese knife handle, he pressed a little basin into the middle of the cheese on each. With the steady hand of a marksman, he carefully filled the tiny basin to the brim with the same liqueur, and then he took two slices of stem ginger out of its thick, sugary syrup and popped it on the top. In contrast to his careful preparation, he finished it off by dousing his creation with the ginger-and-honey liqueur before passing one of them towards me while he took the other, raised it as if it were a glass, and put it whole into his mouth, indicating for me to do the same.

The alcohol burned and so did the ginger, even if it was also sweet, but the creaminess of the cheese mixed in with these contrasting flavours was the best thing I'd ever tasted. With my eyes watering, I was ready for another.

"That's all, my boy. Too much of a good thing *is never a good thing*," he said, chuckling.

This became a regular occurrence. So regular that it still happens now. Whenever I make this cracker, cheese, ginger preserve, and liqueur snack, fond memories of my grandfather are immediately stirred.

Every now and then, my granddad gave me half a small liqueur glass of The King's Ginger, and instead of "Cheers," he would say, "To the gods of indulgence! Let's indulge."

I later found out that half a glass was actually just a quarter of a glass because of the trumpet shape. I discovered this to my detriment, losing a bet when he took two glasses, each three-quarters-full, and poured one into the other without spilling a drop.

I have never really taken my drinking habits further than that, apart from the odd glass of champagne.

I loved the story of how The King's Ginger came into existence. Granddad even remembered how in 1903, King Edward VII used to take his topless Daimler, something he referred to as his horseless carriage, for joyrides around the English countryside. This was evidently quite a nerve-racking experience because this horseless carriage exposed him to the elements, where he ran the risk of "getting a chill." The royal physician sought to address these concerns by commissioning a London merchant, Berry Bros. & Rudd, to formulate a "warming, fortifying beverage," and hence, the brandy, ginger, honey, and lemon elixir came into being. It soon became very popular, extending beyond royalty and nobility to commoners as well, as a drink for not only when one was driving but also when one went shooting. "A clear case of the British government promoting 'drink driving' in the early years of motoring," Granddad said, chuckling. I could just imagine a panel discussing it, and it making perfect sense to them back then. Luckily though, they eventually did come to their senses and made drink driving illegal in 1925.

A few nights after the shoe exchange in Winston Cottage, Granddad, my mum and dad, and I had been sitting around the table in the family dining room, about to have a light dinner, when Hamilton walked in. He was looking very smart except for his shoes, which did not match his formal attire. On seeing this, I watched in amusement as my mum's mouth opened, about to say something, but then she closed it again, having realised what was going on. She clearly knew Granddad well.

On this occasion, Fabrizio had made his famous tomato soup. Famous only because he had declared it so, as he humorously did with many of his dishes. He was quite happy to stretch the truth on this classification when trying to encourage me to eat more.

At breakfast on a Monday morning before I had to go back to boarding school, he would say something like, "You must have more of my famous scrambled eggs."

Thinking about it, they were *pretty famous*, using his definition. Fabrizio said the secret to good scrambled eggs was double cream. He would cook the egg mixture on low heat, folding it over and over until they slowly turned into the consistency of scrambled eggs. Once they were plated, he added salt and pepper, finely chopped parsley, a little grated parmesan and, splashed artistically on the side, his own tomato sauce made from, of course, Roma tomatoes, his secret herbs (all his herbs were secret), and a little honey. On my dad's encouragement Fabrizio had an adult version of his tomato sauce—it included peperoncino chillies from Tuscany. Hot and sweet. "*Ti morderà*. It will bite you," he often warned me. I quite liked testing myself, and my friends, getting *bitten* by his adult sauce. Alongside would be *roasted* bread—not toasted, an important distinction according to Fabrizio. His tomato soup was also quite exceptional, if not famous. He would fill two large trays of what he insisted had to be Roma tomatoes, *obviously*, preferably from Italy, with red peppers, garlic, and herbs, and then place them in the wood-burning pizza oven. Once roasted, he'd put it all through the food processor before he added clotted cream. He served this with sourdough bread, which, yes, was also roasted in the wood-burning oven.

On this occasion, my mother had been serving the piping-hot soup from the tureen, allowed on the family dining room table but not in the main dining room, into our soup plates when Granddad placed a brown paper packet on the table in front of me.

"A surprise for you, Charles," he said with a twinkle in his eye.

I opened the package and was delighted to discover that my surprise was a large frog.

"Dad! Do we have to do this at the dining table?" was my mother's sharp reaction.

He smiled mischievously, expecting his daughter's rebuke.

She looked on disapprovingly as the frog jumped straight into my bowl of piping-hot soup, only to depart as hurriedly. "Now look what you've done," my mother said, her annoyance with her father having shifted up a gear.

My dad chuckled. My grandfather winced, not having expected that outcome. I loved how he seemingly put his tail between his legs when his daughter tore a strip off him for doing something wrong. I was smiling at this interaction, wondering what Granddad's comeback would be.

"Fran, darling," he began, "I am just giving young Charles here a lesson about life."

This had everyone confused and my dad and me chuckling.

"Charles, did you notice how the moment the frog landed in the hot soup, he leapt straight out again?"

I nodded my head in agreement.

"Well, that was precisely the correct response to the abrupt change to his circumstances." Nobody could deny that. "Now, consider this," my grandfather continued. "Had he been in the pot of soup when it was cold and it had slowly been brought to the boil, it is very likely he would have been cooked into the soup." All eyes were on Granddad as he finished by saying, "So, this lesson is that you shouldn't be lethargic about changing your circumstances just because the changes are happening slowly."

Not bad, Granddad, I thought with a smile.

An unforgettable day in my life was when my grandfather gave me my first shotgun, a Browning 410. I listened and learnt intently as he taught me and then practiced with me the principles of shooting game birds in flight.

"You have to shoot where the bird is going, not where it has been," he continually reminded me. "Start behind, move slowly onto the target and then ahead. Judging the speed, the distance, and how it is moving while keeping a steady hand are the differences between a palooka and a professional."

I smiled. So did my granddad. He had chosen his words purposely, knowing I would do whatever possible not to be a palooka.

One of the exercises he made me do was to balance on a large, rounded boulder at the bottom of the rolling lawns below Winston Cottage, the same rock he liked to sit on and watch some of the wildlife around Rockwell Manor or just enjoy a sunset.

"Always set your feet for where you will shoot your target, lean into the shot, nose over toes, and the rest will follow."

When winter came, he set up a portable clay trap and we would do clay-pigeon shooting. Following his instruction in picking up this three-and-a-half-inch clay disc as it catapulted out of the trap had me hooked in an instant. Slowly but surely, I got to the stage where I was hitting almost as many as I was missing. Watching the pieces breaking off the flying projectile pleased me no end. As I improved further, thereby hitting the targets with the centre of the pellet pattern, the clay discs would disintegrate into a thousand pieces in a cloud of clay dust. No guessing which captured my imagination more. "You smashed it," were words I loved hearing my granddad say.

I will never forget on one occasion when I had foolishly missed a couple of clays and been quite forthright in admonishing myself. My grandfather turned to me and gave me this sage advice. "What's behind you is behind you. Let it go. There is nothing you can do about it. Learn how to do that and it will free you to concentrate fully on the next clay."

This boulder, which he called our "shooting rock," had another use. It is where I often read with my grandfather, my mother giving him instructions about what she wanted him to cover.

On one occasion, we began speaking more broadly about my schoolwork.

"Granddad, Mum says I should concentrate more on the things I am weak at. What do you think?"

I knew his reply was important because of the extra time he took deliberating his answer. Then, in a hushed tone, he said, "I have a different idea to your mum. I think you should concentrate on the things you are good at and only do what is necessary on those subjects that don't interest you."

This contradicted nearly everything I had heard around me. "You need to work on your areas of weakness, young man," is what I was familiar with at school. My mother would say, "Leave the maths and science, Sunbeam. You can do that like falling off a log. Concentrate on your weak subjects like geography, anthropology, and English."

I couldn't get out of my mother's English lessons but almost certainly followed my grandfather's advice on the remainder. Like my mother, he reminded me that success comes more easily on a foundation of success, a simple family philosophy. Do something, no matter how small, and once you have successfully completed it, use it as a foundation and move on.

Edward Charles Featherstone

I enjoyed an incredible life with my granddad until shortly before my thirteenth birthday.

It was a Sunday afternoon, and I went down to Winston Cottage to chat with him, but very unusually, he had been taking an afternoon rest. The next morning, I still remember thinking I should run down to his cottage to say goodbye before leaving for school for the week. I didn't act on those thoughts, a decision that would trouble me for many years to come. I never saw my grandfather again. He had woken up ill on Monday morning and remained in his pyjamas and gown, even agreeing to see a doctor the following morning. He died in his sleep in the early hours of Tuesday morning.

When my mum collected me from school on Friday, she said I should sit in the front seat, and on the way home she told me that Granddad had gone to Heaven on Tuesday morning.

She continued, trying to explain the cycle of life to me, but I didn't want to hear that. None of it made sense to me. I asked "Mummy, does this mean I am never going to see Granddad ever again?" The last few words were barely audible as my tears and remorse enveloped me.

I curled up into the corner of the seat facing the passenger window, and quietly wept all the way home. We drove into our gates up the long, winding driveway, past the spot where I could see Winston Cottage, and I couldn't help the choking sobs that immediately resurfaced. My mother stroked my leg trying to console me, until she stopped the car, and I jumped out and ran up to my room with Osric meekly following. There was none of the typical welcome home we shared and no spring in his step. He understood my feelings. I needed to be alone, to share my sadness with my pillow, something I knew all too well from West Buckland.

Granddad had left clear instructions that he wanted to be cremated. One handful of his ashes was to be sprinkled into the earth at the base of our shooting rock and another at the centre point of the polo field once it had been scarified (mowing the grass to its roots). "Ashes to ashes, dust to dust, darling Fran," he had instructed my mother. The remaining ashes, in their urn, were to always be kept next to the one containing the ashes of his beloved late wife.

I didn't attend the cremation or church service. Not wanting me to experience the austere church ceremony, my parents arranged our own little family send-off that I could be a part of. My father had gotten our groundsman to scarify a one-yard-diameter circle in the centre of the polo field, the bare earth ready to receive a sprinkling of Granddad's ashes.

It was the saddest day as the three of us, hand in hand, walked to the middle of the polo field and sprinkled Granddad's ashes on the exact centre point, then bowed our heads and my dad read.

"From the *Book of Common Prayer*: 'We therefore commit these ashes to the ground, earth to earth, ashes to ashes, dust to dust; in sure and certain hope of the Resurrection to eternal life.' "

We then walked to the rounded boulder below Winston Cottage and repeated the little ceremony. As my dad finished reading the prayer, I looked at the boulder and burst into tears. I no longer had a granddad to learn how to shoot pheasant with. To play chess with. To read with. To drink The King's Ginger with. I could not stop sobbing no matter how my parents tried to comfort me.

We went into the cottage, and I was given the responsibility of putting my grandfather's urn alongside his deceased wife's in the old glass cabinet. I then instinctively realised what I had to do.

Taking the other urn out of the cabinet, I told my parents, "We have to do the same again." I could see they weren't sure what I was getting at, so I put it another way. "Granddad will want Nan's ashes with him, so they can always be together."

They then understood my naive point of view and agreed with it wholeheartedly. With my father holding his wife's mother's ashes, we walked back to the middle of the polo field, sprinkled a handful of her ashes, said our prayer, and then went back to our shooting rock, repeating what we had done before.

This time it was my mum who was sobbing, feeling the loss of never having had a mum and now also losing her only parent, and it was my dad and me trying to console her.

The loss of my grandfather made me think about what he had lost when the mother of his children had died. Seeing them side by side, I realised the only thing I had ever had of my nan was sitting in an urn. I didn't get to call her my nan.

My grandfather was born and died at Rockwell Manor. He knew no other home. My mother was born at Rockwell Manor. Would she die there too? I shuddered at the thought.

I had the most special relationship with my grandfather and have even wondered if he subconsciously made an extra effort with me, attempting to make up for the three grandparents I didn't have. It is quite possible, and certainly the sort of thing he would have done. In many ways it put me in a very fortunate position. Except of course, when I lost him I lost all four of them. Along with my parents, especially my mother, he taught me many things that guided me all through my life and that I have often used in the course of teaching my own children.

As an adult, I couldn't help reflecting that for all of my grandfather's good intentions in appointing a governess to make sure my mother and uncle had a suitable substitute for a mother, clearly there had still been shortcomings. Mrs. Kearns, having been a schoolteacher, was clearly of the stricter kind. The way we addressed her seemed to confirm it. So, whilst she may have been very caring and a good teacher, I couldn't imagine her having a warm, motherly side. I could understand where my mother got her propensity to teach me from, but what about her softness? Was my mother's gentle, loving nature a looking glass into the character of her own mother, the grandmother I never had?

CHAPTER 3
GAME-BIRD SHOOTING

G RAYSTON HOUSE SCHOOL was one of the standout memories of my teenage years.

I loved playing sports, and our school was well known for its many and varied offerings. The moment the bell rang for the end of class or prep, I would dash off to play cricket in the summer, rugby in the winter, and athletics in the spring. If not that, I would be found playing squash, doing gymnastics, or even practising karate. Given my family's sporting background, it was perhaps unsurprising that I did well in all my sports activities.

On the academic side, I had already shown an aptitude that suggested I would achieve distinctions in maths and science, and that I would struggle with almost everything else, especially if it required studying. Also no surprise. What was a surprise, especially for me and clearly thanks to the perseverance of my mother, was that slowly but surely, I started getting better marks in English. I was never to overcome dyslexia, but I was learning how to work with and around it.

It was during my teens that I really advanced my game-bird shooting and polo-playing interests as well, fitting them into my very busy weekends at home. I also learnt to drive, mostly illegally, not that anyone really worried about what took place on our remote country roads.

By the time I was sixteen, Osric and I would go rough shooting at every opportunity. He had become a seasoned gundog, accomplished in the two primary disciplines of flushing and retrieving. At times, I would watch him flush large quarry, even ducks, and I couldn't help but marvel at how steady he was. When a gundog flushes birds from the thicket, there is a great fanfare of wings flapping as they take flight. This can be distracting, but a well-trained dog holds its ground and stands immobile and intense, only breaking when the birds are clear, referred to as "steady to flush." This was Osric.

When we went rough shooting, we never returned home empty-handed. I always aimed to shoot at least a brace of birds. Whenever my mother admonished us for being late, I'd explain that we'd needed one more pheasant or partridge to complete our brace, because one pheasant was not enough to feed our family, including Osric.

An important thing to remember is that one never carries one's game-bird quarry by the feet, but rather the neck. This is to keep the blood in the carcass, which adds to the flavour of the meat. I tied some twine between their necks to make a convenient handle.

After several hours, with English weather being what it was, we would arrive home wet and covered in mud. Osric and I were oblivious to this until my mother refused us entry into the boot room, let alone the kitchen. We were required to clean up outside, to make ourselves more presentable before dashing into the scullery. We usually ended up showering together, and being a water dog, Osric absolutely loved it.

While Osric's name came from a minor character in Shakespeare's *Hamlet,* he was by no means a minor character in my early life. He was, for a long time, the main supporting actor. We did everything together. He shared my food, and much to my mother's chagrin, he shared my water bottle, hardly spilling a drop as I held it up to his mouth for a sip. It was when I absentmindedly took a sip myself just after him that my mother would react. At night he slept on my bed, my mother having given up trying to keep him out. She used to tell me how he would mourn my departure on Sunday nights or Monday mornings when I went back to boarding school, and how he only came to life when I arrived home on Friday evenings. When I was at school, I missed Osric almost as much as I missed home.

Like so many pastimes—modern polo, football (soccer), rugby, cricket, tennis, golf, boxing, even baseball and many more—game-bird wing shooting had its origins in Great Britain. Accordingly, it had some interesting British idiosyncrasies, all quite normal to me, although I would discover this was not the case for most foreign visitors.

My Rude Awakening

Once, we had an American, Logan Gates, come and stay because of a polo tournament he was playing with us. He mentioned he enjoyed turkey shooting in Kentucky, USA, so my dad decided we should include him in our own formal shoot.

"Charles, please help Logan get kitted out. Between us, we should have him looking presentable," my dad mused. "And while you are at it, you should explain the proceedings to him. They do things quite differently on the other side of the pond," he said, smiling.

I started by explaining that once we were at the first stand, there would be beaters to get parcels of pheasant to take flight for the first drive of the day. Highly trained retriever dogs would recover anything we shot.

When Logan explained that the turkeys they shot were on the ground, I started chuckling because I was sure he was taking the mickey out of me. Sadly, he was not. My favourite quarry were pheasant and especially grouse because the speed at which they flew made for a great challenge. Shooting a bird that was on the ground—especially a turkey, which I thought of as slow, cumbersome, vulnerable, large, and chicken-like—was a strange concept for an Englishman and brought to mind something I had once read that described perfectly why one should not do this.

Damned be the man, so unsporting, that he shall put a bird at the mercy of his shot without giving it the chance of flighted freedom. Let his pot go empty before breaking this unwritten rule.

—*Anonymous, 1904*

I should add here that years later, when I did go on a turkey hunt in Kentucky, I discovered it was nothing close to what I had imagined. They were crafty little critters, and even using the best decoys to attract them didn't always work. Sorry, Logan, for my judgemental thoughts.

Luckily, he was much the same size as my father, so I didn't expect any difficulty in fitting him out for his first shoot.

"Logan, I'm sure we will find something in my father's wardrobe for you. You seem to be a similar size; what are you, fourteen, fourteen and a half stone?"

Logan looked at me bewildered.

I realised that he had no idea about our stone weight measurement system. "About one ninety or two hundred pounds?"

He nodded his head, still looking confused. "So how much is a stone?" he asked.

"Now it is set at fourteen pounds," I replied.

"What do you mean *now*?" he inquired.

"Oh, don't worry about that. It's just that the system dates back to the fourteenth century when a stone was used in early scales for trading and measuring produce. It's straightforward now, but back in the day, a stone was a different weight depending on the region you were in," I told him, hoping I was making sense.

"Straightforward, you say. And why on earth do you still use such an antiquated system for measuring body weight?"

On reflection, it probably was a bit confusing to a foreigner, especially in a world of the metric system. I supposed it was a case of old habits die hard.

I put together tweed plus fours (much like knickerbockers), a fine wool shirt, a sporting-print tie, a tweed jacket, a woollen cap, leg stockings with bright, ornate woollen garters, and brogue shoes. He would be able to attend our breakfast and luncheon dressed like this, and then just swap the shoes for boots and his tweed jacket for a shooting jacket before heading off for the next drive.

Since ours was a bespoke shoot, we would each need a matched pair of two identical shotguns, so that regardless of which was being shot, they were indistinguishable from each other. I would be taking my early 1900s side-by-side James Purdey & Son matched pair, which had been handed down to me by my grandfather. Logan's guns were a more modern over-and-under identical pair, as they were easier to shoot and more accurate. Experienced shots were more inclined to stick to age-old tradition and not make things easier for themselves with the over-and-under shotgun variety.

I went on to tell him that he would have a loader who would quickly load the one gun while he was firing the other. All he had to do once he had fired his first gun was reach back, and the reloaded twin shotgun would be swapped for his discharged one. This would continue until the quarry had finished flying overhead.

My Rude Awakening

I turned to Logan and asked, "So, what do you think?"

Reeling at the pomp and ceremony, he looked at me incredulously and said, "You must be blooding joking!"

The conversation carried on with Logan asking, "Do we stop for tea?"

"We don't, but you shouldn't worry," I said. "Between drives there will always be time for a snack and a sloe gin, or whatever you prefer in your hip flask."

"What is sloe gin? Surely not gin?" he asked.

"It is actually a liqueur made out of gin," I told him.

"You must be kidding me," Logan said in an incredulous tone.

"Why?" I asked innocently.

"Guns are almost outlawed in England. I know it is very difficult to get your licence, but when you finally do, you have no problem mixing alcohol and firearms." Logan looked at me as he finished making his point.

I looked back at him blankly. What he said was true, and I suppose, looking at it from the outside, it was a bit unusual. It was what I'd grown up with, so it seemed completely normal to me. My answer was a shrug of the shoulders, which didn't help Logan much.

As I now write about this, nothing has changed.

Whilst Logan was right about the stringent attitude both the government and society had towards guns, after that little harangue I chose not to mention an even more curious thing about English gun laws. Although guns are regarded as completely unacceptable, handguns even being illegal—not even policemen are armed unless they are in a special unit—sporting guns are more than acceptable, especially shotguns. Even so, when you apply for a sporting-gun licence in England, it is a lengthy process. It starts with a specialist officer coming to your home, forming a firsthand opinion of you, checking your gun safe, getting character references, speaking to your shooting club, and doing whatever else he deems necessary to confirm that you are an upstanding member of society and a genuine sport-shooting enthusiast before recommending you for a licence. The process could take up to a year.

When it comes to children and shotguns, the law is quite bizarre and even surprises most people in England, and that is, there is no minimum age for applying for a shotgun certificate. The law does prohibit children from using the weapons without supervision of an adult though, up until they are fifteen years old. That suited Osric and me just fine, and there were lots of adults around when I needed one.

Pheasant carried by the neck.

I loved game-bird shooting, and we found ourselves cramming in as much as we could during the short season, starting with grouse on the twelfth of August, known as the Glorious Twelfth, and going through to January or early February. We didn't seem to even notice the cold and often gloomy winter days because of shooting, especially when I was rough shooting for pheasant or partridge with Osric.

We often visited Scotland and the Scottish Highlands on the Glorious Twelfth for the start of the season. Cold, gloomy weather set the scene as we walked the Scottish moors with pointer dogs in search of grouse. It always amazed me how the dogs would go "on point," having almost miraculously detected these game birds, with us looking on disbelievingly. Then suddenly, grouse would rise above the heath and beautiful purple Scottish heather, and dart away at high speed. Even with the assistance of our furry friends, grouse would often evade us.

The frenetic shooting season didn't give us enough time to even think about polo, let alone miss it. Come March, we began thinking about spring and summer sports, the first of which was golf.

Game-bird shooting, something of a tradition in our family, would continue to be an important part of my life's journey, and at times it also played a part in my growing up.

CHAPTER 4
GOLF

GOLF WAS ANOTHER sport I carried all through my life. This is not surprising, given that my mother was an exceptional golfer who competed in numerous pro-am tournaments and often won against the professionals. Her having a scratch handicap, I referred to her as being semi-professional.

From when I was about the age of six, my mother coached me on the home polo field. I was able to confidently hit all the clubs in my bag, including the sand wedge, using the horse exercise sandtrack around the perimeter of the field as a bunker. She would place horse water buckets at different places around the expansive 300- by 200-yard polo field and have me select which club to use, then practise until she was happy with the result. I can still hear her words, "Get five balls in a row within ten yards of bucket number one, and we can move to the next. Groove your swing and your distance and you will be halfway there."

"What's the other half?" I once asked, a little perplexed.

"It's the most difficult part, Sunbeam. It's your mind. That is the difference between a good golfer and a top golfer."

It made perfect sense why she was a top golfer.

The best part of my game was undoubtedly my driving. If you knew me, you would understand why. Apart from the satisfaction of watching a good drive sail into the distance, there was another reason.

I was about fourteen or fifteen years old when I asked, "Mum, what distance would be considered a good drive for a man?"

"Around three hundred yards," was my mum's reply.

"Do you think I will one day drive that far?" I asked.

My Rude Awakening

"Of course, but only five percent of male golfers can achieve that distance," she said as a matter of fact.

Coincidently, that was the length of a polo pitch. From there on out, driving the full length of our polo field was a goal that beckoned me every day. I was not going to stop trying until I achieved it.

A story that epitomises my early introduction into golf started with my mother and me speaking about polo and how one practises for it, which is to "stick and ball," something often not understood by people not involved with polo.

"Stick and balling is similar to what one does on a golf driving range, except you are mounted on a horse when hitting your ball," my mother remarked.

I responded, "Yes, but you are cantering, often galloping, using a longer stick, holding it with just one hand because your other one has a fistful of reins, trying to control your leaping horse, *and* it is a moving ball that you are trying to hit." I grinned. "And don't forget, Mum, if you're in a match, you have to try and do all of that while someone is either attempting to obstruct your shot by hooking your stick with his or riding you off with his horse." I said, trying to make the point of how difficult polo was, even though my mother knew very well the intricacies of the sport. "No comparison, Mum," I finished off smugly.

"Oh, all right then, smart aleck. If it is so easy, then I challenge you."

"Okay," I said, still smiling.

By the time of my mother's challenge, I was in my late teens and had achieved my goal of driving the length of the polo field and could comfortably out-drive her, even though we had never actually played against each other.

I was looking forward to our challenge.

Interestingly, I had never played at Wentworth Club and couldn't even remember when we had last been there. It may have been for a lunch when I was much younger, and I was not really paying attention. Given the contest that lay ahead, I was paying full attention now.

The first thing that struck me was the green lawns on each side of the road leading up to the grand entrance. A fitting lead-in to the imposing buildings beyond that looked more like a castle, complete with gun turrets rather than a golf club. As my mother neared the big gates and guardhouse, she slowed down slightly, and when the gatekeeper recognised her, he promptly lifted the boom. She drove through the full car park, and my chest expanded another inch as she turned into a reserved prime parking spot that read:

Ladies Captain

F. D. E. Featherstone

Smiling, I looked at my mother's initials for Frances Dulce and Edwina, the feminine for two of my grandfather's names. *She must've been his favourite.*

We had no sooner parked than a caddy was at the back of the car.

"Hello, Marcin," my mother greeted him. "We will be taking a golf cart today."

"No problem, ma'am," Marcin responded in a thick Polish accent. "It will be a pleasure to take a cart and your golf bags down to the first tee, ma'am."

"Thank you, Marcin," my mother replied smiling happily.

As we went about our preparation, she was greeted by other members who clearly held her in high regard. I'd never really understood my mother's captaincy or scratch handicap status until this moment. I was seeing her in an environment where she reigned supreme. Feelings of admiration and pride permeated through me as I absorbed it all.

Walking down to the first tee of Wentworth's West Course, golf cart with golf bags parked to the side, I was feeling a little less confident about our challenge. *Oh well,* I thought. *If I win my fair share of holes, it will be fine.*

"Take it away, Sunbeam," my mother said with her 3 wood in hand.

I looked at my yardage card, wondering why she was not going for her driver. No question, it was a par four with 420 yards tee to pin, no obstacles for the next 350 yards, and a rough on the right. I confidently took out my driver and addressed the ball. My mother's coaching voice crept into the back of my mind. *"Check setup and direction, relax your shoulders, breathe, don't look up to see your wonderful shot. That's the best way to leave your ball on the tee box."* And then I remembered her last bit of advice before I began my backswing. *"If you're going to force, rather take a 7 iron. It goes farther than a forced driver."*

I was feeling good. My confidence was not unfounded. I executed one of my best drives, coming up short of a water obstacle, probably 110 yards from the pin. I looked at my mother and was surprised she wasn't more impressed.

She hit her 3 wood perfectly, as I'd seen a thousand times before. *A little too far left,* I thought. I remembered one of her little mantras, *"Groove your swing, groove your distances, engage your brain. Your confidence will grow, and that's what makes a great golfer."*

Right then, I was around 60 yards ahead of her ball. If that meant I was in the lead, I would soon discover it would last for just that one ball.

For my second shot, I was faced with a water obstacle between me and the elongated green. It ran from my left to right, where it dropped off aggressively, and behind it lay an arrangement of bunkers. With my next shot, I landed close to the pin, but with so little green to work with, my ball rolled into the bunker.

For my third shot, I nearly knocked myself out. The ball fired back at me after hitting the high lip of the bunker. Rockwell Manor's sand exercise track had nothing like this. Still in the bunker, I knew I had to blast my ball out of the sand and over the raised edge, temporarily forgetting about the water obstacle beyond. No prize for guessing where I ended up.

In contrast, my mother managed the hole beautifully. Having played a little shorter and on the left, her approach to the green was far more strategic. She had the full length of the putting surface to work with. She was on for two, a 5-yard putt lipped out, and then a knock-in for her par.

I very quickly learnt what a bogey was. Pity I had to start with the double variety.

When we finished the first nine holes, I was fourteen shots over par. My short game had let me down enormously. I could hear her voice in my head saying, *"Drive for show, putt for dough."* My mother was two shots under par.

I was so hoping we'd be going home, but I knew my mother. We never ended anything on a note like that.

At the halfway station, a large Cornish pasty with gravy and Worcester sauce, washed down with a Steelworks drink, made me feel slightly better. My mother had a tuna salad and a rock shandy—soda water and bitters.

Between bites she said, "I left you to your own devices for the first nine holes, Sunbeam."

That was obvious and I knew why. I had been precocious, and my first lesson today was to be more humble.

Then with a thoughtful expression, one I knew well and that it usually meant she had something prophetic to say, she continued, "Sunbeam, there was something I noticed that definitely added a few extra strokes to your round."

"What was that, Mum?" I asked, more than happy with any advice to improve my score.

"Well, you need to always remember what's behind you is behind you. Let it go," she said. "Doing so will free you to focus and commit to the next stroke or hole, unburdened by what happened in the past."

My mother did not understand the smile that crept onto my face, so I answered her inquiring look. "That's what granddad used to say to me, Mum."

Now she smiled. "That's because it's the truth, Sunbeam, so practice it." She wasn't finished there. "Master that and it will make the world of difference." She looked at me as I absorbed her words. "And when you have done something silly, don't admonish yourself for more than five seconds. Then work out where you went wrong. Common sense really."

That made me think about something else she would say. *"Common sense is the least common of all sense, so much so it is sometimes mistaken for genius."* I was smiling again.

She carried on. "You can do that for your successes too. A quick mental pat on your back and then analyse what you did right. It is a lesson of life. Learn from your failures and successes, then move on. Always remember, there is nothing gained from dwelling on the past. But I don't mind telling you, I saw enough to know that you could become a really good golfer," she said reassuringly. "If you want it badly enough. Now let's go and have some fun on the second half."

The second nine was very different. My mother started by saying I had remembered most of her coaching, except just one thing. Then, after explaining to me how each hole we arrived at should be played and why, the words that became the mantra for the rest of the afternoon were, "Engage brain, Sunbeam, and manage your mind, your emotions."

Her view was that anyone could hit a golf ball (a bit of an exaggeration), but few people had the mental capacity. Her words were, "Don't overestimate yourself. Don't be too brave. But you can't be too timid."

Crikey, I'm lost.

For the second nine holes, I scored six over par, which included one birdie. That birdie would definitely have me coming back for more. I couldn't help thinking if I had done that for the first nine holes, it could've, should've been a good first round even if I were being coached. A difficult lesson in behaviour, and a wonderful lesson in golf.

Added to that, I got an appreciation for some avian life. I was familiar with partridge, pheasant, and grouse, but now I could add birdies to the list. I saw them on the second, ninth, eleventh, fifteenth (mine on a tough par four), and the last one was on the seventeenth hole, but my highlight of the day was when I saw an eagle, my mother's, on the par five twelfth hole. She said *her* highlights were my halving (drawing) two holes with her on the back nine and beating her with my birdie on the fifteenth.

But my mother refused to show me even one bogie of her own. Yes, she shot five under for the round.

I had been humbled and then coached and uplifted but not humiliated. For my mother, the former were fine, but humiliation was not. I had a feeling that was the reason she had opted not to take golf caddies that day but our own golf cart instead.

I had discovered in no uncertain terms that hitting a golf ball perfectly was not enough to do well at golf. And unlike a perfectly flat polo field, no hurdles to surprise one, a golf course is a very different proposition designed to challenge players in every which way, using all the obstacles in its repertoire and tempting you to do precisely the wrong thing.

It is fair to say I enjoyed my mother teaching me the craft of golf and it did become one of my sports, giving me a lot of pleasure all through my life, especially in my business career. Secretly, I think she had hoped I was going to be a top golfer, but the allure and adrenaline of polo was just too strong. I was never going to put in the time required to reach her level. I did discover later though, that a single-digit golf handicap, which I did achieve, was more than respectable.

I didn't play often, but when I did, I had no difficulty beating my friends. And no matter that I could out-drive my mum, I had to admit that the next time I beat her would be the first.

CHAPTER 5
POLO

For as long as I can remember, my greatest love has been polo. One of the world's oldest-known team sports, polo had been in our family for generations, so it was only natural that I would also adopt this sport from an early age.

Few sports are as widely recognised but fundamentally misunderstood as polo. Even people who have been around horses their entire lives know little about the sport. Many have suggested there is nothing subtle about the game, describing it as "in-your-face" aggressive horsemanship at its best.

For those of us who love the sport, polo epitomises many things. Power. Balance. Grace. Skill. Coordination. Reflexes. Teamwork. Decision-making. Strategy. Poetry in motion perhaps, and chills and spills aplenty.

Polo looks crazy and intense because it is. It is said that it takes years to learn, decades to master, and a lifetime to perfect. It is truly a horse sport all of its own. I cannot begin to think of anything, in any sport, that is more complicated, challenging, or engrossing.

At a full gallop, shoulder to shoulder, your opponent trying to get the better of you, and you hit a perfect shot—the ball no bigger than one used in cricket—that is an adrenaline rush like no other. The combined athleticism of horse and rider, unavoidably sharing each other's sweat in this dangerous, high-contact sport, is exhilarating.

I embraced it with a fearless passion despite my mother often sternly telling me, "Don't do that, Sunbeam. You will break your neck."

Our family's generational interest in polo started with our home, Rockwell Manor in Berkshire, the middle of polo country in England. It was feted as a rather grand establishment while quite a new estate in

English terms. It was built by my great-grandfather and completed in 1880. Granddad was born there in 1889 and responsible for remodelling part of it after the First World War, around 1926.

It was a vast 36,000 square foot, two-storey Georgian Palladian manor house complete with twelve bedroom suites overlooking its own polo field on extensive grounds bordering a forest.

It was before I was born that my retired grandfather handed over the reins of Rockwell Manor to my dad, perhaps literally and figuratively, and the estate moved from being the Apsley residence to being the Featherstone residence. By then, with the changing times, it was superfluous to have nine guest suites, three of the twelve suites used by our family, but ideal if you were intending to accommodate a polo team and their manager. My father undertook a remodelling and further development of Rockwell Manor that included turning the one wing into polo player and manager accommodations; upgrading the field into a world-class surface and adding a number of sporting elements, including squash, tennis, and beach-volleyball courts; and developing two staff houses for estate grounds and house staff. But the most wonderful element he added was a stable block that housed forty horses.

This was the start of Rockwell Manor becoming a more serious participant in the burgeoning world of professional polo. It then became a Rockwell Manor tradition to invite a team from a foreign country like the USA, Australia, South Africa, or Canada, or an eighteen- to twenty-goal team—always tough competition—from Argentina. Once, there was even a team from Barbados. We would arrange a series of matches against various teams, the highlight being the matches against Rockwell Manor on our home field.

This became ever more exciting as I progressed through my teenage years and was able to enjoy all that the new Rockwell Manor had to offer.

It was when I turned sixteen that I began to realise I was advancing along the Featherstone cycle of life. History had already quite clearly laid out the progression. My parents would eventually move into Winston Cottage, and I would take over the main homestead. Hopefully, my children would have a similar relationship with my parents as I had enjoyed with Granddad. But as they say, only time would tell.

My Rude Awakening

In proving this point, on my sixteenth birthday we were at the dinner table and my mum asked, "How does it feel to be sixteen?" A rhetorical question that had an obvious answer.

I didn't have a chance to even attempt to reply before my dad asked, "How would you like to move into the polo manager's suite in the north wing?"

I was ecstatic and could easily answer my mum's question now. It was *great* being sixteen! Were they allowing me to spread my wings and start the transition into young adulthood?

Apart from its expansive extent, Rockwell Manor had two enormous upstairs and downstairs patios. We could easily accommodate 200 or more people on game days, overlooking our polo field. Visitors were often amazed at the size of the field at roughly five football pitches. This is necessary, of course, because polo horses can gallop up to forty miles per hour in play, traversing up and down the 300-yard length as the teams attack and then counterattack. Whilst it was mostly used selectively for high-goal matches, on weekends we often invited friends to use our home field for practises or a bit of stick and ball.

My mother's inclination to be hospitable meant there was always a breakfast buffet set out on one of the expansive patios so visitors could conveniently get something to eat before or just after riding or practising.

For invitation matches at home, special attention was paid to the catering for our guests, with the finest cuisine and vintage French champagne, none of which was of any interest to me. Our guests would typically come for breakfast or brunch beforehand. Fabrizio and his kitchen staff, sometimes with complementing outside catering, would lay out a delicious buffet and be on hand to provide all aspects of the meal.

It was all quite normal, until before a practice match my father came in asking for lobster frittata, complete with beluga caviar, fresh spring onions and chives, and Dom Pérignon champagne to wash it down. That took it to another level. While it would only be late morning, flowing champagne was quite normal for us.

"An effervescent start for a sparkling day," was his toast.

By the time I was seventeen years old, I was already a competitive, rising player. I spent endless weekend hours at the stables when not playing polo.

45

As much as I loved rugby, cricket, and track and field athletics, polo had somehow gotten under my skin like no other sport. A large part of that was the horses, which I was passionate about.

The top polo horses, also referred to as "ponies" in days gone by, are nearly all thoroughbred ex-racehorses of which more than 70 percent are mares, purely because they are nimbler-footed and a lot braver than geldings. My dad would say it was as if geldings, "do not have the balls for the game," the depletion of testosterone production ultimately weighing on the courage and ability of these equine athletes. A literal and figurative statement if ever there was one. On the other hand, stallions cannot be used because they are far too strong and powerful and do not normally succumb to the demands of the rider.

My father and I each had our own string of ten high-goal horses—the most superb equine athletes imaginable—plus twenty other top horses so that we were able to mount a third, and sometimes even a fourth, polo player.

We would seasonally bring in a top player from Argentina with a six- to eight-goal handicap. As I got older and my dad started stepping back, we brought nine- and even ten-goal players to Rockwell Manor. My father was well handicapped as a two-goal player and, as a teen, I was rated at two, going on three. The fourth team member would invariably be our polo manager unless the goal level of the tournament meant we had to find a local player with the right handicap to complete our team.

Speaking of our polo manager, Guy Watkins was a very valued team member, a combined role that was not uncommon in polo. He was playing off a handicap of four, had just turned thirty-two, and was well on his way to attaining at least the six-goal level. Apart from being a top manager and a very solid polo player, his greatest attribute was his expert ability in working with horses, something he did whenever he had completed his other duties. We would regularly see Guy on the polo field either schooling and bringing on a young horse or working on a weakness he had detected on one of the older horses, or just practising to improve his own game. He took great pride in "his" string of our forty horses and was always watching their every move, whether it was in a match or in training.

"Who are you riding, Guy?" I'd ask.

"It's Noble Wine. Lew played her in the fifth on Saturday. She wasn't stopping and turning to the left as fluidly as I would've liked," he explained. "Just doing some schooling before Grace gives her a bit of physiotherapy."

As I got older, I took an ever-increasing interest in the behind-the-scenes activities of the Rockwell Manor Polo Team. It was probably no coincidence that this was around the same time my father began stepping even further back.

Once when I was around seventeen years old, I sat down in front of him while he was reading his newspaper, wanting to go through all the daily activities around the stables. "Dad," I said a little louder than normal.

He lowered his newspaper to listen to what I had to say.

"Have you ever analysed all the things Guy does during the course of the day?" I asked him pointedly. "Do you know that he is up at about five o'clock, checking on the horses' early-morning preparation, feeding, et cetera? Then he begins the exercise routine on the sand track. After that he goes through the veterinary list with Grace, which, as you know, takes one to two hours every day. Sometimes the farrier is there. Then he moves on to schooling horses. He has amazing skills, especially with the young ones. And it doesn't stop. I think he has his first break at about two in the afternoon, *nine hours* after he started." I stopped rambling for a moment, before deciding to add, "He takes it easy for about two hours and then he's back again to begin the evening preparation." I looked up to see if I was making an impression.

My dad had listened intently to what I'd said, but his short answer surprised me. "Son, you must not lose Guy."

I was a little taken aback. Was this the first sign of him handing over the reins to me? An excited little tremor reverberated through my stomach. It was completely normal that I should continue the tradition and one day take over from my father, as he had done with his father-in-law before that. There would be a difference though. Under my stewardship, I would want Rockwell Manor Polo Team to compete at the very highest level and win, hopefully often.

Then moving on to something else, I had noticed how Guy interacted with our young female vet, Grace Brayers. She didn't work in our yard full time, but with our having such a big string, she spent a lot of time with us.

Nobody was complaining, especially Guy, because she was so good at what she did. He had recently given her the responsibility of our horse nutrition programme as well. What with top-grade rolled oats, bran, wheatgerm, full-fat soya, pine nuts, and sunflower seeds, there was no reason to go to the main house for breakfast. *If you're a horse, you can't do any better than ending up at Rockwell Manor,* I thought happily.

"You know, Dad, I wouldn't be surprised if Guy and Grace got married one day."

My father lowered his newspaper and said "Gosh, I have had the same thought! They'd make a good team." And then he got back to his *Financial Times* again.

Clearly, I wasn't the only one who had seen the spark.

I loved it when Guy sent the entire string of forty horses out for their morning exercise. Ten of his grooms, each riding a horse and leading three others, would do a strong trot around the perimeter of the polo field on the custom-built silica sand track, giving each horse a thorough workout on the heavy surface. This routine normally started at around six-thirty in the morning and lasted about twenty-five or thirty minutes, finishing off with the horses being hosed down—weather permitting. Guy would often ride a younger horse on the polo field, just inside this cavalry, conditioning the younger one for when she would begin exercising on the track with the others. At the same time, he would be keeping a beady eye on how each of the main string was responding to the exercise.

Doing well in the sport nearly always boiled down to horsepower, and having so many good horses was one of the reasons for our success in fourteen- to eighteen-goal-level tournaments, the sum of the four players' individual handicaps. This was just slightly below the twenty-two-goal level that we would need to compete in the Queen's Cup, one of my secret goals for the future. My father decided that when I achieved a four-goal handicap, we could start planning our entry into that most prestigious competition. I loved the thought of Rockwell Manor fielding a Queen's Cup or Gold Cup team and playing alongside an Argentinian ten-goaler, the top handicap.

I have said how important the polo horses were and how they contributed to our success; however, I should include a note about Argentina,

My Rude Awakening

Argentinian polo players and grooms, and the influence they have had on the modern game.

Polo's origins trace back to 600 BC to AD 100 in central Asia before migrating west to Persia (modern Iran). It was part sport, part war training and later used extensively to prepare army cavalries. Introduced into England in 1834, it only made its way to Argentina just before the 1900s and was played there exclusively by British aristocrats. It was only in 1921, with the formation of their association, that polo became available to Argentinians.

It is fair to say that the rest of the world—wherever polo was played—had a significant head start on the Argentinians. But now here's the rub, which will go some way towards explaining the dominance unparalleled in any other sport, that this country and its players have had on the game of polo. Today, if Argentina were to field six teams, each with four players of Argentinian origin only, the team that came last in that six-team event would beat a "rest-of-the-world-combined" team by such an appreciable margin that it would not be a game worth watching. The first thing one asks is, "Why?" That's both impossible to answer and very easy. It's everything. Firstly, the incredible Argentinian Criollo horses, in recent times crossed with thoroughbreds. Then take their never-ending flat grasslands, especially in the centrally located La Pampa, with rich, fertile soil and an ideal grass species that most often only needs to be mown and you have a polo field. The value of this should not be underestimated, considering each polo field is roughly five football pitches. This amounts to a polo industry probably as big as the rest of the world combined, resulting in an abundance of professional participation. Then add to that the athletic flair of Argentinian men—just think of soccer for a pointer—and it begins to make sense. The moment you have Argentinian influence in your team, you are *in the game*. Importing players from Argentina always gives a team an advantage. I can still hear my father saying excitedly, *"Son, I have found a brilliant young six-goal player, going on eight. I think we should get him."*

It was always a highlight playing against Highgrove Polo Team—the team of the then Prince Charles and very young Princes William and Harry. Not that it was ever a very competitive game. As much as they may have liked it to be played in the "normal" competitive manner, it never was.

Competing teams could not help but approach ride-offs more tenderly and generally give the Highgrove Polo Team the benefit of the doubt in the various phases of the game.

Speaking about the royals makes me think of a story I once overheard my father telling some friends.

He had gone to a luncheon and was listening to a conversation an American gentleman was having with someone sitting across the table from him, about the popularity of polo in England. Evidently, appalled at the costs involved, the visitor said in a pompous, facetious tone that it was clearly only a sport for "kings and clowns." Not wanting to let on that I knew what they were speaking about while he recounted the story, I feigned ignorance, keeping a deadpan face. My father was not going to just sit there quietly and take this indirect abuse, so he tapped the man on the shoulder and told him that he, in fact, played polo. Without any hesitation, the American turned to him and said, "Oh, what country are you the king of?" They both laughed raucously and ended up becoming good friends.

To some, polo's appeal is the exclusivity, the fancy showboating, the champagne, the bling, the fancy cars, the mystique of dashing professional polo players with foreign accents wearing tight white jeans. There is a strong scent of money around this "sport of kings," as it is among the most expensive to play, especially competitively, and it always seems to attract the attention of polo groupies.

It was different for our family. Having been involved in polo from its earliest days in England when it was primarily a military or farmer sport, we were not in polo for the glitz and the glamour. For a time, my father and especially my grandfather would look on in bemusement at where the modern game had gone with its newfound professional elements and, even more so, the trendy socialite tag that was now part of the game.

Whether it was Guards, Cowdray Park, Beaufort, or any of the other clubs around Berkshire, Surrey, and Gloucestershire, they were all familiar to me and I was comfortable at all of them.

I suppose it wasn't all perfect though, and there is a saying that explains some of the frustrations. It goes like this:

> Polo is a gentlemen's game played by hooligans, on the
> far side of the field, on a horse called Bloody Bitch.

Right or wrong, 'bloody' is a commonly used word in England, even for young adults. Not so for what was being described in this sentence.

"Bitch may be the correct name for a female dog, but it is very unfortunate that it is such an accepted word in the wrong way," my mother said. "That's more than just rude. It's so very disrespectful."

A word often heard around polo is *ridiculous*. Two conversations that had taken place over two consecutive weeks with my good polo-playing friend Malcolm Barwick (Malcs), the captain of the Balthazar polo team, will explain one of the reasons the word *ridiculous* fits so well.

"Good morning, Malcs. Are you up for tennis this morning?" I asked him.

"Absolutely, Charles. The usual, Wentworth tennis courts in an hour." Malcs knew they also played tennis at the famous golf club and that my mother was an honorary life member. "Perhaps afterwards we can have lunch in the clubhouse with whoever is able to join us," he said, making sure the logistics were clear.

"Perfect. I'll bring two tubes of balls," I added, not wanting us to forget anything. We were ready.

Then, the following week I asked him, "Is Balthazar up for a game of polo?"

"Absolutely, Charles," was his same reply. "When would you like to do it?"

In stark contrast to the ease and quickness of arranging the tennis match, we began planning our polo encounter.

"Well, it is a little short notice for tomorrow, so how about Sunday?" I replied, already thinking about the logistics.

"At Rockwell Manor, I assume?" Malcs asked.

"Of course," I affirmed.

"Since we are saving the £5,000 green fee, Balthazar will arrange the two umpires and goal judges and pick up their costs. I think it is about £2,500 for them," Malcs replied. "And I know your mum will do some great catering, to say nothing of your dad. He's always so generous with his champagne stocks. Yes, a good deal for Balthazar."

"So how many horses will you be bringing and what vehicles?" I asked, thinking about parking and paddock allocation.

"The normal. For the six chukkas, we will have eight or nine horses for each of our four players, plus two for one umpire we mount. You can mount the other umpire. So, let's say thirty-eight, maybe forty horses for us," Malcs replied.

"And they will all fit into your two pantechnicons?" I asked, needing to confirm these arrangements so I could advise our estate staff and they could make parking arrangements.

"Oh yes, and we will probably manage with six to eight grooms, but I will let our polo manager, Phillip Sergeant, worry about that. Oh, and, Charles, please don't forget our two drivers and co-drivers, just so your gate house has the numbers."

"Okay, got it," I replied, tallying up the head count. "I have fourteen Balthazar support staff, including your manager, and I guess you'll be bringing your vet?" That reminded me to ask Grace Brayers to make a note about the nutrition preparation for Guy, not that he was a forgetful manager but that I was being thorough. "Will you have a safety vehicle ahead?" I asked as an afterthought.

"Yes, I think so. I will let you know and confirm. Oh, and Charles, do you have rolled oats and chopped dry lucerne? It will save Phillip having to organise feed for the horses as well."

"Yes, no problem, and we have all the electrolytes and supplements to replenish them after the match. Maybe get Phillip to check with Guy. Ah, and don't forget your kit, Malcs," I said teasingly, because he once did exactly that and we hadn't let him live it down. "Remember, two helmets, two pairs of gloves, your boots, knee guards, probably twelve polo mallets, four each of fifty-one inch, fifty-two inch, and fifty-three inch, the three common sizes."

Anyone listening to these two friends arranging to play some sport together would concur that for this reason alone, polo was "ridiculous." Perhaps my dad's new American friend had a point about polo only being for "kings and clowns."

So yes, polo too was another family tradition, perhaps the most noteworthy along with business. Not only did this tradition continue unabated with my generation, but unquestionably the level and competitiveness of our involvement advanced considerably during my adulthood and under my stewardship. To say it played a leading role in many of my adventures would be an understatement.

CHAPTER 6
EIGHTEEN

MY OTHER OBSESSION was flying. I just had to fly, which was no surprise since my family had flown for generations. With my uncle and great-uncles having served in the Royal Air Force, there was always a sense of inevitability that I would develop an interest in aviation.

Thanks to my father's willingness to traipse me around the country, I never missed an air show. By the time I was fifteen or sixteen, I knew all the aircraft museums and could identify most fixed-wing aircraft and helicopters (or rotary-wing aircraft, as they were also known). Apart from accompanying me to the Farnborough Airshow in England, my parents took me to Le Bourget Airport for the Paris Air Show every alternate year. I really enjoyed this, even if it meant I would also have to take part in a few cultural activities.

"Right, Sunbeam, you can't have planes and helicopters every day. We are in one of the most exciting, artistically rich cities of Europe. Today we are going to take in the Louvre," my mother would say.

As much as I didn't like looking at paintings all day, I knew it was our agreement and so did not say a word. I remember on one occasion I saw an amazing exhibition of Leonardo da Vinci's works. I found his drawings of flying machines particularly astounding because even though he lived in the early 1500s, he seemed to understand rotary-flight aerodynamics.

When I was old enough, my parents would leave me at Le Bourget to consume the world of aviation whilst they went shopping on the Avenue des Champs-Élysées, sending a car to collect me from the prescribed place at the prescribed time. I would get back to the Four Seasons Hotel George

Cinq, having done a fair amount of shopping of my own, which included models of aeroplanes and helicopters that I couldn't wait to build once I got back home and add to the rest of my collection.

I started my private pilot licence (PPL) on a small aeroplane trainer when I was sixteen, having to wait until seventeen to get the licence, but it was helicopters that held a real fascination for me. I remember my first experience of flying in a Bell 47G as if it were yesterday. Mid-flight, the instructor allowed me to take the dual controls of cyclic, collective, and rudder pedals. I already had a good understanding of the flight controls, basic aerodynamic principles, and several technical aspects, and I was driven by an insatiable passion for these machines. I gingerly tried coordinating the opposing forces, a feature of helicopter piloting, and as I relaxed, my tentative approach gave way to my feeling like the aircraft was an extension of me. When I began to control the Bell 47 that day, I knew right then that I would not stop until I became a helicopter pilot.

Whilst I grew up in a family where there was wealth and success, as I progressed through my teenage years it became more and more important for me to find my own identity. Was that my reason for wanting to go into the RAF and become an attack helicopter combat pilot, where success came down to just one thing—one's performance? Very likely.

No amount of money can buy you a career in the RAF. You are judged purely on your ability, your courage, and your appetite for facing danger.

I loved my family and respected and admired the traditions and benefits of our privilege, but I was determined to make my own way in life. It was probably this that drove my ambition, that made me push myself harder than most people.

By the time I was sixteen I yearned for my first car, seeing it as the key to unsupervised independence. Anything would do. Give me a Volkswagen Beetle, anything, but it was still two years away.

Then, on my eighteenth birthday, my mother lectured me even before I knew what my gift was. "If you are not responsible and don't behave like an adult, we will take it back," she said.

With that, my parents gave me the most wonderful gift—a beetle, but not the Volkswagen variety. I was given my father's old Porsche 911 Carrera 4S, with its amazing race pedigree. Even if it was something my mother referred to as, "Dad's midlife crisis"—which my dad downplayed by saying his Bentley and Range Rover were far more to his liking—it was unquestionably the most exciting gift I had ever been given. It was midnight blue, which added to its understated look. It really was very low-key, but it performed like a true race car. With Porsche's newly introduced four-wheel-drive feature, it stuck to the road as if it were on railway tracks.

Looking at the instruments, I figured I had racked up more than half of the low mileage registering on the odometer. It had started with my dad teaching me to drive in it, pretending not to notice my mother scowling at my lessons being done in a Porsche. Thereafter, he allowed me to drive his car on the country back roads, without a licence, mind you. In fairness, it had always been way beyond my father's scope of driving ability.

Oh yes, and I did behave like an adult. An *eighteen*-year-old adult. It is safe to say that I loved driving…fast.

It is also safe to say that my mother hated me driving…fast.

My parents also gave me another very special gift that day, handmade Argentinian Fagliano polo boots made of horsehide. These boots were coveted by every polo player, and now I understood the foot and leg moulding my dad had put me through almost a year earlier.

Another amazing gift was a Breitling Navitimer watch from Aunt Edwina and Uncle Alexander Apsley, my mother's twin who was a pilot in the Royal Air Force during the Second World War. He had always been quite circumspect about telling me "war stories," but he did give me a feel for Air Force life that resonated with me. Because of this, from an early age I imagined that I'd one day go to the Air Force as well. My mother often spoke about her brother and the Air Force with an amount of reverence, which was probably why she ultimately agreed to me going into the RAF, albeit with some reservation. And for his part, Uncle Alexander loved the thought of my "continuing the family tradition" and becoming a pilot.

A Porsche, Faglianos, and a Breitling. What a birthday! Was that cool or what?

Sadly, I felt I fit into the "or what" category. If a girl looked at me, I would immediately blush and look away, sometimes peering over my shoulder to see who she might have been looking at, never believing it could've been me. A symptom of going to an all-boys school, I guess.

One morning, I had been at Royal Berkshire doing a little early-morning clay-pigeon shooting before I was to attend a polo practise at the Guards Polo grounds. Heading over to the club, I chose a route of endless twists and turns. I loved racing my Porsche through the narrow, winding country roads heavily shrubbed on both sides with thick, emerald-green vegetation, sometimes overhead too, which gave the impression of driving through a tunnel of hedges and trees. I had not quite gotten to the exciting part when, in my rearview mirror, I noticed the unmistakable sleek, angled lines of a rather gaudy lime-green Lamborghini Countach. I was driving along at some speed, a magnet to its macho driver, complete with his slicked-back hairstyle, muscles bulging from his tight T-shirt, and Barbie-doll lady friend alongside.

Not from these parts, I thought.

It was no surprise that, with a show of his car's impressive straight-line speed, he overtook me. I often attracted these would-be street racers who I typically ignored but not always. This was to be one of the latter occasions. As he drove by, his lady friend stuck her hand out the window and gave me a, "We are better than you, you silly little Porsche," wave. While his car was notably quicker than mine, that was in a straight line and you would be hard-pressed to find even 200 yards of straight line on the country roads of western Berkshire, especially for the next eight to ten miles. And I knew these roads like the back of my hand.

I came up behind him, making as if I were trying to overtake him when, in fact, I was just biding my time while getting his racing spirit going. We had not yet gotten to the really twisty, winding stretch I knew lay ahead. I grinned, thinking this could be fun. In less than a mile, there would be an ideal place for me to look across an open clearing to check for oncoming traffic. You wouldn't know a road was there unless you saw vehicle rooftops. If the coast was clear, then three bends beyond that, I could nip past him at the start of some treacherous twists and turns.

He was loving that I could seemingly not get past him, with his lady friend glancing over her shoulder as if to really make the point. As I came up alongside the opening, I looked across the field and saw no moving rooftops. *All clear. Brilliant,* I thought. We rounded the next two bends, and he lifted off the gas pedal, wary of oncoming traffic. I pressed hard, knowing it was unlikely, and passed him in a flash. *Too easy.* I didn't immediately draw away from him, making him think he had a chance of regaining his lead. I watched his lady friend egging him on, then tired of watching them, I started ripping through the corners, a tightening in my gut and adrenaline pumping through my veins. With the unmistakable sound of the Porsche flat-six engine singing in my ears and my four-wheel-drive traction responding to my demands, I drew away effortlessly and put more and more distance between us.

I couldn't help thinking about an article I'd read in a motoring magazine in which the journalist reviewed several high-end motor vehicles. What I enjoyed most about this particular reviewer was that he would close by including an all-encompassing throwaway line. I remembered for the Rolls-Royce Phantom, his closing remark was, "Get out of my way, little man," which did seem to describe the character of the vehicle, with its oversized front grille, and perhaps it was a reflection of the owner's character as well. *Probably the reason my father preferred Bentleys,* I thought idly. The funniest one though, was for none other than the Lamborghini Countach. Here, his closing sentence was, "Gentlemen of the adult entertainment industry, your car has arrived."

Touché. I chuckled.

Just outside Calcot, about fifteen miles up the road, I pulled into a petrol station. Once I had finished refuelling my car, I strolled into the quick stop store to get a bottle of water and pay my bill. As I was returning to my vehicle, who should arrive but the unmistakable garish green Lamborghini. I glanced at my watch and smiled, neither consciously intended nor missed by the occupants of the new arrival. As I sped off, I couldn't help very consciously jutting my hand out of the window and giving them a reciprocal wave.

It was no surprise that the moment I had completed my A-levels, I applied to join the RAF. Because I was not yet eighteen, I needed my parents' consent. My father did not hesitate, knowing it was my passion, and that little would stop me anyway. My mother knew this too, and even though the Soviet-Afghan and Iran-Iraq War was escalating conflict in the Middle East, making her very hesitant, she finally agreed.

In the intervening time before basic training started, I enrolled in university to start an undergraduate degree in economics, business science, and management information systems. Although normally an ambitious undertaking—simultaneously starting a bachelor's degree and an Air Force career—I felt confident about it. On all fronts, I would be learning about subjects I enjoyed and found interesting. In just under a month, I would be going to the RAF.

Having gotten my driving licence and going to the Air Force, I felt that I had now grown up. While this was clearly debatable, there was no question that my learning years lay ahead. The Air Force and university were clear indicators of that. What I didn't realise was that there would be a whole lot more education in store for me.

CHAPTER 7

RAF SHAWBURY

THERE WAS A long way to go before I would get to RAF Shawbury. First up was RAF Halton to begin my basic training shortly after I had turned eighteen. Looking back now, the first three months in the military were a blur. It was a tough fourteen weeks of rigorous emotional, mental, and physical stress, with the objective of making sure recruits had the mettle to "cut it" if ever they should end up fulfilling an operational role. For example, we would have to wait for permission to eat or go to the toilet and were woken at all hours of the morning, sleep deprived, and told to prepare for inspection in an hour. A lot of the chaps really struggled with this, but I took it all in my stride because I understood they were merely trying to test us. I thought of the part in "If—" where Rudyard Kipling says, *"And so hold on when there is nothing in you—Except the Will which says to them: 'Hold on!'"*

I would not let them break me.

One of the incidents I remember was on the parade ground, when I mistakenly referred to my rifle as my gun. The corporal taking us for drill instructions seized on this as an opportunity to make an example of me. With my rifle in my left hand, I was required to run around the entire parade ground shouting, "This is my rifle, this is my gun. This is for fighting, this is for fun," and each time I said "rifle" and "fighting," I would raise my rifle, and each time I said "gun" or "fun," I was required to grab my crotch. After thirty-odd minutes of this, I was finally allowed to rejoin the company and continue with the drills. Even though I was exhausted, a smile crept onto my face as I thought about how my friends would laugh

My Rude Awakening

when I told them. I just had to make sure the drill instructor did not see my smile.

Basics over, I went on to do several assessments at every level so I could be put in the running for an RAF pilot career. The entry requirements for pilot school were top A-level results, as well as a myriad of other assessments, including medical, and—most importantly, it seemed—a psychometric assessment. I'm not sure of the statistics, but what I do know is that very, very few candidates were selected. Once I jumped through every imaginable hoop the RAF could dream up, I was finally accepted into the programme.

My years at boarding school—the discipline, the need to be organised and often self-reliant and courageous—held me in good stead. I'd hated being away from home in those early years, always keeping a stiff upper lip. But everything had led up to my taking the Air Force challenges in my stride. Perhaps my biggest challenge was finding an obscure parking spot for my Porsche, not wanting my peers to be aware that it was mine now that I was able to start using my own car.

It is safe to say the RAF continued to develop my character, and later on in life it would be the foundation of my work ethic and determination.

I was enrolled into the officer's course at RAF College Cranwell in Lincolnshire to become a pilot officer, the lowest rank. Initially it seemed to be a continuation of basic training, but later it took a different direction. Referred to as Initial Officer Training (IOT), the course lasted about six months and was designed to develop our leadership and management skills. It included fitness development, military training, and academic study, as well as practical outdoor challenges. We learnt military field skills such as first aid, weapons handling, and protection against chemical weapons. We then went on to specialist training before we were streamed into fast jet, multiengine, or helicopter flight training. My time there flew by, and my nineteenth birthday passed without even a thought of celebration.

It was on the IOT course where I first met James Blackwood. As if singling me out, he walked across the room and extended his hand to greet me. "Hi, I'm Jamie Blackwood," he announced confidently.

"How do you do? Charles Featherstone. Nice to meet you," I replied with unintended inbred haughtiness, immediately kicking myself at my formal response.

Judging by his smile, it didn't go unnoticed. He was a slim, athletic chap, standing a little over six feet tall with a thick mop of black hair sweeping back from his temples; hazel-green eyes, under thick eyebrows; a sharp nose; a broad smile revealing large, straight white teeth behind cherry-red lips; and a cleft chin giving him a roguish grin. Tall, dark, and handsome, and he carried it well. He had an air of confidence, bravado even, in a most endearing way though. Unusually for me, I had felt an immediate connection to him and his natural charm and found myself hoping that we would both make it to 60 Squadron.

As it transpired, a few months later I did indeed receive the amazing news I would be going to 60 Squadron at RAF Shawbury for helicopter flight training. My dream had come true. I soaked up the feeling, barely containing the excitement that threatened to explode inside me. Much to my delight—not that I would say anything—Jamie Blackwood was going there too.

RAF Shawbury is a Royal Air Force Helicopter Flying School near the village of Shawbury, Shropshire, in the West Midlands of England. Founded in 1917, it provided helicopter crew training for the tri-services of the United Kingdom.

Along with the usual en-suite apartment accommodation for airmen, non-commissioned officers, and officers, RAF Shawbury boasted enviable sports facilities. This included a gym, sports pitches and courts, a sports hall, weights bay, cardiovascular fitness suite, two squash courts, three tennis courts, five-a-side indoor football pitch, grass pitches, indoor hockey pitch, and high ropes. There was even a highly rated golf club just six miles away, Hawkstone Park Golf Club. But it was looking over at the airfield and the lineup of different helicopters that captivated me most of all. I was in my element.

By the time we began our *ab initio* pilot training at RAF Shawbury, a solid friendship between Jamie Blackwood and me had begun to develop.

This was the start of a completely different phase of my Air Force career. I went into a programme where I would learn about flying, engines, airframes and instruments, aerodynamics, navigation, military air law, and a

My Rude Awakening

whole lot more. I'd thought my private pilot licence on fixed-wing aircraft would help me a little bit, but I was about to enter a vastly different realm. The very first meeting we went to confirmed this.

We shuffled into the presentation room, Jamie and I taking seats next to each other, and the senior officer walked in.

"Welcome to RAF Shawbury, gentlemen. I am Captain Gallagher. To start with, if any of you have previous flying experience or a PPL, raise your hands."

I hesitantly raised mine, one of three fellows to do so.

"Right. What you have learnt is of no consequence here. In fact, it may even be better if you forgot everything you have learnt. Make this a new beginning."

Far from this having disappointed me, I was thrilled at the thought that I would be learning new things. I was consumed and enthralled by it all.

Our helicopter training was initially on the Aérospatiale AS350, commonly known as a Squirrel, or in French, *Écureuil*. There was a clearly laid out syllabus for each day of the eighteen-month schedule, and the classroom programme was as demanding and relentless as anything we had done previously. Admittedly, the hours and hours spent in lectures did get me down a bit, but I knew we would eventually be flying "until you are sick of it," the lecturer had promised.

The flying was even more intense, with the trainees being expected to make noticeable progress every week or face ejection. We were required to advance at an astounding pace towards mastering our skills on these single-jet-turbine helicopters.

Flying a helicopter is a matter of coordinating three primary controls—the cyclic (or joystick), the collective, and the pedals. Straightforward enough. Before that though, you have to learn how to hover.

For the trainee pilot, hovering the helicopter is arguably the most difficult thing to master. Using all the controls to balance opposing forces is easier said than done. It feels a bit like trying to balance on a large ball whilst patting your head and rubbing your stomach. Much to my delight, I discovered there is a great similarity between flying a helicopter and, would you believe, riding a horse. A good horseman feels his steed in his seat and thereby becomes a part of his equine companion. Flying helicopters is about feel, and a lot of that feel is in the pilot's seat, feeling the movements and then controlling the forces with hands, feet, wrists, and even one's fingers, the helicopter becoming an extension of them. Mind you, I felt a lot of that in my seat behind the wheel of my cherished Porsche too. Seems I may have enjoyed doing things that had me "flying by the seat of my pants," you might say.

Whilst many of the trainee pilots took four or five lessons to conquer just this, I got the knack of it after my very first lesson. With my right arm resting lightly on my thigh, steadying my right hand as it caressed the cyclic control, my left hand on the collective, feeding in small power adjustments, my feet gently controlling the tail rotor, countering the torque effect, I smoothly and gently responded to her every move, as I accomplished the motionless dance against opposing forces, that was the hover.

As I completed the exercise, my instructor remarked, "Humph, we don't see that every day," which had me beaming.

As we progressed, so we began to do more and more complicated flight manoeuvres. Unquestionably, the single most exciting aspect for me was the autorotation—landing without an engine. I understood the mechanics perfectly, having gone over it countless times. There was nothing I had looked more forward to. After a thorough final briefing, we headed off to Ternhill Airfield to do the practical.

When it was my turn, the instructor and I climbed aboard the Squirrel and initiated a well-versed start-up. Then, when we had ascended to 1,500 feet AGL (above ground level), he cut the single engine of the helicopter. I wasted no time lowering the collective, removing all angle of attack on the rotor blades as we purposefully started dropping like a stone. As a result of our high rate of descent, the increased airflow through the rotor blades allowed me to maintain flyable rotor rpm. I had to be quick in establishing a glideslope and 60 knots of airspeed to give me some manoeuvrability to get to the area where I was to land.

"Good show," murmured my instructor.

With the ground fast approaching, I readied myself to flare the helicopter using the cyclic control before pulling the collective for maximum rotor angle of attack, thereby arresting my fall. I gently slid her on to complete my autorotation.

My Rude Awakening

"Just don't tell me this is the first time you have done that," said Captain Gallagher.

I was beaming again, but I didn't say a word. Autorotations became the exercise that I most enjoyed doing. After progressing through hovering, basic flying, and autorotations, we stepped it up with tail-rotor and hydraulic failure.

Finally, it was time for a decidedly big occasion in every pilot's life—we flew our first solo flights. This was followed by the customary Shawbury ceremony, which involved being unceremoniously dunked into the duck pond and, occasionally, smeared with duck droppings.

I remember phoning home, asking after Osric first and then excitedly telling my parents I had reached this important milestone. My mother, after congratulating me wholeheartedly, asked quite sheepishly if that was not what I had already done when I got my private pilot licence, and why so much fuss was made of a solo flight.

"Mum, flying a helicopter is an entirely different thing, and doing it on your own for the first time is a *big* achievement."

My mother went quiet on the other end of the line.

I wondered if she was feeling apprehension at the thought of her only son flying alone or contemplating the day I would move into a combat role, which was where all of this would hopefully end up. I thought it best to address her fears directly. "What is the matter, Mum?"

"No, nothing's the matter…but isn't that what you are meant to do? You know, fly it on your own?"

I had to smile. I had clearly misread that one. My mother, never one to over emote, thought I should best be getting on with the job at hand and focus on the end goal, not the little steps in between.

The next step was a big transition to the Bell Griffin HT1. Just the complex start-up procedures of this twin-engine helicopter let you know you were progressing. It turned out to be simple for me. I just reduced it to a logical pattern, only needing the long list of steps outlined on the start-up checklist for the first couple of days.

As my knowledge of the helicopter advanced, so my opinion of it increased. It was in many ways, battle ready. It made sense, considering the Huey, its predecessor, had a proud history as a combat helicopter.

The conversion went uneventfully and in no time at all, we were all certified to fly it. We knew this was just the first stage, as we would later be transferred to 60 Squadron (R) for advanced training, still on this twin-jet-engine machine. This would include weapons systems and tactical flying—all aspects we would need once we moved into active service.

We were always under extreme pressure because of the ongoing scrutiny, which resulted in a trainee pilot being dismissed every other week. There was nothing I dreaded more. To top it all, my ongoing university studies took up an appreciable number of hours every week. I was at times really under the whip. Somehow I managed to get through it all, albeit on a lot less sleep, something that would become a feature of my life.

On the subject of losing sleep, one evening while we were in the officers' mess, one of the orderlies handed me a small package. I would often receive letters but not packages, so I was naturally excited and curious to see what it contained. I resisted opening it until I got to my sleeping quarters but was barely through the door when I removed the brown wrapping. Inside was a curious-looking cube made up of numerous haphazardly coloured smaller cubes in red, green, blue, yellow, white, and orange.

My interest was immediately piqued as I read my father's note.

> Hello Son.
>
> I thought this would interest you.
>
> It's called a Rubik's Cube and was invented by a Hungarian professor of architecture who used it to help him teach algebraic group theory to his classes at university.
>
> What it calls for is to mix up all the colours by swivelling the planes around the central axis, and then to return it to a 'single colour per surface area'.
>
> You can see I've got the first part right without any difficulty. Ha ha. I've left the second part to you.
>
> Let me know when you have done it.
>
> Dad

My Rude Awakening

There were no instructions in the box with the Rubik's Cube, just a description that read something like, "Consists of twenty-six cubes that rotate on a central axis; nine coloured cube faces arranged in rows of three by three to form one side of the cube."

I was fascinated.

Fortunately, I had the foresight to complete a university assignment for submission the next morning before I did anything more with this little challenge. Forty-five minutes later, I was ready.

I looked at my bedside clock as I began. 9:02 p.m. I started by understanding the mechanics, twisting the small cube planes in the two possible directions. It took just moments for me to realise that getting a single colour on a surface could not be done sequentially, because as I began solving one dimension, it would undo what I had done elsewhere. I was engrossed. At a glance it looked like I had it half done, only to undo it again when I tried to progress. I had another look at the packaging, making sure there weren't any clues of how I should go about solving this three-dimensional puzzle. Nothing.

I had a sip of water and glanced at the clock. 10:22 p.m. An hour and twenty minutes, and I was nowhere. I wondered why I kept looking at the clock. I wasn't competing with anyone. Then I remembered—oh yes, I was. I never stopped competing with him. Me.

Going around in circles figuratively but also literally, I continued rotating these groups of little cubes around a mechanism in the centre of the block. *Wonder what it looks like.* No question, I would find out. *It may involve a hammer.* Another sip of water and a glance at the clock. 11:29 p.m. The only thing preventing frustration was that I was beginning to see a pattern. Yes, there *was* a pattern. And a formula.

My yelp of excitement in solving the Rubic's Cube happened at 12:12 a.m. I did the time calculation. *It will be a lot quicker next time* I thought as I began jumbling it all up. Big mistake.

I finished my second attempt at 1:26 a.m.

Done, and bedtime. But first, a quick note to my dad. Pity I can't attach a photograph. Actually, no problem. I went down to our study centre and photocopied the six sides in colour to include with my little note that said:

Thank you, Dad.

Amazing little challenge. First attempt—3 hours, 10 minutes. Second attempt—1 hour, 14 minutes. I will tick the box once I have figured out how to jumble it up the way you did.

Ha ha.

Charles

Knowing my dad would appreciate my little dig, I mentally ticked the box and happily went to sleep, something that would have been impossible had the box remained unticked.

Two days later I received a letter from my dad—thanks to the Royal Mail being amazingly efficient at times. His flowing longhand on the envelope was something I was very familiar with. The note read:

Hello Son.

Well done. Have a look at this little cutting.

Dad

He'd sent me a newspaper cutting about the Rubik's Cube. Apparently, it was set to take off around the world. The part that had me sitting bolt upright was that there were people doing it in under five minutes. The record was under two minutes. There was also a bit about how best to orient the cube and move the planes with something they called "triggers," which require using your wrists and fingers in a coordinated fashion (as you do on a helicopter's cyclic control) to quickly get through the moves and achieve these unbelievably quick times.

"Jamie, sorry, chum. I have some university work to attend to," I blurted as I hurried to my quarters that night.

So my excuse to Jamie wouldn't be a lie, I did twenty minutes of economics homework before taking the Rubik's Cube in hand.

At a little past midnight, I switched off the light, feeling a little disillusioned. I was still in double digits. Five days later I achieved six minutes and forty-six seconds and ticked the box, disregarding that I had been appreciably slower than the record. I had helicopters to fly.

As our flight training advanced, so the numbers of trainee pilots started stabilising, with fewer and fewer ejections as opposed to what we had seen in the early part of the course. I wondered whether a lot of potentially good pilots had been mistakenly dropped in those first weeks because of the immense stress. The more I thought about it though, the more I realised the approach was most likely by design and little had been left to chance. One of the most important things we would learn in the years to come was how crucial it would be to be able to operate under the most extreme pressure.

We soon realised that the RAF had seen enough skill in our group to continue investing in us. This led to a noticeably positive change in each of the fellows, and I felt we had finally got to the stage where we could start enjoying our time more and certainly with more confidence. As it transpired, those feelings were short lived.

We were introduced to the Grouping System. How it worked was that we would start with a grouping examination that would determine where we were placed on a ranking ladder, strongest to weakest. Not unlike a player ladder you would see at a tennis club. Then each time we completed an important aspect of the flight training course or did a ranking examination, the instructors would adjust the rating board. The top ten were Group A, the next ten Group B, and the remainder were Group C. We never got to see the actual ladder, but from time to time we were told which group we were in. In the early stages, it was an ever-changing table, the primary goal being to stay out of Group C as this was from where ejections from the course were made.

Up until the time we had been introduced to the grouping system, it was us against them, doing our best not to be ejected. The grouping system changed that and overnight we were now competing against each other. It wasn't a big thing initially, but in time we would learn the powers that be were quite happy to up the ante.

I loved RAF Shawbury for many reasons, but none more so than that I was finally flying helicopters. Overall, this training would last just under two years, during which time I would be commissioned as a flight lieutenant, something I had dreamt about since childhood. The only downside was that it was up to a four-hour journey to my home in Berkshire, which would make it nearly impossible for me to get home when I had a military pass for the night or even the weekend. As it transpired, this was not as big a negative as I had imagined.

Just over four months into our training at 60 Squadron, we had the first of five exciting days when we went onto the range and fired the 30mm Browning machine gun, or chain gun as it was also known. At the end of this weapons training introduction, one of the trainee pilots—William Granger, a really decent fellow—emerged as the top shot, setting himself up for becoming a Copilot-Gunner, or CPG, and earning the nickname Great-Shot Granger.

During this time, Jamie and I had become good friends and admitted to each other that we would prefer a Pilot-in-Command role over a Gunner role.

As it turned out, Jamie's home was around thirty minutes from the base, about five minutes outside Shrewsbury—the county town of Shropshire in the West Midlands of England. There he lived with his divorced mother and slightly older sister. It offered me a lovely place to go with Jamie for our nights and weekends off. A lovely place indeed.

CHAPTER 8
SHREWSBURY

I WILL NEVER FORGET the first time I went with Jamie for an overnight pass. He had asked his mother if he could bring a friend, and she had agreed. His sister would also be coming home from the University of Birmingham to see him. We were in Jamie's car, allowing me to take in the surroundings on the short trip to his home. The area around RAF Shawbury was very picturesque, and I'd heard that Shrewsbury was even more special.

As we left the base, dressed in our Number Two's, standard pass out attire consisting of Air Force blue trousers, light blue long-sleeved shirt, tie, and jumper, I began to feel a little pensive. In the Air Force there is very little way of telling the social standing and affluence of the various people you meet, and therefore, I had no idea what lay in store for me. I so wanted our burgeoning friendship to endure, but I knew it would be more difficult if we were from wildly different levels of affluency.

Enjoying the drive between Shawbury and his home in Shrewsbury, nestled amongst the rolling Shropshire hills and just a few miles from the Welsh border, Jamie began to give me a commentary of the surrounding area, which I enjoyed.

"On the left is Attingham Park," Jamie pointed out as we drove past a sprawling wooded area. "And I'm going to take you through the town, just for you to get a feel. We live about five or ten minutes southeast from the centre," Jamie advised.

"What is the population of Shrewsbury?" I asked, trying to get a feel of the town.

"There are around 62,000 Salopians, which is what we are called. You know, inhabitants of Shrewsbury."

Unusual, I thought, *that they should want to give themselves a name. Well, you get Londoners, New Yorkers, why not Salopians?* I had to smile.

As we approached a bridge, he said, "This is the Iron Bridge over the River Severn. It dates back to the late 1700s. The town centre is in the loop of this river." Jamie went on with a twinge of pride in his voice, "You will recognise Shrewsbury's Saxon roots. It has a largely undisturbed medieval street plan with over 600 listed buildings, some possibly going back to the eighth century. Shrewsbury is one of the oldest medieval towns in England."

While he was speaking, we passed rows of half-timbered Tudor homes. We rounded the next bend, and he pointed to a church. "That's St. Chad's Church."

I noted its distinctive round shape and high tower.

"It has a long history with Charles Darwin, who was born in Shrewsbury. This was where he was baptized in 1809. A statue of him stands outside the town library, which was once a school where he was educated," Jamie continued.

"This little town is amazing," I replied, genuinely impressed.

"And over there is St. Mary's Church, with its well-known stained-glass windows. If you really want to appreciate it though, you need to go inside and look out through them."

Unusually, I found myself wanting to do just that but instead made a mental note that I would do so at some time in the future.

Jamie was not finished there and as we drove a little further, he pointed to a red-bricked medieval structure on the hill. "And that is Shrewsbury Castle, where I must definitely take you. It houses the Shropshire Regimental Museum."

"Bloody hell, Jamie, that is amazing. And it looks really old." I enjoyed learning about the early days of England and the British Empire and appreciated his little guided tour.

"Yeah, AD 1067 old, and it has a whole bunch of military artefacts, old uniforms, and some really old weaponry. You will love it. But if you want to see even older, I can take you to see the Wroxeter ruins."

"I would really like that, Jamie," I said without hesitation.

My Rude Awakening

"Wroxeter is an amazing spot for Roman history. It was founded in around AD 55, and the excavated ruin was once one of the largest towns of Roman England, comparable to the size of Pompeii."

I was astonished at all of these 'early England' little gems and couldn't wait to explore the town and discover more about it..

As I watched Jamie, I couldn't help but think there was something so familiar about him. I just couldn't put my finger on it.

We drove a bit further, and I imagined we could only be a few minutes from his home. The mixture of period England attractions and the obvious affluence of the area now made me curious about where Jamie lived, the pensive thoughts having dissipated.

"So, you're about to meet my sister and mother, old chap. I hope you like them. I'm quite certain they will like you." With that, Jamie turned into a pillared entrance and announced, "We're here."

We navigated a two-hundred-yard meandering driveway, and as we rounded the last bend, I took in the typical Tudor-style home fronting a manicured lawn that rolled down to the bottom of the garden. It was a lovely home that suggested the Blackwoods were more than just comfortable.

What a relief, I thought, now feeling very guilty about my earlier concerns, or even having had them.

As Jamie opened the front door, I was met by a wide passage, a spacious drawing room over on the right-hand side. A mixture of antiques and contemporary furniture pieces. *Just like my mum. Auspicious,* I thought happily.

We wasted no time going inside and dropping our bags in Jamie's room. I followed him out to the back garden where we found the two women on the tennis court, finishing a game. I could not immediately make out which was his mother and which was his sister. All I saw were two extremely attractive, athletic women, clearly proficient tennis players, having a ding-dong rally and neither one immediately able to get the upper hand on the other. It turned out to be Mrs. Blackwood who eventually won the point with a grunted effort.

Seeing us, they walked over to where we were standing and greeted us warmly.

"Hi, I'm Georgina, and this is Charlotte," Mrs. Blackwood made the introductions, both ladies not hesitating to kiss me on both cheeks, making no excuse for being out of breath and quite sweaty.

I was taken aback by how warm and informal they were, something I was quite unused to but rather enjoyed.

I was surprised at how attractive Jamie's mother was, as she removed her cap and undid her ponytail, letting her dark blonde hair fall to her shoulders. She had Jamie's features, or more accurately he had her large hazel-green eyes, high cheekbones, an aquiline nose, and cherry lips. Had I tried to guess her age, she would have had Jamie when she was about twelve years old!

Charlotte was the proverbial "hot blonde with large blue eyes" who surely turned the heads of most men. With straight golden hair, the same cherry lips, and a peaches-and-cream complexion, she had a tall, athletic body. It was obvious where she got her looks from.

Most unusual for me, I blurted out, "You and Charlotte look like sisters!"

"Ooh, flattery will get you anything." Mrs. Blackwood chuckled. "Yes, I had my children young, just twenty-two when Charlotte was born."

I quickly calculated that Mrs. Blackwood was forty-three, though I could not believe she was that old.

"Come along, let's go to the house and have a fresh lemonade," she invited.

We sat down at the kitchen table with both mother and daughter being ever so friendly and demonstrative with me. I blushed and struggled to string sentences together, my awkwardness due to my rather sheltered upbringing. Going to an all-boys school and never having attended socials or dances—always being far more interested in playing sports, learning to fly, or just rough shooting with Osric—made me very shy around women.

"So, you are a polo player?" Mrs. Blackwood asked.

This was something that came up regularly after meeting anyone new, which immediately seemed to frame me as either having money or being a bit of a "player." Either way, I didn't like it.

"Charlotte and I both had our own horses right up until Charlotte went to university and we decided to sell them. Jamie used to do a lot of riding as well," she continued. "Has he mentioned it to you?"

I vaguely remembered Jamie having told me something about this and now welcomed the common ground I shared with he and his family as we continued chatting about what sort of riding they did and where.

"You don't have any sisters, Charles," Mrs. Blackwood stated rather than asked.

"No, I am an only child. I guess having me changed my parents' minds about having another," I replied in a feeble attempt at being humorous.

My mind was wandering. Did Charlotte have a boyfriend? *God, she was beautiful!*

I did later learn that real beauty is found beneath the skin, as the cliché went, but right then, I was face to face with someone who could surely qualify as one of those centrefolds. Looking at Charlotte and having these thoughts made me feel guilty and added to my bashfulness. I was certain she wouldn't have any interest in her younger brother's friend.

Jamie and I made ourselves comfortable in the drawing room while the ladies freshened up. "Let's open some wine and relax a bit. God, it's good to be home," he said, putting his feet up. "So now you've met Charlotte… and my mum. Not sure, but I don't think Charlotte is seeing anyone," he offered even though I hadn't asked.

I looked at him with the proverbial mouthful of teeth and said nothing. I didn't even know where to begin, I was so unused to dealing with matters of the opposite sex.

The ladies returned wearing loose-fitting summer dresses, open sandals, and tousled wet hair they were attempting to dry with hand towels. Jamie poured them each a glass of wine, and we settled in for a lively chat, something not normally easy for me in the company of people I had only just met. It was different with Jamie's mother and sister though. They were animated and demonstrative, and I felt at ease in their presence. Of course, they were anxious to catch up on all Jamie's news, having not seen much of him since he'd joined the RAF, and they also wanted to know about me and my home, which I played down. Jamie had no such sentiment. At the first opportunity, he enthusiastically told his mother and sister that Rockwell Manor was a polo estate, and I had invited him there so he could try polo.

"Ooh, that sounds like wonderful fun," Charlotte enthused. "I would love to come and watch a polo match sometime."

"Yes, yes!" I said, excited at the thought of Charlotte being there too, even though I was sensitive about her seeing my home too soon. I would have preferred her getting to know me first, before meeting my family and seeing our grand homestead. I had this notion about one day meeting *the* girl and wanted to be sure that she was with me for me and did not have her judgement clouded by the Featherstone trappings. Surely I wasn't already thinking, hoping, Charlotte could be *the* girl, or was this just hopefulness because of my insecurities and naivety? I dwelt on this possibility for a long time afterwards, not altogether sure how to reconcile my feelings but still wanting certainty.

We chatted about all the goings-on at the Air Force base, with Jamie touching on some of our training programme. Then Charlotte told us about her days at university. They reminisced about their childhood, Mrs. Blackwood enthusiastically providing context.

Through it all, I consumed every detail about these women: their looks, their mannerisms, every word spoken, their ex`pressions, their little chuckles and ripples of laughter, the scent of their perfume. I was riveted. Not that there was anything unusual about this evening. It was just that I was seldom, if ever, in such intimate company with ladies who weren't members of my family.

The longer we sat, the more enamoured I became with Charlotte. My mother often said everyone has beauty and it is just a matter of seeing where it resides in a person. She also reminded me of the adage, "Beauty is in the eye of the beholder." Charlotte was unquestionably beautiful, and on top of that, I could see she had "made an effort," as my mother would say. I looked at her, thinking how one day she would be as beautiful as her mother. They both had the same physical loveliness.

Once we finished our predinner drinks, Mrs. Blackwood summoned us to the annex dining area set in a bay window extension of the kitchen, in preference to the larger formal dining room. It was a pleasant, cosy little space with a table for four, and the aroma of their cooking had my stomach grumbling in anticipation. Looking forward to having dinner and sitting between Charlotte and Mrs. Blackwood, I first assisted the ladies with their chairs before taking up my own place.

"Ooh, Berkshire manners! I hope some of that rubs off on Jamie," quipped Mrs. Blackwood.

By this stage, there was a very relaxed and warm atmosphere, no doubt the predinner aperitifs having contributed to everyone's good mood. Sitting in such wonderful company, the occasional demonstrative hand on my arm, even the odd squeeze of my hand as either Charlotte or her mother expressively made a point during conversation, was all quite unfamiliar. I loved the Blackwood ladies' unreserved affections, and it was having a marked effect on me.

Mrs. Blackwood and her housekeeper, Suzie, had made an extra effort with our dinner for Jamie's first visit home. After our starter of pan-seared sea scallops with lemon and chive butter and a little wine, Charlotte turned on the hi-fi as she and her mum went back to the kitchen area. They busied themselves grilling some vegetables to accompany the roast Côte de Boeuf, Yorkshire pudding, and roast potatoes, evidently Jamie's favourite and the source of my stomach's growling. Then I heard the unmistakable voice of Bruce Springsteen singing "Cover Me."

"Cover Me" – Bruce Springsteen & the E Street Band

| YouTube | Spotify | Apple |

I watched as Charlotte and Mrs Blackwood spontaneously started dancing to the rhythm of this popular song. I had never previously paid attention to the lyrics, but it suddenly hit me. *Surely this is not about what our stallions do with mares.* Realising this rude song was unquestionably about just that, made me blush in embarrassment.

As they danced, they looked over to us, trying to entice us into joining them. They were no doubt oblivious of the effect they were having on me as their hand and body gestures became an element of their dance moves.

My stomach tightened at the thought of joining them, and I was mesmerised. But this was evidently normal behaviour in the Blackwood household. I was far too shy to do anything except laugh it off as if it were a joke, while Jamie rolled his eyes and ignored their suggestions completely.

This was so different to what I was used to at home. Mrs. Blackwood's trendy, relaxed way of dressing, her music choices, the way she spontaneously danced—her warm and demonstrative charm was simply amazing. Smiling, I wondered if Jamie sometimes thought he had two sisters, not a mother and a sister.

"Excuse their behaviour. They are just trying to compete with Goofy and doing a bloody good job of it," he said, teasing me in a haughty tone.

Goofy to Jamie but tantalising to me. *An example of one man's meat being another man's poison,* I thought wryly.

They finished grilling the vegetables and headed back to the table.

Then Jamie's mother asked me with a glint in her eye, "A penny for your thoughts, Charles."

I looked up in mild horror and chuckled nervously. "Uh, n-nothing, Mrs. B-Blackwood."

"Oh no, call me Georgina—or Gigi if you like—but not Mrs. Blackwood. That ship has sailed, or rather sunk," she said, referring light-heartedly to her failed marriage.

"Aah, umm, okay, thank you, Georgina," I replied shyly.

It was the distraction I needed to stop my mind from drifting into thoughts of Charlotte and bring me back to the present. I also felt quite awkward because in our circles it was unheard of that I should use the Christian name of one of my friend's parents, unless I knew them very well.

Our dinner continued, and with the occasional sip of wine and the enchanting company, I felt incredibly happy. Jamie's mother was the perfect hostess, and Charlotte was charming and attentive. As the evening drew on, I paid increasing attention to Charlotte. By the end of the dinner, I was feeling wonderfully comfortable and alive.

Unfortunately, we eventually had to excuse ourselves from the table, as we were already going to bed far later than we should have, considering the busy programme we had back at Shawbury the next day.

As I stood up, Charlotte put her hand on top of mine and asked, "Where did you leave your bag?"

"In Jamie's room."

"No need for that. Let me show you through to the guest suite."

Her mother nodded her head in agreement.

Even though I was more than happy to bunk with my friend, I appreciated this little bit of spoiling. I said good night to Georgina, waved good night to Jamie, and followed Charlotte as she led the way upstairs to the bedrooms. I was very aware of her every touch on my shoulder and arm, or her hand brushing against mine as she chatted about her and Jamie having grown up in the house, while we continued our way to collect my overnight bag and then on to the guest suite. The tightening of my stomach was palpable. My physical attraction to her was astonishing. I had never been so confused in all my life.

The guest suite was a lovely, spacious room with a king-size bed that had a fluffy goose-down duvet, extra-large pillows, padded headboard, and an ottoman at the foot to complete what were extremely comfortable sleeping arrangements that rivalled Rockwell Manor's. Quite the opposite of what I had become accustomed to in my officers' quarters at RAF Shawbury.

I decided to have a quick shower before going to bed. I was particularly aware of the corrugations of my six-pack as I looked in the mirror before stepping into the shower. While I soaped myself, I was conscious of my toned body. I had always been fit and strong from my very active lifestyle. With my burgeoning maturity, my muscular development was more pronounced than ever. I found it interesting that I was suddenly paying attention to my body. Perhaps I was trying to reassure myself, given my shyness around women. It hadn't mattered quite so much before, but something about Charlotte and how she made me feel was different than when I'd been around other girls my age before that night.

I finished showering, dried myself off, pulled on boxer shorts, jumped into bed and switched off the light, delighted to finally have a moment to reflect and relive some of the evening's activities. It had all been intoxicating, though not just from the wine and port. I thought again about Charlotte—the scent of her perfume, the feel of her touch on my arm or hand, her looking into my eyes as she spoke to me.

We were up early the next morning for our drive back to RAF Shawbury, and I was disappointed to discover that Charlotte had already left for university. Georgina more than made up for it though, giving us a wonderful breakfast and sending us on our way after planting kisses on our cheeks. *That was so warm and affectionate,* I thought, blushing and beaming at the same time. Jamie's mum really was "cool," as he would say, but that was an unusual reference for me. I felt warmth and acceptance, home away from home, and maybe a little unsure as to whether thinking about Charlotte quite so much would be okay with her mother.

Back at RAF Shawbury, the frenetic tempo of our training threatened to extinguish my memories of that wonderful first night in Shrewsbury. Amazingly, after a couple of months, a pattern emerged where we were going to Jamie's home every fortnight, even several weekends in a row, and this alternated the ardours of the RAF and the relaxed comfort of Jamie's home perfectly. What a contrast. What a relief. Jamie would let me know when he was getting an overnight or weekend pass, so I could do likewise and accompany him to Shrewsbury. I really appreciated the way he included me. I had a feeling Jamie and I would soon become the best of friends.

CHAPTER 9
OSRIC

THOUGH I WAS not able to visit home very often due to the distance from our base, there was one trip I will never forget. My mother had phoned me on a Wednesday evening and quite unusually almost insisted I come home for the weekend. She ended the call with a seemingly casual, "And Osric is missing you." I put the phone down, thinking my mother was just wanting to see me and included the Osric bit for some added enticement.

I looked at my diary. *Bloody hell.* I had two days left to submit a university paper on IBM marketing strategy analysis that had to be in by Friday. I also had at least an hour of RAF study on turbines and transmissions that was for tomorrow! Just as well I wasn't a big sleeper.

The next day I used the same emphatic approach my mother had used on me and requested a weekend pass from the officer on duty. As it turned out, the officer was Captain Gallagher, who had been pleased with my flying, which probably paved the way to him happily signing me off for the weekend.

Before I knew it, it was Friday afternoon. With more than just a twinge of excitement at the thought of going home I jumped into my pride and joy, my Porsche 911, and headed off. Three hours and twenty-one minutes later I stepped through our front door. Osric was the first to greet me.

"Osric! Osric! Aw! Come on, boy! There's a good boy."

He lumbered towards me grunting and whining, his rear wiggling with joy as I fondled his head and kissed his soft, wet snout.

"There's my good boy. Ooh, I've missed you." I chortled at his wet, eager licks to my face. "Helloo? Mum? Dad?"

Osric walked beside me as he always did, guiding me to the study.

"Sunbeam! Welcome home!"

My parents greeted me warmly while Osric, not wanting to be left out of the homecoming welcome, wagged his tail furiously.

That night, over an early dinner in our family dining room, my parents got onto the topic of the RAF, eager to hear how I was getting on.

"Tell us about Shawbury," my father insisted.

"Oh, Dad, I am just loving it. You can't believe how quickly we are progressing. I've already done some autorotations—you know, landing without the engine," I blurted, hardly taking a breath. "But first we had to learn how to hover, which funnily enough, I found quite easy. I basically got it right on the first day. And you will never believe what helped me."

"What, Sunbeam?" my mother chipped in.

"My polo. You have to feel these machines, just like riding a horse," I continued excitedly, not sure I was even making sense.

We carried on speaking for some time about the Air Force, my father interested in the aircraft and my schedule, my mother more interested in my accommodations, the food, and officers' quarters and how my studies were getting on.

Then my mother asked, "And what about your new friend…James, I think you said?"

Only then did I realise I had completely forgotten to tell them about meeting Gigi and Charlotte. "Yes, that's right, James Blackwood. Oh, Mum, how could I forget? I have now met his family, well his mother and sister, and they are so nice."

This was especially interesting to my mother, and she was thrilled to hear that I was able to use my passes to "enjoy some home comforts" as she put it. "Be sure to invite James to Rockwell Manor at the first opportunity," my mother instructed.

"That will be wonderful," I replied. "We have become such good friends."

Having caught up on all the news on both sides, we were ready for bed. As I went up to my room, I couldn't help noticing the effort it took for Osric to get up the stairs. He was getting old. Of course, there was no question where he would sleep.

"Come on, my boy. Up you get!" I helped him onto the bed, and he settled down in his usual spot at my feet. *He really has gotten old.* I shut the thought out as quickly as it had come.

The next morning's plan was a given, a rough shoot starting at one of our favourite spots, Crow's View. There were always pheasant in the thickets above the open ground where I would be at the ready. Once we were done there, we would go down to the brook. We loved this route. Was duck on the menu?

I packed a tasty snack of a few crackers, cheese, sliced ham, cherry tomatoes, fried Cumberland sausages, a peach, and water and placed it all neatly into my haversack. I fetched my Joseph Lang twelve-bore from the gun cabinet, perfect for a relaxed shoot.

"Osric, sausage? Sit! Good boy." And we were off.

Now behaving years younger, Osric bounded out of the door.

We walked almost two miles, around thirty minutes, and arrived at our favourite shooting spot. Osric knew the drill. While I took up my position in a wide, clear area, he went into the woods on the high ground above my position. He flushed a bevy of pheasant. Staying clear of the trees, they flew overhead in clear shot. That first flush yielded six birds, but I missed them all. *Goodness, I'm rusty.* I looked at my gun accusingly anyway.

A short while later, Osric perfectly flushed another parcel before emerging from the hedgerows and looking at me expectantly. This time I got one and he retrieved it and dropped it at my feet. *Perfect shot.*

Encouraged, I decided we would take a break and share a snack. I could see Osric was a little tired.

While we ate, I freely shared my thoughts and felt completely understood by my furry friend. Satiated, we set off again.

Osric headed back into the thicket and flushed four more birds. I missed with my first barrel, hit with the second. This time, Osric was slower to retrieve. Very slow. I tied a piece of twine around the pheasant's necks and hooked it through the loop on my belt. With our brace of pheasant secured, it was time to head down to the brook and try for a wood duck, one of my favourites.

After the creek, it was another forty-minute walk home and Osric had had enough.

I looked down at my faithful companion and asked, "Should we go home, my boy?"

The wag of his tail and the droop of his head said it all.

It was one of our shortest shooting days but in retrospect, the most rewarding. After a few minutes, noticing he was struggling, I picked him up. He licked my face a few times and I chuckled. I carried Osric that way for a while longer, with him snuggling into the crook of my neck. Carrying him was a first.

When I stopped and sat down to hydrate, he turned his nose away, not interested in sharing my water. I put him on my lap, his head resting in the bend of my arm, and stroked him gently.

After some time, he went limp in my arms.

My beautiful, faithful Osric had stopped breathing. His eyes were closed…peaceful.

For a long while, I continued stroking him, holding his head gently and trying to absorb what had happened, the welling of tears in my eyes beginning their gentle stream down my cheeks.

I had lost my best friend.

Eventually, with an aching heart, I organised my gun and haversack and picked him up again. Cradling him in my arms, tears blurring my vision, I trudged home.

I had already decided where his resting place would be and went straight to a spot in the garden that would be in clear view from my north-wing bedroom window.

I laid him down gently and set about burying him. I found a tall rock in an adjacent flower bed and used it as a temporary headstone.

I will get you a proper one later, my boy. I promise.

When I finally came inside, my mother was waiting for me.

"Oh, Sunbeam…Sunbeam…" was all she said and then she just hugged and held me, both of us sobbing gently.

"Thank you, Mum."

She had insisted I come home in the nick of time.

For the first time ever, my dad also hugged me. Hugging was just not our way.

Dinner was sombre. Our little family of three sat very quietly in our

My Rude Awakening

family dining room, Granddad's empty seat making our loss feel even greater.

There was no room for anyone else, not in any sense of the word. No one else could understand the grief we were all feeling. There wasn't anything to say. We had all lost a beloved family member.

After picking at my food, I went up to my room. I thought perhaps the best way to distract myself would be to study aspects of helicopter aerodynamics, critical conditions, and height-velocity ratios, also known as "dead man's curve." It didn't work. Every few minutes, I looked up from my desk towards the rock beneath which Osric lay. I couldn't concentrate. That night I tossed and turned, waking every hour or so, desperately hoping to feel his comforting presence at the bottom of my bed.

The next morning, I awakened to a cold, dreary day. Not so much because of the grey weather, but more because it was the first morning after one of the saddest days of my life. I went down to our oversized kitchen where the Aga stove was stoked and generating warmth, and Fabrizio, our Italian chef, had the pizza oven going, baking fresh bread rolls, bacon, sausages, and an egg frittata. Breakfast was especially good when done in a wood-fired oven, and he knew I loved it. Fabrizio was just doing his bit to make me feel better, and this wasn't lost on me.

"Thank you, Fabrizio," I said as I put an arm across his shoulders. Being Italian, he appreciated the physical gesture.

My mum and dad stepped into the kitchen, our favourite eating spot, so that we could all have breakfast together before I left for the Air Force base. I was sipping on a mug of cappuccino—no prizes for guessing who made it—as I watched Fabrizio reach into the oven with the pizza peel. My mother's words, *"It's not a shovel, Sunbeam,"* came to mind. He retrieved about ten crispy bread rolls, dusted them with flour, popped them into a breadbasket, covered them with a napkin, and brought them over to our rustic kitchen dining table. He pushed the French *beurre* towards us and just the thought of the butter melting into the warm bread roll had my stomach grumbling. There was already an assortment of possibilities to accompany the fresh bread rolls on the table, but I ignored them all.

"Prosciutto?" Fabrizio asked, trying to push his Italian wares.

"Nooo, Fabrizio," I said, frowning. "My normal, please," which was a few rashers of bacon and fried banana with maple syrup. A variation of an English butty roll. I looked up and saw his mischievous expression, realising he was gently teasing me. He then produced his wood-fired-oven breakfast of baked eggs and shredded potatoes, which we had all been smelling since we arrived in the kitchen.

I hated the idea that I was already feeling better. Life shouldn't carry on so close to normal after the horrendous day before.

We had our breakfast, making sure we spoke about anything other than shooting, hunting, the countryside, and the myriad other things that always involved Osric. It did not leave much to talk about, not even polo, because Osric loved that too. My mother held both my hands and, speaking very softly, tried to explain that this was all part of growing up.

God, I didn't like growing up right then.

"You are a man now, Sunbeam…a wonderful man."

I gave her a kiss, shook hands with my dad as he told me, "Take care, son," and then I headed back to RAF Shawbury.

More than ever, I needed the distraction. I understood that an aspect of my life had changed, and it was by far the most difficult. The radio offered no comfort at all as a song came over the airwaves that put Osric straight back on the centre stage of my mind.

"Fire and Rain" – James Taylor

YouTube	Spotify	Apple

Yesterday, Osric hadn't yet gone. I'd come home just in time.

My eyes welled up with tears as each line of the song bored into my soul.

I thought of Osric as a pup, a soft, spotted bundle of cuddles, ears, and thumping tail. Osric in his prime, bounding in the woods alongside me was a vivid picture, now just memories that I knew I would never forget. The thought of never seeing him again sent a tear down my cheeks. I had never considered that Osric wouldn't be around one day, and the sadness of my new reality felt almost unbearable.

"Sweet dreams and flying machines in pieces on the ground…" as the song went.

I had to get my chin up, so I wiped my cheek, blew my nose, and pulled myself together as I continued a very quiet, sad and lonely drive back to RAF Shawbury.

On the passenger seat was a flask and two aluminium-foil-wrapped parcels. It was the work of Fabrizio, and I knew the contents, which made it even more welcome. In around three hours and twenty minutes just before arriving at RAF Shawbury, I would enjoy a hot latte and two bread rolls with Camembert cheese and mixed-berry jam.

Osric would have had a bite of the bread roll and then looked for the bacon.

After a muddy, rough shoot, Osric cleans up good.

I didn't get Osric a headstone because no matter what I had inscribed on it, it wouldn't say enough. Deciding what I should do was simple. The artist did a fine job of transforming a photograph of two pheasant taking flight into a solid brass sculpture.

Well, I'd promised Osric a proper headstone, and now he was lying under a perfectly flushed brace of pheasant. How could he not be happy with that?

Two pheasant perfectly flushed.

CHAPTER 10
AIR FORCE LIFE

LOSING OSRIC WAS like losing a special friend. He had been my companion all through my childhood, and no longer having him seemed to shut the door on my youth and mark the day I became an adult, if not yet a man. My thoughts had to turn towards continuing my journey into adulthood.

It seemed just the other day that my dad was assisting me with the lengthy application process and then giving consent for me to go into the RAF. None of that now. More than having reached the age of consent, I was in my last teenage year. This transition also reflected in my efforts at RAF Shawbury as I became more determined than ever before to succeed. I *badly wanted* to become a "top pilot," not just "the best pilot I could be," as the less demanding narrative went.

Everything was different after that sad day. Okay, maybe not the driving. Driving at breakneck speed had always been a form of escapism for me and would probably always be.

Another change, perhaps because I was attracted to his quiet and sincere nature, was my making a friend of the other tall, dark, and handsome William (Will) Granger. Over six feet tall with a statuesque broad-shouldered frame, he was a big athletic man. Large, generous hands with well-trimmed nails. His thick black hair, piercing blue eyes, strong jaw, a Grecian nose, full lips, and slightly overlapping front teeth added plenty of character to his charming face. Will smiled easily, which caused his cheeks to dimple. Standing tall on muscular legs and with his "could get any girl" good looks, he was surprisingly reserved—quite the opposite to Jamie who flaunted his attractiveness. And when you looked at the pair of them, you would have sworn that the RAF had recruited for a talent contest. Jamie had an inch on me, and Will had an inch on Jamie. I once remarked that from behind, there was little to tell between them right down to their light olive skin tone. When they were in civvies, they were only distinguishable from each other because Jamie mostly wore white T-shirts while Will preferred navy. We all seemed to wear jeans and flip-flops when we were off duty. I was the odd one out. Blonde and not quite as tall. But while they may have been slightly taller than me, because of polo and riding spirited horses and hours of holding a polo mallet, my torso and upper body were more developed.

Will and Jamie—so similar on the outside, so different on the inside. I loved Will's very sanguine approach to life, truly refreshing. And whereas Jamie could be described as "the life of the party," Will was a lot more like me, preferring to be in the background. I enjoyed our quiet times together. Oh yes, there was another difference. Will was a one-woman man. Jamie wasn't.

I liked them both and ignored that Will was inclined to call me Charlie, which I hated.

Then there was Shrewsbury. Nothing could be compared to our excursions there and how it contrasted life at the air base in every way. The tantalising prospect of seeing Charlotte, and Georgina and Suzie, always making an effort with our delicious dinners, putting the predictable and mundane menu of the officers' mess to shame. One of my favourite meals, which reminded me of home, was the slow-cooked pheasant pie prepared during shooting season. Regardless of the menu, we'd always end with cheese and crackers, including baked Camembert in pastry, served with an assortment of preserves and accompanied by a vintage Madeira port. It was cosy and comfortable to sit with Jamie's family around their small dining table, though I made sure I was careful not to drink too much wine. The comfortable guest suite with its soft bedding engulfed me, and I was able to easily drift off to sleep. It was such a luxurious comfort compared to the rudimentary rooms and hard beds of the officers' quarters.

I loved the idea of seeing Charlotte and that, in time, I would win her over. But sadly, our visits to Shrewsbury often didn't coincide. Totally inexperienced at relationships, I was blinded by the illusion I'd created about her, enjoying my thoughts of "us" regardless of the reality.

Several months into our training, we received our first long weekend pass. Four nights instead of the usual two. My first thought was to take Jamie to my home, Rockwell Manor, something that I knew he was looking forward to. I understood it was not unusual for people to be interested in their friends' homes, especially if they were as unique as Rockwell Manor. So there was no real reason for me to be self-conscious. It also gave me the opportunity to reciprocate his family's hospitality towards me, something I was looking forward to doing. By then, broadly speaking, Jamie had a fair idea about my life, polo, shooting, my parents, and the like, even though I had avoided going into too much detail with him. My idea was to balance the few occasions I was able to take Jamie to my home against the regular visits to Shrewsbury by ensuring I crammed interesting and enjoyable activities into our time at Rockwell Manor, especially shooting and polo. He was quite an experienced horseman, and a capable one, and I was quite certain the polo bug would bite, as it often did with new entrants to the game.

"Jamie, are you up for spending the weekend in Berkshire?" I asked him after hearing the news about our pass.

"To your home? Rockwell Manor? Is the pope Catholic?" he asked, a typical quirky reply from Jamie.

A few days later, we stashed our weekend bags in the front of my Porsche and were on our way.

Jamie thought the drive to Berkshire was a good time to catch up on some of the details that I had avoided. Not inclined to do that, I told him a resounding, "Wait and see," preferring him to make up his own mind when we got there.

We carried on chatting amiably, enjoying each other's company, when Jamie asked in a mock-serious tone, "So are there any girls in Berkshire?"

Grinning broadly, I replied, "Who needs girls when you have polo and game-bird shooting?"

"Me." Jamie chuckled.

He was going to have a field day. There were always any number of girls at the polo club, often disparagingly referred to as "polo groupies."

"Don't worry, Jamie. I am sure you will be fine," I assured him.

God, he was incorrigible. I couldn't help laughing though. How were my parents going to deal with this *rude* friend of mine? I simply replied, "Jamie, we're about twenty minutes out. Start getting your bearings because this is our neck of the woods." And I meant our neck of the woods in the literal sense as we drove along the winding country roads of a densely forested Berkshire.

We turned into 1 Polo Drive and soon arrived at the two oversized gate pillars. The signage cut into a large sandstone slab indicated the estate roads to the Manor House, Polo Stables, and Staff Accommodations, which was two large houses, one for the equestrian staff and the other for the housekeeping and ground staff.

I had that old familiar feeling of self-consciousness as I ignored the intercom and touched the remote. The heavy black wrought-iron gates swung open, and we made our way to the homestead entrance. Jamie said nothing as we drove up the mile long tree-lined driveway towards the house with its own entrance and guardhouse. With a little acknowledgement to the guard I drove the final three hundred yards that ran parallel to the polo field, giving Jamie a clear view at the lush green expanse of grass and the undeniably large homestead. There was no getting away from it, fronted by sandstone pillars Rockwell Manor was an imposing stately home.

"Jeez, is this grand or what?" was Jamie's drawled response.

Both my parents were on hand to greet us warmly, my mother taking an instant liking to Jamie and what was coming across as his boyish charm, as opposed to the Jamie I was more familiar with. I was secretly pleased. It was important to me that my parents liked my friend. Jamie was given one of the guest suites in the north wing next to me, which became his room from there on out.

My objective for Jamie that first weekend was to get him started on polo and shooting, and much to my relief, he did both admirably. Nothing like his disastrous attempt at playing golf. Having the benefit of our own home polo field, he quickly got the knack of stick and ball. We were similarly able to get him started with clay-pigeon shooting, using the same clay-pigeon launch trap my grandfather had used with me. Very quickly Jamie got the idea of starting behind the flight of the disc, then advancing ahead to establish a lead, then firing so that he was shooting into the space where the clay pigeon was going, as opposed to where it had been. It was quite cumbersome trying to handle the trap and give Jamie instructions, so I made a mental note of organising a trap operator the next time we attempted this.

By the end of his first visit, two things stood out for me. The first, Jamie was unquestionably a ladies' man. The second, far from my mother thinking he was a "rude young man" and that she may have to influence him differently, both my parents thought Jamie was the most delightful, charming, respectful, wonderful house guest, and well done to me for making such a good friend. The superlatives bordered on my mother gushing about his virtues, something she never did.

By Jamie's third trip to Rockwell Manor, he was already into the swing of things. On polo days he enjoyed playing as much as he enjoyed all the glamorous goings-on. There was no doubt that his contribution to these weekends was his charisma, dashing good looks, and RAF pilot image, which drew a fair amount of attention. My lack of confidence when it came to females made me oblivious of the fact that I too evidently portrayed a similar profile, especially to the polo-groupie set. Jamie had no such insecurities.

As we got closer to the game-bird shooting season, I was eager to prepare Jamie for his first pheasant shoot. Once again, I decided to do this in an opening in the woods alongside Rockwell Manor, but this time I was not going to make the mistake of trying to handle the clay-pigeon trap while also trying to coach Jamie myself. I contacted a local shooting range, and they were happy to give me a couple of names of university students who could do the job.

"Jamie, to help me with the trap I have two contacts. Samuel McGinty or Kelly Peppard. I don't know either of them, so who do you prefer?"

"Kelly's the one," Jamie said without hesitation, as if he knew the girl.

That afternoon, an attractive brunette arrived to assist us.

I chuckled. *Trust Jamie.*

Kelly was lovely, with a pretty face, undoubtedly one of the reasons that after the shoot, he invited her to join us for a pub dinner.

"Ooh, I would love that!" she gushed.

"I hope you don't mind, Charles?" Jamie asked in a way that showed he was not really concerned whether I did or not.

I had to endure a shamelessly affectionate, excited girl hanging on Jamie's every word all evening. I had to admit that her striking good looks made it somewhat enjoyable. It was clear that *I* was the third wheel encroaching on *their* fun, so I happily bid them good night soon after our meal. "Jamie, well done today. I'm awfully tired, Squire! I am going to head off back to Rockwell. I hope you don't mind."

"Oh, okay, chum," Jamie said rather enthusiastically. "I will follow shortly. I also want an early night."

On one occasion Jamie had been confiding in me, admitting that he sometimes marvelled at how easily he attracted the attention of the opposite sex. He then said to me knowingly, "You're just a blond version of me, aren't you? But you just keep it all to yourself."

Little did he know. We may have had a similar look, a fair versus dark version of each other, but that was where it ended. Shy and introverted around females, I was the furthest thing from a ladies' man. Jamie and I could not have been more different. It made no difference—I liked him anyway. I guess you never really know what it is that draws you to another. A clear case of opposites attract, or was there something else?

It was when Jamie and I were driving back to RAF Shawbury that he voiced his views about us in the ladies' man department. In a forthright manner, he asked, "Charles, have you, you know, gone out with any of the girls at the polo club?"

I could literally see the cogs turning in his head, and when I did not immediately answer, he did so for me.

"So, you haven't." Then he continued, "I always thought you and I were similar when it came to girls, but now that I've gotten to know you better, I realise how different we are."

I said nothing, knowing he had more to say.

"You certainly have the looks and all the trappings…polo, Rockwell Manor, the lot. You could go out with any of them."

That was the last thing I wanted to hear.

"You are such a gentleman. Surely you aren't going to wait until marriage?"

My Rude Awakening

I was clearly far more circumspect than Jamie, but the gentleman and marriage parts were not what grabbed my attention. It was "having all the trappings" that really did it. Jamie had inadvertently touched on something that was most certainly a contributor to why I had never had a serious girlfriend. It was in the romance department too that I wanted to be wanted for who I was.

"So, if you and Charlotte get together, she will be your first girlfriend. How cool that would be." Jamie wasn't asking a question, so I didn't answer.

Imagine that, flicked across my mind.

With my self-consciousness about not having had a girlfriend at almost twenty, I gingerly broached the awkward subject with my parents, only to receive conflicting advice.

"Just wait until you meet the right girl, Sunbeam," was my mother's simple reassurance.

I could have guessed that would be her response. She was quite unconcerned that I had not yet had a girlfriend, as if it were the most normal thing.

My father had a different point of view. "I think around about now, you know, nineteen or twenty, is a respectable time for a young gentleman to have a few girlfriends," he had ventured.

I smiled at the thought of them comparing notes later, which they invariably would do. No doubt my dad would get a sharp pinch from my mother. She often teased that my father had been "quite the ladies' man" before they got married, and his response to me would have been consistent with his earlier behaviour, which probably irked her a bit.

One afternoon when I walked into the officers' rec room, Jamie handed me the phone and said, "Charles, my mum would like a word."

Giving him a surprised look, I hesitantly took the phone.

"Hello, Charles. I was just telling James that Charlotte will be home tomorrow night. I'm sure she'd love to see you, and it'll be lovely for us all to get together. Be sure to get a pass, all right?"

I was excited. It seemed Mrs. Blackwood—Gigi—was trying to advance things between Charlotte and me? *Fantastic!* To temper my enthusiasm, though, I would have to do some work on instrument navigation and

95

vectoring, but that was easy. It was economic theory, higher secondary, that would be the bugbear that night.

The next afternoon we jumped into my Porsche and headed off to Shrewsbury. We were five or ten minutes into the trip when Jamie turned to me and asked, "So, what do you think of Mum insisting we get together this evening with Charlotte?" It was the "with Charlotte" part of the question Jamie was interested in.

"Umm, not sure," I replied thoughtfully. "What do you think?"

Jamie didn't immediately give me his more carefully considered reply. "Mum may think you and Charlotte are a good match, but I'm not sure about it."

Even if his views were a little guarded, my stomach tightened at the thought. I was imagining things again. I wanted more information.

"What do you mean?" I pressed.

Then after a little more thought, he concluded, "To be honest, I wouldn't want it to change anything between us." He flicked a sideways glance at me.

I couldn't help thinking what my mother would say.

"Oh, so you're not always honest? And are we to assume that if you don't start your sentence with 'to be honest' or something along those lines, there is a good chance that you're not telling us the truth?" I had long stopped using phrases like that as my mother would not hesitate in pulling me up on it. But I also appreciated Jamie's openness about how he felt about our friendship. I was starting to see a different side to him, and I liked it.

We carried on chatting the rest of the way to his home, Jamie doing most of the talking. I learnt how his mother and father had drifted apart. "I think they stopped loving each other about six or seven years ago," he said. "And then when I was sixteen, they got divorced. Very civil and amicable. Charlotte and I have a good relationship with him, but in truth, he is preoccupied with his work, and since the divorce, he hasn't played a big part in our lives."

Upon our arrival Gigi gave us each a kiss on the cheek, saying, "So lovely that you both came. Charlotte should be here any minute."

We went inside to our respective rooms to quickly change into our normal casual attire—jeans, T-shirt, and flip-flops—and set down our overnight bags. No sooner had I done so than I heard Charlotte's car arriving. I quickly headed outside to greet her. She seemed to have a little more spring in her step, which delighted me no end that she'd be as happy to see me. I approached her, thinking about giving her a kiss on the cheek, until I caught a glimpse of a fellow coming around the corner.

"Hi, Charles, this is Alex, my boyfriend. I don't think you've met," came the bombshell.

"Er…h-h-hi!" I stammered. Alex was probably in his mid-twenties, and I felt very much his junior as he confidently put out his hand and shook mine.

"Hello, Charles. You must be Jamie's pal."

That was all it took to demolish months of endless fantasies. Thoughts of weekends to Rockwell Manor, introducing her to the Berkshire lifestyle, all evaporated in an instant. It was the first time I had felt downright glum at Shrewsbury.

Charlotte was doing everything she could for Jamie and me to engage with Alex, but it was the last thing I wanted, and evidently Jamie was not receptive to him either, judging by his lack of interest in Alex. At the same time, Charlotte was showing a very definite coolness towards me, making sure Alex didn't get the slightest idea of any possibility between the two of us, which I certainly wasn't enjoying.

"Wow, I never expected this," Jamie whispered to me while the others were engaged elsewhere. "Do you think Mum was just trying to give you a heads-up?"

As much as Jamie may have been concerned that Charlotte and me being together could affect our relationship, I was touched by his concern for me learning about Alex.

We squeezed around the little table in the annex dining area, Jamie on my right and Gigi on my left, which put Charlotte and Alex next to each other on the other side.

We started with salmon roulade, followed by a "bird in a bird," which was a deboned pheasant in a wild, deboned duck covered with a cranberry glaze. Gigi had specially ordered it from the Provenance Butcher in Chelsea, in London, along with a baked cheesecake. This was complemented with a French red wine from Bordeaux. We finished off with our usual cheese, crackers, and port. Once dinner was over, the evening seemed to come to a rapid close, everyone appearing to be lost in thought about the day ahead.

I walked into my room and immediately noticed a little parcel sitting on top of my pillow. On closer inspection, I discovered that Gigi had left me a treat from Charbonnel et Walker, the London chocolatier. Opening it, I discovered some lovely chocolates. That little gesture made it clear. I realised then that Gigi had orchestrated the pass out, wanting me to be aware Charlotte had a boyfriend before I got my hopes too high. I couldn't help but think that it was something my mother would have done.

Just before my twentieth birthday, Jamie and I took a weekend pass out and once again headed to Shrewsbury for what Gigi had decided would be my birthday dinner. Charlotte joined us for this celebration without Alex.

"Not sure *I've* ever received this treatment for *my* birthday," Jamie protested.

"Oh, nonsense! It's for all three of my favourite people," Gigi replied.

Jamie and Charlotte seemed happy with that. This interaction was interesting, showing just how accepted I had become into their family. And perhaps their mother felt that I might be the better suitor for Charlotte after all, or at least I thought hopefully that this could be true.

With no rushing back to base or university the next morning, we were all settling in for a fun, relaxed evening. I was assigned as cocktail waiter and given the task of mixing dry martinis, because that was evidently ideal for the meal that lay ahead. Drinks flowing and music playing, the ladies danced to the rhythm, and the mood immediately replicated what we had enjoyed so many times before.

The contrast in Charlotte's behaviour towards me could not have been more obvious. The coolness that I had experienced the last time we had been together was replaced by a warm, affectionate, fun girl that had me forgetting the previous occasion with her and Alex in an instant.

Who's Alex? I thought wryly. Her joviality warned me though, that she did not necessarily have any intentions for the two of us but was just making sure I didn't drift away. It worked. My dreams and fantasies about the two of us swamped back into my mind effortlessly.

With the four of us happy and relaxed, the martinis fuelling our feelings of euphoria, Gigi enthusiastically beckoned us to the candlelit table in her cosy annex dining area. "Come along, darlings! Dinner's ready."

The sumptuous seafood meal set before us was enticing. The starter was Kumamoto oysters on the half shell—with plenty of lemon, Tabasco sauce, and shallot mignonette with freshly ground black pepper—served on a bed of crushed ice on a large silver platter. This was followed by a platter of king crab legs, a selection of dipping sauces, and grilled giant tiger prawns.

Charlotte, helping me extract the flesh from the legs using a nutcracker and then dipping it in one of the sauces and every now and then feeding me, was a first. I was very aware of her hands and long fingers. *They are so beautiful.* Normally, I would've pulled back, or at least been self-conscious about what others may think, but not this time. It was as if I were in the room alone, enjoying this closeness, this intimacy. I felt lightheaded, my stomach in a knot.

As was often the case, we didn't have dessert but instead, Gigi brought a large cheeseboard to the table, with various crackers, cheeses, and preserves. This would be a perfect way to end the meal, washed down with her favourite Madeira port.

I watched as Jamie took a cheese biscuit, a swipe of butter, and a neatly cut segment of cheese that he placed squarely on the cracker, and then from its jar of thick, sweet syrup, he put a sizeable piece of fig preserve atop his creation. It was when he popped the entire delicacy into his mouth that it hit me. His cheese-and-cracker ritual may have been a coincidence, but the similarity between Jamie and my granddad was unmistakable.

Did this have something to do with why I felt so connected to him? Right then, I felt very close to not only Jamie but also my deceased granddad. Both tall, handsome men. Both with wicked senses of humour. It made me wonder if Granddad had also been a ladies' man. Why not? He wasn't even married. Then I wondered if my mother had seen any of her father in Jamie when they first met. It would have explained her instant liking for him.

CHAPTER 11
A NEW EXPERIENCE

ONE MAY HAVE thought the distraction of going to Shrewsbury would have a detrimental effect on my demanding flight training and studying towards an undergraduate degree. In fact, it had the opposite effect, except for a few overly long telephone conversations. What may have proven to be a distraction actually enhanced my calmness and concentration, two vital ingredients in dealing with the challenges at RAF Shawbury. Over the next few weeks, we began the most complicated part of our syllabus, yet I was flying with more confidence and competence than I'd ever experienced before.

"You are certainly on it, Lieutenant," complimented one of the instructors, words that had previously been used by Captain Swales.

It seemed there was consensus. Even the other trainees began to hold me in higher regard. That included Jamie, who on one occasion asked me quite pointedly, "What has happened to you, chum?"

"I dunno," was my lax reply, not wanting to get into that conversation.

A few days later, Jamie announced, "Get a pass out, Squire. Shrewsbury is on tonight."

My heart jumped and I immediately looked at my watch. 11:58. *Just five hours to go.*

Finally, it was five o'clock, and we were officially on pass. We jumped into my car and sped off. At five thirty-five, we drove through Jamie's gates. Charlotte arrived alone soon after us. In good spirits, she bounded into the drawing room, gave her brother a quick kiss on the cheek, and then hugged and kissed me… on the lips! For the entire evening, she was decidedly even friendlier and warmer towards me than before, casually touching my arm, squeezing my hand, and being far more animated when she spoke to me. This was a clear continuation from my birthday dinner, and I was lapping it up as I began responding more comfortably to her easy charm.

Just before dinner, Charlotte and Gigi gave Suzie a hand with the meal. Jamie was in the hallway on the phone, so I decided to see what the ladies were up to. Just as I got to the kitchen door, I heard Gigi say to Charlotte, "You have been awfully friendly towards Charles this evening. What's up?"

I couldn't help but notice the protective tone in Gigi's voice. Even though it was her daughter she was speaking to, I realised she was making sure that Charlotte was not misleading me. *My mum would do that*, I thought, feeling a special closeness to Gigi for caring like my own mother would do.

"I like Charles, always have. I think he is cute," came Charlotte's reply.

"Oh, and how does Alex feel about that?" was Gigi's sharp response.

"Oh no, of course he doesn't know," Charlotte said in a hushed tone. "Anyway, I think Alex and I have run our course, Mum."

"Hmm, and you don't think Charles is a bit young for you?" came Gigi's pointed reply. "He doesn't deserve any insincerity, darling."

"He may be a little young, but he is very mature. I may just have to teach him a thing or two," she said with a giggle. Then, seeing the serious expression on her mother's face, she added in a solemn voice, "Don't worry, Mum. I like Charles…a lot. I really do. I have got to know him, and I'm not being insincere."

I didn't want to be caught having overheard such a telling discussion, so I quickly turned around and headed back into the living area.

Charlotte's newfound interest in me continued unabated through dinner, having stepped up a gear as if telling her mother her intentions gave her licence to openly pursue me. Jamie seemed to be taking it all in his stride, which made me think he had known Charlotte and Alex were ending things.

I retired to bed, warm thoughts bouncing around my head. *Is something about to happen between Charlotte and me?*

The next morning, the ladies were preparing breakfast and, whilst Charlotte was finishing off the eggs, Gigi came through with plain yogurt, berries, pumpkin and chia seeds, and granola. Maple syrup as a sweetener.

As she leant over to place it on the table, she whispered, "I am pleased to see Charlotte and you getting on so well," followed by a little wink.

Once we had all eaten, everyone in good spirits, we gathered our overnight bags and headed for the door. There were kisses all around as we said our goodbyes. Again Charlotte kissed me on the lips, this time even more fondly, and my uplifted feelings had me reciprocating warmly.

As we sped off with Jamie having a go in my car, the only thing on my mind was how long it would be before we could return to Shrewsbury. I relaxed into my seat, wind blowing in my face as I looked out across the countryside, lost in my thoughts of the previous night and that morning.

The drive was noticeably quiet. I knew why I was not chatting, but I was not too sure about Jamie.

"All good, Jamie?" I asked.

Jamie did not reply immediately, as he was focussed on his new driving experience. "Yeah, absolutely. I never imagined these Porsches handled like this." A mile or two farther down the road, once he had started relaxing, he glanced at me and said, "I must admit, I am quite worried about selection this week."

That was the first time I had given any thought to what lay ahead for the day. It was our first grouping examination, a particularly important event as each trainee's all-round competency, theoretical knowledge and practical flying skills were tested. After this, our initial grouping would be determined. Getting into Group A was the minimum requirement for you to choose your streaming and later on, your squadron. Whilst it was not something the trainees would typically speak about, perhaps for fear of not getting into their desired wing, we had a good idea which squadron posting each of us wanted. Jamie and I knew exactly where we wanted to go. Thinking about that it dawned on me I didn't know what Will's preference was.

There were a few possibilities. Bottom of the list was general transportation. *Please God, no.* There were other equally unexciting noncombat roles such as dignitary transportation, troop carrying or medical evacuation. Medevac was not a bad posting, as you would still be in the fight but just on the outskirts.

We had attended several lectures about flying medevac helicopters and,

My Rude Awakening

because spinal cord and head injuries are all too common in polo, this was something that had grabbed my attention. My mother's voice crept into my mind. *"Don't ride like that. You will break your neck,"* and, *"Stop being such an adrenaline junkie."*

Appropriately termed "the Golden Hour," the first sixty minutes after a traumatic accident mostly determined the patient's outcome. What is required in these circumstances is to do everything possible to get the patient into hospital critical care treatment inside the Golden Hour, to counteract the far-reaching consequences of spinal cord or neurological injury, and especially brain swelling.

Flying medevac helicopters—especially the Chinook, also used for troop movement—with its huge twin-rotor blades, would always be an important and meaningful role with much appeal. But for Jamie and me, our minds were made up. We both wanted to be at the very sharp end of Joint Helicopter Command (JHC) postings, and that was none other than the Apache attack helicopter squadron.

In the past fortnight, it had become generally accepted that I would get the posting of my choice. Will Granger was also looking pretty good to choose his posting, but it wasn't all that certain for Jamie though.

"Don't worry, you will be fine," I assured him.

"All very well for you to say. We all know *you* will be fine," came Jamie's curt reply.

"I will help you if you like," I offered sincerely.

"Really? Will you?" enquired Jamie.

"No question, chum. Imagine, we may even end up in the same machine together, Pilot-in-Command and Copilot-Gunner," I said.

"Fantastic, let's shake on it."

My thoughts drifted off into wondering where we would end up. The Middle East was hot. If the Iran-Iraq War was not enough, Iraq was shaping up for military conflict involving oil with its neighbour, Kuwait. And if it involved oil, it somehow involved us—the USA, NATO, and British Forces. The writing also seemed to be on the wall with Afghanistan's becoming another military conflict zone. In fairness, it was a lot to try to understand, and we didn't spend much time thinking about it. All I understood was that we were needed in a combat zone, and I was up for the task. Correction: I *couldn't wait* for the task.

The mood in the car had changed noticeably. I wondered how much of my offering was because I wanted Jamie and me to be together well into the future, and how much of it was a way of ensuring that Charlotte and I would be together in the future. Was I just being selfish?

Then I thought about Jamie and me. Even though he could sometimes be crass and inappropriate—rude, as my mother would have said—we had become really good friends, and I was no less a gentleman for it.

CHAPTER 12
WINGS

NEVER MIND HOW quickly being twenty flew by, my twenty-first birthday was already a distant memory. This important milestone in civilian life was a nonexistent luxury in the middle of flight training in the Air Force. And the next seven or eight months at RAF Shawbury was no different. Soon our eighteen-month initial flight training course seemed to be over no sooner than it had begun.

True to my word, I spent a significant amount of time working with Jamie, coaching him on the practical aspects of flying and our classroom subjects, which was also excellent studying for me that unquestionably improved my flying too. The instructors had become fully aware that we were working together and realised that I was taking a lead role, but they didn't seem to mind.

Even though our programme was demanding and frenzied, we found time to go to Jamie's home at least every fortnight and sometimes several weekends in a row for what became a regular weekend pass.

On the weekends when we stayed at the base, Jamie, Will, and I would often go to the gym, play tennis, and generally keep ourselves busy with the many activities available. It was also the time that I used to catch up on my university work and go over the previous week's Air Force syllabus with Jamie. On one occasion, and I say *one* pointedly because I only ever took Jamie to Hawkstone Park Golf Club once. My mother's assertion that "anybody can hit a golf ball" was proven wrong. No matter how I tried, Jamie *could not* hit a golf ball. Luckily, Will Granger was a solid 12 handicap, having played regularly with his father, William Senior. As a result, he became my golfing partner. We would enjoy spending the best part of a day at the club, nine holes before lunch and then another nine in the afternoon. There was one other person as pleased as me that I had a regular golf partner, and it was Jamie. He was thankful being spared me trying to drum the game of golf into him.

I won't easily forget the first time I played against Will. We had started on the back nine, the term used for the second nine holes. As it transpired, the 10th hole at Hawkstone Park was their longest, a par 5 of over 500 yards. After a short warmup, Will invited, "Take it away, Charlie."

I stepped onto the tee box to start the game. I knew the 10th hole quite well and confidently took out my driver. Not a bad effort as I estimated my ball had gone quite a bit past the 310-yard mark. *Better that,* I subconsciously said to Will. I smiled at his setup routine, which in his case had him moving his feet as if looking for grip, while he wiggled his bum. He looked quite gangly as he unloaded his relaxed swing. I stopped smiling as I watched the flight of his ball before it landed where mine had come to rest. It would roll at least ten to twenty yards past my ball. My mother had told me that only 5 percent of men drove the ball more than 300 yards. I wondered what the statistic was for men who drove the ball over 330 yards! Well, I wasn't going to outdrive him, so my round would have to rely heavily on my short game. Thank goodness my mother was not Will's coach, or I would've been in trouble.

At the end of almost eighteen months of flight training, we finally reached the closing stage of our programme.

It was around this time that Jamie and I started talking about the two-week pass we would get after the wings and commissioning parade. He was intent on going to Rockwell Manor while I was looking for any reason in the world to spend some time in Shrewsbury, wanting to see Charlotte during this break. There seemed no way this would happen so I slowly resigned myself to the fact that we would be in Berkshire, at my home, because there was "so much more to do there," as Jamie had insisted. One consolation was that at least my parents would be pleased.

We had just one ground-school class and two practical flight sessions left to do before our final flight tests, and then it would be the Wings Parade and our Flight Lieutenant commissions. All the pilots were feeling quite confident about passing, but less certain about which group they would be in for the next phase, the advanced helicopter training programme. It didn't end there. Our intake was now down to eighteen pilots, and now only the top eight would be in Group A and likely get the posting of their choice. In Groups B and C, the choices became less interesting. There was still a lot of training ahead, during which time we expected to perpetually be moved up or down the ladder and hence the risk of losing one's place in the group. I reminded Jamie there was still plenty of time for him to cement his place in Group A, as he became increasingly nervous about where he would end up.

Both Jamie and I had no problem with the ground-school examination. The time we'd spent together, going through every aspect of every subject, had prepared us perfectly for the first part of the week, and we came out of the exam room giving each other high fives. The big one lay ahead though—next week's flight test.

Jamie and I were scheduled to do ours on the Tuesday. One advantage was that we'd have a chance to watch some of the other pilots and critique their flying, hopefully learning something from it. But I was also worried that the other pilots giving their feedback would make him more anxious about his own test.

Jamie's flight examination was going to be first, and then mine. I couldn't wait, feeling confident that I already had one leg inside an Apache attack helicopter.

To really get me in the mood, I turned on my Walkman and selected a song that always got my adrenaline going.

"Eye of the Tiger" – Survivor

YouTube   Spotify   Apple

I had never felt so good. *Combat missions, here I come.* Life was great. I just wanted to live while I was alive.

I watched Jamie's flight test intently. There were a few areas needing improvement. Once or twice, I saw his helicopter's tail swooping as a gust of wind caught him off guard. It was not the smoothest touchdown when he attempted to land without hydraulics, never an easy thing to do anyway. I would have liked to see a more positive flair, arresting his rapid rate of descent before he slid on after the autorotation. I smiled inwardly. What was I thinking? That I was his instructor or something? I had really taken the role of helping my friend with his flying to heart. It felt good. Overall, as far as I could tell, it was a good test.

Next, it was my turn, and it went more smoothly than I could have hoped. Captain Swales's words, "You have got a lot to look forward to Lieutenant," seemed to confirm it. And once again, I knew that having watched Jamie as closely as I had was very much to my advantage.

We both passed our examination and had finally qualified. I say *finally* not because of the time it had taken, which was less than two years, but because of the constant pressure and ongoing demands of the course and numerous flight tests. Now we'd suddenly reached the pinnacle of the mountain.

It took only a day or two for us to get comfortable with this new accomplishment and very soon we started seeing T-shirts and the like applauding our achievements. A couple of the inscriptions that tickled me were:

> I didn't say I was smarter than you.
>
> I said I was a "helicopter pilot."
>
> It's implied.

In reality, the attack-helicopters squadron was the most difficult RAF squadron to get into.

> 24 months ago, I couldn't even spell heliploctor pliot,
>
> now I are one.

My Rude Awakening

That one was more my style. Not that I had one, but it was certainly how a lot of the trainees felt.

There was certainly a lot of truth in this tongue-in-cheek plaque that Jamie put up in his room:

> The thing is, helicopters are different from airplanes. An airplane by its nature wants to fly and, if not interfered with too strongly by unusual events or a deliberately incompetent pilot, it will fly. A helicopter does not want to fly. It is maintained in the air by a variety of forces and controls working in opposition to each other, and if there is any disturbance in this delicate balance, the helicopter stops flying, immediately and disastrously. There is no such thing as a gliding helicopter. This is why a helicopter pilot is so different a being from an airplane pilot, and why in general airplane pilots are open, clear-eyed, buoyant extroverts, and helicopter pilots are brooders, introspective anticipators of trouble. They know if anything bad has not happened, it is about to.
>
> —Harry Reasoner

Dressed in our Number Ones, pretty much the same as our Number Twos—Air Force blue trousers, light blue long sleeve shirt, Air Force tie, with the addition of our tunic and cap—we all felt very smart and by all accounts looked it too.

It was a special multi-squadron occasion attended by most parents and family members. There was the customary flyover, followed by an aerial display. Then came the actual presentation of wings and officer's commissions to each of the now graduated pilots.

Jamie and I were very pleased with ourselves, having heard that morning that we were both confirmed in Group A. So had Will, which was what I had expected. My excitement was mostly about Jamie's rather than my own success, and our still being together…or was that Jamie, Charlotte, Gigi, and me still being together? He'd become like the brother I never had, and Gigi was something of a second mother to me, so different to my own mum. And, of course, Charlotte, even though there had been little opportunity for us to date. Having my "second family" while so far from home made all the difference to my Air Force career. The one thing I was clear about was that I had finally qualified in my RAF flying career, and that sat very comfortably with me.

The one thing that could be said at this stage was that I had finally qualified, not only in my RAF flying career but in life too—if that was what you called it when you had a girlfriend. It may have been just the beginning, but even though I was still very inexperienced, it sure felt like *life* to me.

With the ceremony having come to an end, everyone was milling around, trying to team up with family who had come to attend the event. Jamie and I were looking around, seeing where our parents were, and just as I was thinking it would be a difficult task finding them, we saw them, standing just several yards apart in the swilling crowd. Jamie made his way over to his mum and Charlotte, and I went over to my parents. After making our way to a quieter spot, we were finally able to formally introduce them to each other.

My parents were looking forward to meeting Gigi and Charlotte, and there was already a familiarity because of the times Jamie had been to Rockwell Manor.

"Oh, how wonderful. You must be Georgina, and you are surely Charlotte. I am Frances," my mother said as she took Gigi's arm and Charlotte's hand. "So lovely to finally meet you both. This is my husband, Arthur. Thank you for taking care of Charles on so many evening and weekend passes."

"Yes, thank you. We appreciate your kindness," my father chipped in.

"Frances, Arthur, lovely meeting you too, and thank you also for having James at your home. He thoroughly enjoys his time with you," said Gigi, reciprocating their greeting.

It was customary to give gifts to mark the occasion of pilots' receiving their wings, the most popular one seemed to be none other than the Breitling Navitimer watch, like the one I had received on my eighteenth birthday from my aunt and uncle. I also came to understand that sales of

My Rude Awakening

this Breitling model experienced an unusual surge after the release of the popular film *Top Gun* starring Tom Cruise. Was this because there were suddenly more Air Force pilots being trained? *Me thinks not.* Far more likely is that it became a fashionable accessory for wannabe pilots who likely didn't understand half the functions of this timepiece. This alone was almost a good enough reason for me to stop wearing mine.

To mark my wings occasion, my mother gave me a small cushion in RAF navy blue with white trimming and an inscription that said:

> You get old pilots,
>
> And you get bold pilots,
>
> But you don't get old, bold pilots.

That summed up my mother and her very controlled emotional disposition to a tee. She was far from starting a profusion of emotional narrative about me being her only son, about how I should be careful and look after myself or, perhaps, about how much she loved me. No, that was not my mother's way. It was not that she was devoid of deep emotions. Not at all, and quite the contrary. She was a very loving and caring mother who played an incredibly special role in my life. In her world though, it was not necessary to put one's feelings on public display. In her mind, it was far more practical and made better sense to give me some sage advice instead.

That cushion has been and remains an important part of my decor. It can always be found in my study, even to this day.

My father gave me his own gift, the latest ASA electronic flight computer, capable of calculating groundspeed, time, fuel and almost any aviation calculation one would need. They are essential to pilots, with nothing fashionable about them.

After a surprisingly good lunch in a marquee set up under the trees, where we had managed to seat the Blackwood and Featherstone families at the same table, it was time to say our goodbyes. I still had mixed feelings about the two-week pass that lay ahead before we were to report back for duty to begin our advanced helicopter training course. I had resigned myself to our going to Rockwell Manor to enjoy his new favourite pastimes, polo, and shooting. Undoubtedly, Jamie would also hope to have some of the polo-groupie "birds" succumb to him. I did need to spend some time at Rockwell Manor because we were playing in an important twenty-goal polo tournament, the Barrett Cup, but that hadn't stopped me from tentatively suggesting to Jamie we also spend a bit of time in Shrewsbury.

"You know, just for you to be fair to your mother and have some time with her and your sister," I'd suggested.

Jamie looked at me as if I had lost my mind. "What in God's name could we possibly do in Shrewsbury?" he asked, even though I was quite certain he knew full well what my reason was.

My forlorn expression because of me not being able to see Charlotte over the two-week pass as I had hoped was making no difference to Jamie. He had chosen not to register that Charlotte and I had become far more than just good friends, were at the start of a more serious relationship.

With a good measure of insistence, he'd said quite pointedly, "Don't go arranging anything now, Charles."

With him so set on spending these two weeks at Rockwell Manor and Berkshire, I gave up trying to convince him otherwise.

Everyone standing around getting ready to say goodbye had put a dampener on what should have been the most wonderful day.

Jamie was heading over to say farewell to his mum and sister before we were to make our way down to Berkshire. Right then, as I was thinking about going over to say my goodbyes to Charlotte and Gigi, I suddenly had a thought. *Charlotte and Gigi should come to Rockwell Manor!* My mother would be thrilled at reciprocating for all the time I had spent at the Blackwoods'. So would my dad. Jamie and I had been friends for around two years. I had been visiting the Blackwoods for around twenty months. Jamie had first visited Rockwell Manor about eighteen months ago. It was way overdue for the Blackwood family to come to my home after all the wonderful times I had enjoyed at theirs. While Jamie and I were playing polo or shooting, the ladies could do some exploring in the area. No doubt, my mother would try to rope our two female guests into all sorts of activities in and around Berkshire. My mind began to race. Nothing like a last-minute change of plan.

I turned to my mum and dad and, in a lowered tone, said, "Don't you think it would be a nice gesture for us to invite Jamie's sister and mum to join us at Rockwell Manor for this extended leave?"

My mother's face lit up. "That is a really wonderful suggestion, Sunbeam," she cooed. She clearly loved the idea, as she was not prone to cooing.

My father's grin confirmed he felt likewise.

"Mum, it'll be nice for you to extend the invitation?" Such was my mother's enthusiasm, I thought she should do the selling to Gigi, and I would just sidestep Jamie by making it look like it had all been my mother's doing, not that I thought he would mind.

"Of course, that is entirely appropriate," came her reply.

"There they are, over there," I pointed out. "Mum, don't take no for an answer."

My mother went over to where Charlotte and Gigi were standing. As expected, Gigi was no match for my mother's persistence or, as it turned out, for Charlotte's, who readily accepted the invitation on behalf of her mother and herself without any hesitation.

I smiled, now looking forward to having a wonderful time in Berkshire. My dad gave me a knowing smile, probably realising that Charlotte was my primary interest in inviting the Blackwoods to Rockwell Manor.

Jamie, oblivious of what was going on behind his back, stepped over to where we were standing and chatting, and I told him the good news. "Jamie, my mum has invited your mother and Charlotte to Rockwell Manor."

Jamie gave me a blank look, which made sense because I knew he wouldn't mind as long as we were going to Rockwell Manor.

This sudden change of plan delayed our departure and resulted in some animated chatting to Gigi and Charlotte. No doubt my mother would rope our two female guests into all sorts of activities in and around Berkshire. I wondered what else they were speaking about. Was my mother already assessing Charlotte's and my suitability for each other?

"And, son," my dad said, getting my attention, "don't forget you have a big match in the Barrett Cup semifinals." Then smiling broadly, he said. "Bloody hell, I forgot to tell you. We won our quarterfinal match and are playing against Cambiano."

"Wow, and I believe he's just been rated the best player in the world!" I replied, not able to conceal my excitement.

Jamie listened intently. The moment he heard the word *polo*, his ears always pricked.

My dad carried on, "Our new pro, Nic Aroldin, is fitting in so well. Incredible player, and he couldn't be more match ready. He played a brilliant game in the Coronation Cup and was a key member of the Argentinian team. I'm so pleased they lifted the Barrett Cup to twenty goals this year, out of my league now, but it allows us to contract players like Nic."

It was a pity my dad had started stepping back a bit, but it did pave the way for Rockwell Manor to compete at a higher level.

"I can't wait to meet him" Jamie said spontaneously.

"You will meet him soon Jamie, as my dad has invited him to come and stay." I updated Jamie.

"I think we will change that arrangement until after the Blackwoods have left Rockwell Manor." My mother interjected. "Let's first have a bit of family time," she added.

Does she already have ideals about us? I wondered.

We returned to discussing the logistics of Charlotte's and Gigi's visit to Rockwell Manor. They decided to spend the night in Shrewsbury and drive to Berkshire the following lunchtime.

With kisses on cheeks from Gigi, and me on the lips from Charlotte along with a little squeeze, we said goodbye to the Blackwood ladies and we went our separate ways. I wasn't sure if the look on my parents' faces was one of happiness or relief. Goodness, I had grown so close to this family.

I'd been so completely absorbed with my flight training and degree, it was as if without warning, I'd graduated from university and received my flying wings. A strange thought given that I had been doing nothing else for an appreciable amount of time. This officially meant I was now a helicopter pilot and would one day be suitably qualified to go into the commercial world with my economics, business science and management information systems degree. And I had a girlfriend. Looking back now, it's funny how that felt like my greatest accomplishment.

CHAPTER 13
ROCKWELL MANOR

I WAS ALREADY FEELING uncomfortable, and the Blackwood ladies hadn't even left Shrewsbury yet. I tried to imagine how my home would look through Charlotte's eyes and whether I would be judged for it.

Once they arrived at the home guardhouse, under the watchful eye of the gatekeeper, the heavy timber and wrought-iron motorised gate would slowly swing open. They would then pass a row of trees and a gravelled area for guest parking before arriving at the garage forecourt and six garages arranged in an L shape. These of course had been for horse drawn carriages when Rockwell Manor was built in the late 1800s.

The three facing garages housing my mum's and dad's Range Rovers and my beloved Porsche would invariably be left open. The other three garages were mostly left closed. Behind the first garage door would be my dad's Bentley, which he seldom drove unless he was going to London. Even then, Hamilton would most often do the driving because of the challenges of London parking.

Behind the next door was my mother's ivory-coloured Aston Martin Vantage convertible, with a tan canvas top and matching interior. It had been a gift from my father, and when she had thanked him for it, in the same breath she had added with a wink, "Is this because of you buying that ridiculous Porsche? You see, your little midlife crisis has cost you two cars."

My dad had replied that he had visions of his beloved Frances driving with the ragtop down, silk scarf blowing in the wind as she sped around Berkshire. Even I could have told him that was never going to happen, and it didn't.

I was very happy with his "ridiculous" purchase regardless of the reasons. Since my eighteenth birthday when it had been passed on to me, it had been my pride and joy.

In the last garage was a red, late-1950s Ferrari Dino my father had restored to concourse condition. *That* was his pride and joy, and he didn't let anyone drive it, a restriction that seemed to include himself since I had barely ever seen it out of the garage.

Out of view behind the vehicle forecourt was an extensive guest parking area for when we staged big events. Then looking as if it were an extension of the garages was another structure. No windows, just vents. People often thought it was an unusual place to have a storeroom and an awfully large one at that. It was only when they descended a steep stairway concealed behind a chest-high wall that they discovered a largely below ground squash court and gym. And there was indeed a sports-equipment storeroom for the myriad of activities that took place at Rockwell Manor. Rockwell Country Club was what some of my friends jokingly called our home. Hopefully Charlotte would be as lighthearted about it as they were.

On the side of the house was a staircase that led up to a separate entrance—the north wing. From there you would have a view of the tennis and beach volleyball courts, some of the horse paddocks, and a silica sand horse exercise track around the polo field. Friends would often bring a couple of their own horses, and because it was such an expansive area, we wouldn't realise anyone was out there until we actually saw them on the field.

On the other side of the house were two oversized patios, one on top of the other, overlooking the field. Mostly used for watching polo matches, the top patio was also a good vantage point to look down at one of my favourite landscaping features, a twenty-foot obelisk with a fourteen-foot triangular steel section that looked like a protractor. It always confused people until they noticed the twelve large sandstone tiles with Roman numerals I to XII and four giant steel balls of the enormous sundial that showed not only the time but also the seasons.

Alongside the downstairs viewing patio was a much smaller and comfortably decorated terrace, a favourite place for our breakfasts. Concealed behind stainless steel doors was an inbuilt barbecue with a rotisserie.

Glancing at it reminded me how much I missed the smell of a ribeye roast and potatoes now that I was in the Air Force.

It also had a very good view of the polo field and beyond that the large stable block. Immediately in front of it was a large all-weather, heated swimming pool with emerald-green tiles so that it blended in with the surrounding garden. My mother's attention to detail of course.

Off the family patio were the "outside rooms," as my mother called them. A changing room, including sauna, steam room and a massage cubicle. A little further along was the bar and game room and my granddads 120-year-old full-size, green-baize-covered slate billiard or snooker table.

I thought for a moment about a stuffed pheasant in a glass cabinet on the one side of the game room and winced.

"When it comes to matters of decoration, I think I should get the right of veto," my mother had suggested after my father and I had voted her out of having it removed. Right now, it was a ballot I was sorry we had won. I knew without doubt that Gigi and Charlotte would not have voted with my dad and me. Hopefully they would like the wooden propeller hanging above it that came off a First World War British biplane, a *Sopwith Camel*, even though they were art effects mostly interesting to men.

From the garage forecourt, the entrance to the house was beneath a Georgian-style portico, flanked by a large flower bed on the one side and a long sandstone drinking trough on the other. Drinking from the water gently lapping over the edge was a string of eight, life-size horse heads and necks magnificently sculptured out of sandstone. Because the Blackwood ladies loved horses, I was sure they would like our entrance.

Once they stepped through the imposing heavy double doors with the seldom-used brass door knocker, they would enter a cavernous triple volume entrance hall—the gateway to the rest of the house. The most notable feature was the imposing staircase sweeping around the right side of the room and up to the accommodations. I can say with confidence I'd never once walked up or down those stairs as an adolescent and seldom even as an adult. I took the stairs three or four at a time. In many ways, it described my character, especially as a young boy.

Looking out through full-height glass panes and double glass doors, opposite the front door was a long, rectangular pond of indigenous fish. My mother's voice saying, *"No koi fish here, please. We are not in Japan,"* came to mind. I smiled, knowing Gigi would agree with her. Looking down the length of the eight-foot-wide, forty-foot-long expanse of water, there was another statue of a horse, again just the neck and head. This one was an early sculpting by Nic Fiddian-Green in bronze, balancing on its nose on a heavy wooden plinth, the familiar pose adopted by this renowned British sculptor.

Underfoot was polished sandstone that swept through the 16,000-square-foot downstairs area of Rockwell Manor, but not the game room and bar area, that had teakwood flooring.

Looking up into the open space, they would see hanging at mid-height an ancient light fitting of some extravagant proportions that came from a late medieval castle, circa 1460. It was made of hand-forged wrought iron of three concentric circles. On top was the smallest ring with three evenly spaced bulbous globes, the middle ring had five globes and the largest circle at the bottom had eight of these sphere globes.

"Do you know what those circles stand for?" my grandfather had asked me when I was about eleven or twelve years old.

I'd never even imagined they stood for anything, let alone what they were for, so I had just shrugged my shoulders.

"They represent the spread of the English language, once we became civilised," he quipped. Then, more seriously, "From the top to the bottom, the first is the inner circle, then the outer circle, and the last is the expanding circle of our language. There must be something to it, though. Do you know that English is one of the youngest languages in the world but also the most widely spoken, when you take first and second languages into account?" my grandfather told me.

"The most widely spoken first language must be Chinese?" I had remarked. "Because of the population."

My granddad nodded, then continued. "So the size of the circles and the number of lights—squat candles in medieval times—weren't the designer's flair. It was all based on Leonardo Fibonacci's number sequences," he said.

"Who's he, Granddad?" I asked.

"He was an Italian mathematician during the Renaissance who deciphered the patterns or proportions of nature, which reminds me that we were once ruled by Rome." This time, he gave me a wry smile.

That immediately caught my attention. I loved mathematical patterns. I made a mental note to read about Fibonacci. Would I one day learn the proportions of life? *Incredible.*

The significant weight of this light was suspended by irregular-sized links of a thick chain that reached down from a large, rudimentary mechanism used to lower the ancient light fitting to a more manageable working height. Luckily, nowadays, one only had to occasionally change light globes instead of sixteen candles, something that would probably have been done daily back in medieval times.

Because of its history, my granddad and dad loved our "medieval chandelier," as my mother put it.

"Just lift it a bit, Arthur. It really is an eyesore," my mother could be heard saying from time to time.

They were both thrilled she allowed it to stay, and so was I as I loved it. Was it a male thing?

I wondered what Charlotte would think, secretly hoping she'd like it too.

An important doorway off the entrance hall was to the guest toilets. *"Water closet,"* I can still hear my mother correcting me. A friend had once teased that our *powder room,* with two other doorways leading to separate Fillies and Colts water closet areas, had clearly been decorated. It was complete with original, now antique, washbasins, brass water faucets, chaise lounges, wingback chairs, artworks, and even a latrine.

"To save us being reprimanded for not lifting the seat," my grandfather had once joked.

Also off the entrance hall was the formal drawing room, my mother's pride and joy. It was decorated in an unusually modern, eclectic style that combined large family heirlooms with a few carefully curated contemporary furnishings. "To add contrast, depth, and character to your home," the interior decorator had said. The walls were adorned with an array of what I understood were important art pieces. The only one that really appealed to me was a large painting with horses and hounds, by a well-known English artist, George Stubbs. *Just as well the Blackwoods like horses,* I thought wryly.

To the side of the entrance hall and fitting in with the medieval chandelier was an interesting heavy steel and timber door that opened to a dark, almost mysterious stairway. It descended to a large, contrastingly modern stainless steel and light beechwood finished wine cellar. It did have a long antique table and bench seats in the middle of the room though, for wine and cheese tastings. It was one of only a few parts of the house where my father had any jurisdiction.

From the entrance hall was a wide passageway that led past the expansive kitchen, the formal dining room with its large Victorian dining table and an alcove in one corner that accommodated my mother's favourite musical instrument, a Steinway grand piano. The passageway continued through the spacious informal living area with a significant wood-burning fireplace, complete with a carved sandstone architrave surround. This room had floor-to-ceiling-height glass doors that opened onto the garden at the front. Wide timber railway sleeper steps were set into the lawn, creating a terraced grass walkway.

At the end of the informal living room was the family dining room, a similar idea to Gigi's annex dining area. No prize for guessing which one I preferred. The wonderful intimate dinners I had experienced at the Blackwoods' home were among my favourite memories. Like Gigi's, the family dining room led off the kitchen, which bordered a large courtyard garden of carefully managed vegetables and herbs.

The informal or family dining area was a spacious room with a central circular table and a seating area with a burgundy velvet-covered sofa often used for predinner aperitifs when my parents were hosting formal dinners. Hamilton would be on hand to take care of our guests, making sure he had every possible accompaniment to make any cocktail. He would enthusiastically show off his bartending skills, but in fairness, he was really just a very proper English gentleman on the other side of middle-aged and was not about to be mistaken for Tom Cruise in the film *Cocktail*.

The upstairs of the house, where all the accommodations were, matched the footprint of the lower level. This comprised twelve bedrooms with en-suite bathrooms, a master study and several private lounge areas, which in modern times were TV rooms. These were set out in three distinct wings. The west wing was our family accommodation—two junior suites, one of which *had* been mine, and a grand master suite, which had been my grandfather's and now my parents'. The east wing, where Charlotte would be

My Rude Awakening

staying, comprised four en-suite bedrooms. These were for family and close friends. I wondered what my parents were thinking. *Are the Blackwoods family or friends?*

When Rockwell Manor was originally built, the north wing was for "other guests," as in *lesser*. Evidence of this distinction from the east and west wings was that they were accessed via the grand staircase off the entrance hall while the north wing had its own separate outside stairway and entrance. Things had changed since then though. In addition to my suite, there were four others for the players of visiting polo teams, each having en-suites with steam showers, and there was a very roomy living area with TVs, stereos, and the like. A clear upgrade from former times and now a very comfortable arrangement, one could say.

That was where Nic Aroldin would be coming to stay for the season, but only after the Blackwoods left, had been the recent change of arrangements.

We may have been a family of just three living in this very large manor house, but it didn't feel that way. To start with, we had a large complement of staff, and we regularly had two or three visitors, and sometimes up to half a dozen if there was a visiting polo team.

Having Charlotte at Rockwell Manor would bring about an array of new emotions. There was another worry though. I had told her very little about my life outside the RAF, and especially very little about Rockwell Manor. The reason was simple, stemming from my age-old insecurity about wanting to be wanted for me and not for Rockwell Manor and all that it represented. Jamie and I had got to know each other well before he had visited my home, and as a result he too had instinctively said very little to either his mum or his sister, and thankfully they had not seemed very interested. It was for this reason that I so loved the Blackwoods. All of them. They had taken me into their home and their hearts without knowing anything of my background.

But were things about to change? Our relationships had a sincere foundation, but even so, I was very still nervous that the overdue trip to Rockwell Manor would shake it somehow.

Having played it over in my mind, I arrived at the conclusion that the Blackwood ladies would no doubt be interested in where I lived but only out of normal curiosity. They already knew and cared about me for who I was, and I let that thought dispel my concerns of anything else.

CHAPTER 14

THE ARRIVAL

JAMIE AND I arrived in separate cars, and my mother was ready to greet us.

"Hi, Fran," Jamie said casually as he gave my mum a peck on the cheek.

"Jamie, you know where your room is," she told him in case he thought he may have been moved because of his mother and sister visiting.

I often reflected on how well my mother and Jamie got on, with him having once remarked to me that my mother was "super cool." This was an expression I felt was far more suited to his mum.

"I think your mum will appreciate the comfort and privacy of being in Winston Cottage," my mum suggested.

The cottage had recently been refurbished and tastefully decorated by my mother. There was a limestone-surround log fireplace in the cosy lounge area, a large L-shaped sofa, beautiful antique tables, an armoire, drinks and display cabinets, and a Persian rug, not to mention all the objets d'art and paintings she'd fittingly placed. The large bedroom housed a king-size four-poster bed made up with a goose-down duvet—or comforter, as it is commonly known in the USA—covered in Frette Italian linen, pillows, and sumptuous cashmere throws and cushions. It led into a spacious bathroom with a towelling-covered chaise longue; a bath, complete with water jets; and a large walk-in steam shower. Two rare instances of my mother allowing technology into her home.

My mother looked at me thoughtfully, and I could literally read her mind. She wanted to make sure our guests were comfortable. They were *special* guests in her mind, considering how well they had looked after me in Shrewsbury and, of course, because of the possibilities they saw for Charlotte and me.

After settling into his room, Jamie accompanied me to the barn to do evening stables.

Guy was already there and greeted us warmly with a broad grin. "You up for a bit of polo this week, Jamie?"

Noticeably excited, Jamie followed Guy through the stable as he pointed out the horses he had selected for him, highlighting some of their characteristics as he went along. Then Guy took me through my string, which was always pretty much the same group of ten horses, unless I had to substitute one or two because of injury.

"They look wonderful, Guy. We are all set for some good polo," I said, now really looking forward to playing in the Barrett Cup.

"Oh yes, and you haven't met Nic yet. Bloody hell, he's good," Guy remarked.

I would've loved to have heard more, but after an exhausting day, all we wanted was an early dinner and to head off to bed.

I got to my room, jumped into bed and, with excited thoughts of Charlotte's arrival the next day, I soon dropped off to sleep.

When I called her the next morning, it was Gigi who answered. "Charlotte is just packing the car. We will leave shortly after lunch, darling."

I loved how informal Gigi was. *She would be such a cool mother-in-law*, I thought, smiling.

"It should take you about three and a half hours, Gigi. Drive safely," I said, barely containing my excitement.

This gave Jamie and me the opportunity to have an early afternoon stick and ball session. We were soon mounted on two energetic steeds and gracefully traversing our perfectly manicured polo field. First, we set about getting our riding legs before going on to practising more complicated polo shots. Then, we slowly increased the tempo until we were close to match pace.

Having just driven the ball up field, I was at a strong gallop to catch up for another shot, when Jamie suddenly rode his horse across the front of me, his horse's hind legs coming dangerously close to my mare's outstretched front hooves.

"Jeez, Jamie," I shouted. "Careful."

The slightest touch could have easily brought both of us down, with bone-jarring, or even limb-breaking consequences for both horse and rider. We stopped our mounts before I continued, needing to remind him of the "right of way" rule.

"Jamie, you must remember, when a player is following the ball on its line of travel, you cannot cross this line if there's any chance of a collision."

I couldn't remember his response, such was my excitement and focus watching out for Charlotte and Gigi as I checked my watch for the hundredth time that morning.

"Your watch will wear out if you keep looking at it!" Jamie said as I calculated again when they would be arriving.

When I finally caught a glimpse of Gigi's car coming down the driveway, I galloped off to meet them. "Come on, Jamie! Your mum and Charlotte have arrived."

Jamie followed me across the field, and when we slowed down, he looked a little disappointed that our stick and ball session had been interrupted just because his family had arrived.

"Only right that I'm there to welcome them, Squire," I said defensively.

My mother had been pottering around the entrance lobby and was close at hand as Jamie and I arrived to greet the Blackwood ladies. I remembered too late that I had taken my T-shirt off and tucked it into the back of my pants. With my naked torso glistening under a thin sheen of sweat, I dismounted and led my horse up to Gigi's car.

They gave Jamie a quick kiss and then me, as he went to help with the luggage.

"What a beauty," Charlotte cooed as she rubbed my horse on the nose. "And the horse isn't too bad either," she quipped. "I hope you don't welcome all female guests to Rockwell Manor in such a state of undress."

My mother then approached, enthusiastically welcoming Gigi and Charlotte to our home. "Oh, isn't this just wonderful, having you be *our* guests for a change. Welcome, my dears." My mother kissed them warmly on the cheeks. "I'm sorry Arthur isn't here to meet you," she continued.

I slipped my T-shirt back on as my mum gave a few instructions.

"Jamie, be a dear and show Charlotte to her room in the east wing, next to yours. Sunbeam, you can show Gigi to Winston Cottage."

Jamie and I handed our horses to Pablo, one of our Argentinian grooms, and we helped the ladies with their bags.

Gigi followed as I led the way to the cottage carrying her large, wheeled bag on my shoulder. I wasn't even tempted to use Fabrizio's perfectly concealed catering-trolley path, even if it was ideal for Gigi's case. Not only because my mum preferred guests to use the scenic route, but I too had suddenly developed an appreciation for this picturesque pathway. I took her down the meandering trail of stepping stones and wooden railway sleepers, carefully arranged to make the hundred-yard walk among the big trees, dense green foliage, and various flower beds an enchanting experience. As we got closer, we reached the part that was lined with peonies in full bloom, as if they were welcoming her. I knew she would notice them, and I was surprised that I did too.

"And here we are," I said, reaching for the door handle. "My favourite place in the world…after Shrewsbury," I quickly added with a wink.

I briefly checked that Gigi had whatever she needed before running off to make sure Charlotte had also settled into her room, guessing she was probably ready to go downstairs. When I knocked, she opened the door whilst brushing out her long blonde hair, looking radiant and pretty in a flowing floral dress and leather thong sandals.

"Oh, Charles, Rockwell Manor is just fabulous. Jamie didn't tell me even the half of it," she gushed. "Just one thing though, can you show me how the steam shower works? Outrageous that I have my own steam shower."

I smiled, and even though she was acting more like one of the polo groupies, I shrugged it off as her just wanting to be nice about my home.

I pushed the solitary button in the spacious steam and shower room and turned the dial to 42 degrees Celsius. "Keep the door closed when you use it, otherwise you will steam out your entire room," I cautioned.

"Ooh, look at that steam! Dreamy. Any ideas who I could test it with?" she said with a giggle.

I didn't answer, as I didn't really think she was expecting one. I was mistaken.

"Well, don't leave me hanging. Are you going to test the shower with me or not?" she said mischievously.

"Come along, let me take you downstairs," I said, feeling a little awkward and not quite sure where this was coming from.

As we walked down the hallway and past the main dining room, Charlotte hesitated, wanting to stop every few steps to look at a painting, an ornament, or just the room. Having never been to Rockwell Manor before, it was not unreasonable for her to be taking in the different aspects with some wonderment. *Not now,* I thought. *You can do that with my mum.* As pleased as I was to have Charlotte at Rockwell Manor, I wasn't about to get roped into a guided tour. The extent of my showing anyone around Rockwell Manor started and ended with, "Through that door on the left is the guest cloak." Even from a young boy, I had reckoned that was one part of my home they needed to know about. But around the stables, I could spend ages enthusing about the horses.

We were at the end of the informal reception room and about to step into the family dining room when she hesitated again.

"Come along, now," I said. "If you want to look at anything, my mum can show you around after dinner."

When she gave me a disappointed look, I took her by the hand so she would not be sidetracked again, and that's how we arrived, hand in hand, to a mixture of responses. Jamie's face had a look of confusion as he took a gulp of his drink, probably thinking things had somehow progressed very quickly with Charlotte and me. There were no such looks from my parents, only ear-to-ear smiles and "our son has a girlfriend" expressions emblazoned across their faces.

I let go of Charlotte's hand, but it made no difference. My actions were merely the result of polite behaviour, not to be holding hands in company.

"Hello, Charlotte. Hello, Sunbeam," my mother cheerfully greeted us as if we hadn't seen each other earlier. She walked up to Charlotte, taking both her hands, and kissed her on both cheeks. "You look beautiful, darling."

My father, who actually had not yet seen Charlotte, greeted her especially warmly. "Hello, Charlotte, darling, so lovely to have you at Rockwell Manor with us," he enthused.

"Oh, Arthur, so lovely to be here," Charlotte replied, as she did not hesitate and kissed him on each cheek. Their behaviour was typical of people that had known each other for ages, not just one brief prior meeting.

Was this all playing out true to form? My father, the ever-charming gentleman, and Charlotte, the perfect future daughter-in-law?

My parents seemed in particularly good form, undoubtedly from what they had just witnessed. I could just imagine the bedroom talk later, enthusiastically speaking about Charlotte and me.

"Charlotte, darling, what would you like to drink?" my dad offered, affectionately putting his arm across her shoulder as he guided her towards the bar alcove. "Hamilton can suggest some of the Rockwell favourites, just to get you in the swing of things."

On that cue, Hamilton enthusiastically started making recommendations to Charlotte.

She turned to my dad and placed a hand on his arm. "What do you think I should have, Arthur?"

"Well, what about a pink gin or a gimlet—gin, lime juice, caster sugar, and lime zest, if I'm not mistaken?" he said, looking at Hamilton for confirmation.

"Not a good idea if you don't like lime," I said.

"Charlotte, dear, why don't you get Kir Royales for you and Charles? It's his favourite" I heard my father say. He really was playing the perfect father-in-law role—laying it on thick.

"Ooh yes, what a good idea, Arthur." Then Charlotte looked across at her brother and my mother sitting on the burgundy bay-window seating, and asked, "And, Fran, what about you and Jamie? Can Hamilton prepare something for you?" She was being the perfect daughter-in-law.

Luckily, what was becoming a rather uncomfortable situation was interrupted by Fabrizio's wanting to make sure he had everyone's dietary requirements.

Just then I heard the heavy brass knocker at the front door, not a familiar sound because ordinarily our guests would be announced by the gatekeeper via intercom way before their arrival at the house. I realised it was Gigi, as no one had yet shown her in. I immediately jumped up to go and greet her, embarrassed that I had not been more attentive. With a quickened stride, I dashed down the long foyer towards the entrance hall as I heard her opening the heavy door and stepping in.

She called out lightheartedly, "Helloooo, is anyone home?"

Arriving hurriedly, I greeted her with, "Hello, Gigi."

"Hello, Charles," she replied in a measured tone as she took in her surroundings. "I was worried I wouldn't find you." She gave me a wink as she stepped into the entrance hall.

We then walked past the formal dining room, and when I saw Gigi look up at the large crystal chandelier set over the Victorian dining-room table, I more quickly led her through the informal living area and towards the family dining room. Gigi wasn't missing much as she took in the wide-open passages, the various pieces of art, the wood panelling, the oversized fireplaces with carved sandstone surrounds, and the antique furniture. That was probably the first time I thought about them having been bought new in the late 1800s and now being over 100 years old. These were probably all the things Charlotte had been looking at just moments earlier.

I became very aware of the exceedingly formal Rockwell Manor decor, which made me miss Shrewsbury and its simpler, more casual, homely style even more.

Walking through the family room towards the family dining room, Gigi looked ahead at the double doors to the outside area. I wondered how she would react the next morning at breakfast when she discovered they opened to a view over the polo field towards the stables. She had probably only caught a glimpse of that when driving in.

I had a sense that Gigi was indeed judging me because of what she had experienced since arriving at Rockwell Manor this afternoon and now this evening. Would this influence her views about Charlotte and me? Would my home and my family once again be my nemesis, complicating the pathway to me having a relationship? *I better take this slowly,* was the thought that crept into my mind.

My parents, still sitting at the bay window of the family dining room with Jamie and Charlotte, got up as Gigi approached. My father also greeted her warmly, seeing her for the first time since she had arrived. *My dad likes the Blackwood ladies,* flicked through my mind.

She sat down next to my mother and immediately remarked, "Oh,

Fran, I just love Winston Cottage. I feel very spoiled." She continued with a hand on my mum's arm, "And the meandering pathway up to the house is so, so special. Those big, old trees, the dense foliage and flower beds, and the way you have lit it all up—it's just enchanting."

I loved all the natural affection between my parents and the Blackwoods, and I imagined a large part of their feelings were based on their hoping Gigi was the mother of their potential future daughter-in-law.

I couldn't help wondering if something could one day come of Charlotte and me. Was she in fact my destiny, or was I just hoping?

CHAPTER 15
THE FIRST SUPPER

MY MOTHER WAS soon ushering us into the main dining room, wanting to get dinner started. Rockwell Manor dinners could sometimes be quite drawn out, and she was mindful that Gigi and Charlotte were perhaps a little tired after the trip down to Berkshire.

It was my mother who took charge of all the dinner plans, including the seating and menu, leaving only the wine selection to my father. One of his favourite quips was that he was the head of Rockwell Manor, having received Frances's permission! Yes, the running of the Rockwell Manor household was entirely my mother's domain.

With just six for dinner, the eighteen-seat table had been reduced by removing two leaves, which then left a table that would typically seat twelve people. In addition to the chairs at each head, two chairs were evenly spaced on each side of the table's length. Outstretched arms would still be required to touch hands, but at least it fit better.

We were a traditional family, which was on full display at dinner.

My place was always at my father's right side, and Gigi, as the most senior guest, was at my father's left. My mother placed Charlotte next to me, certainly to encourage a chance of some intimacy between her and I without compromising English etiquette. Jamie was placed opposite his sister, between his mother and mine, sitting at the other head.

As Charlotte stepped forward, I was a little slow in withdrawing her chair so she could take her seat. My mother give me a stern glance, a visual rebuke. I could just hear her words, *"Manners maketh man, Sunbeam. Manners maketh man."* I hurriedly tried to make amends as I helped

Charlotte to be seated. A flash of white teeth told my parents she appreciated my gentlemanliness. I suspected it was more that she hadn't been treated like that at university.

My father seated Gigi and gave her a kiss on the hand, such a charmer. I was subconsciously taking it all in. *Why is it not as natural for me?*

I surveyed the scene around me and couldn't help noticing how beautifully dressed Charlotte, Gigi, and my mother were. Unusually, this made me feel self-conscious about having dressed in the first items of clothing I came across when I opened my wardrobe. I had grabbed some white polo jeans, slightly stained from my saddles, which I had over a dozen pairs of, a silk navy-blue shirt that at least had a collar and some tan slip-on shoes. I had rolled up my sleeves only to the middle of my forearms, since much higher than that was difficult because my arms were quite muscular from spending so much time holding either horse reins or a polo mallet. Not certain I had remembered to brush my hair, I quickly ran my fingers through the thick fringe.

My mother noticed what I was doing and teasingly turned to our guest and said, "Charlotte, you'll have to keep an eye on Charles and remind him to brush his hair."

Oh, goodness, this is getting worse by the minute! I thought.

"I think his messy hair looks sexy," Charlotte replied, smiling as she leant over and put her hand on the back of my head while she looked me up and down.

I heard the soft rumble of my dad's chuckle, but it was my mother's blushing embarrassment that distracted me. I couldn't help smiling. *Sexy* was not a common word around Rockwell Manor, and mothers, in general, probably didn't think of their sons being described in that way.

Once we were all seated, my dad gave me strict instructions to retrieve two bottles of 1975 Château La Mission Haut-Brion Rouge from his cellar, as he set aside the red wine choices Hamilton had put out. It was not lost on me that my father placed enough importance on this evening that I was to take wine out of his special reserve section in the cellar.

I placed the bottles on the drinks counter so Hamilton could decant the first bottle, allowing it to breathe. There was also a large ice-filled silver bucket with two bottles of Dom Pérignon champagne and two white-wine selections. This looked more like a formal gala banquet than an intimate first dinner with the Blackwoods.

Please take me to Shrewsbury, I thought.

And then there were the place settings. First, the silverware was always set for five courses, which meant there were no fewer than twelve utensils for each of us. Glassware next, we each had four: a water tumbler, a champagne flute, and white and red wine glasses. That was to start with. Cocktail glasses may be required, almost certainly liqueur and port glasses, and brandy balloons could come at the end, especially if there was occasion to bring out the cigar humidor. We also each had our own silver pepper grinder and crystal rock-salt pot, which my mother reminded me was either referred to as a *salt box, salt pig,* or *salt cellar.* It was just as well, because passing these around such a big table would have looked like a baton-passing relay. I was used to this and ordinarily would have thought nothing of it. Right then though, I was cringing. I had never had a formal dinner at the Blackwoods', and so I imagined they didn't care much for them.

And always flowers. There was a tall, elegant centrepiece and then others that were under fourteen inches tall so as not to obstruct anyone's view of someone seated across from them. I used to watch in amusement as the staff took up various places around the table while they were setting up, struggling to find the perfect positions so as not to have any obstructing arrangements. My father also found it quite funny and often remarked teasingly, "Sorry, Fran darling, can't see you. The centrepiece will have to go!" even though said centrepiece stood high and proud so that you could look past the slender vase. Needless to say, the centrepiece always remained.

This evening's centrepiece was thirty or forty very long-stemmed red roses. I didn't think much of it, except that we usually had white lilies. Then Charlotte remarked how beautiful and romantic they were as she leant across the table to take in the scent.

Oh, goodness, I hadn't even realised, I thought. *Red roses! Trust my mum not to miss a trick, I thought, smiling broadly.* And she knew me well enough not to have arranged a pianist.

As I surveyed what lay before me, I couldn't help noticing how quiet and reserved Gigi was, the wine having done nothing to lift her spirits. I was certain she was finding it all a bit overwhelming and couldn't stop my thoughts from becoming sarcastic. *Obviously, all this stuff is necessary for us to nourish ourselves.*

I couldn't blame my parents for our rather formal lifestyle. It was just how they had been brought up, and I guess it was now just continuing in that same way with me. Now having all the Blackwoods here with me, I couldn't help but feel the difference between sitting around the cosy table for four in their annex dining area and what I was looking at now. By now I was missing Shrewsbury more than ever. I would have enjoyed eating in our oversized kitchen, which we only ever did for breakfast and pizza evenings. In fact, among the polo-playing fraternity, pizza evenings at Rockwell Manor were legendary. I made a mental note that we should have one with the Blackwoods and avoid the formal dining room at all costs.

I desperately wanted the dinner to be a success, but realised it was a big ask for it to be comparable to our dinners in Shrewsbury! How could it even begin to compare? Just the formality of the evening, which was so blatantly evident, was the first flaw. I tried to get over my sensitivity and just hoped it would at least be an enjoyable meal. Fabrizio was a top chef, mind you.

Charlotte was as effervescent and happy as ever, even more demonstrative and animated than usual. At least she was thoroughly enjoying the evening and, undoubtedly, also the keen interest my parents were taking in her.

As dinner ensued, Hamilton adopted his usual management position over the "out of kitchen" staff, servers, and so on. I loved how he had assumed the kingpin "elder statesman" role amongst Rockwell Manor staff. It was as though, since he had once worn my grandfather's shoes, he now had the right to *be in his shoes*. This had not suited the younger upstart chef, Fabrizio, who eventually got his own way as far as the kitchen being his domain. "Out of kitchen" staff had been something of a compromise between the two of them.

The staff wore formal, black-tie attire and served each person individually from silver platters or bowls. No platters or bowls were allowed to stay on the table, only out of sight in the kitchen, under the warmers. "Only flower arrangements on the table" was what my mother felt was appropriate, but bread baskets emerged when Fabrizio came and told us what he had prepared for our dinner. My mother tried to make sure he did not get carried away using "flowery language," as she put it, when going through the menu. A chef or maître d' who felt the need to say he had drizzled something-or-other over one-thing-or-another would exasperate her. I found it amusing, watching my mother's expression when Fabrizio would emote about the menu in his passionate Italian way.

Fabrizio came in and wasted no time going through our dinner courses. "*Buonasera, miei cari.*" My mother had given up trying to convince Fabrizio it was not entirely appropriate to be calling us and our guests, collectively, "my dears." In his Italian-accented English he continued, "Tonight, we have beautifully fresh-a asparagus spears, a delicate-a butter sauce, and parmigiano shavings. Or, if you prefer you could have-a *foie gras* with ginger *confit*, prepared for you on a thin sourdough cracker. Then, we have an entrée of baked figs with Halloumi, wonderful Italian prosciutto, and basil. Your salad this evening is a fresh *di rucola e pompelmo*, or as you say in English, e-rocket and grapefruit"—he shook his head and rolled his eyes—"peeled segments of *pompelmo*, not grape fruit, and it is served with a Greek yoghurt, *pompelmo*-juice dressing, and my special herbs."

I couldn't help smiling at his exasperation, so I asked, "Fabrizio, is there something you want to explain to us about this *pompelmo* salad?"

With a lot of hand gesticulations, he began, "There are no grapes in the salad. In Italy, we take this grapes, which is a fruit, grape fruit, and we make wine. In England, you ask for grapefruit, you get *pompelmo*. Santo Cielo, *salvami dagli Inglesi*." Fabrizio enjoyed making fun of the idiosyncrasies of the English language.

"*Io sono con te*," Gigi said, smiling.

Fabrizio's head snapped around in her direction, and he just beamed at her. "*Parla italiana, signora?*" he asked.

"*Solo un po,*" Gigi replied.

Fabrizio had a new best friend. He looked around to see if there were any questions, and when there weren't, he carried on. "For your main course, we have two options. Jamie's favourite, Côte de Boeuf with roast potatoes and caramelised shallots. No secrets in this house, Jamie," he said with a wink.

Jamie was definitely a well-accepted member of our extended family, not only because he had been to Rockwell Manor on a number of occasions, but more because of how he gregariously engaged with everyone around him. Everybody loved him, especially my parents.

"For those who are less, ah, how do you say, ah, red-blooded than our pilots and polo players, we have a lightly pan-fried sea bass with lemon butter. The vegetables that will come around are Jersey Royal baby potatoes, broccoli stems, and creamed spinach."

"What about the caramelised shallots?" Charlotte wanted to know.

"*Bella ragazza*, haven't you realised that nothing *you* ask is too much trouble here at Rockwell Manor? Just look at *le belle rose rosse*," he said cheekily, leaning over and putting a hand under one of the deep red blooms as he looked at her.

Everyone chuckled at his perceptiveness, knowing my mother had selected the red roses for their love message aimed at Charlotte and me. And everyone chuckled. I just smiled.

Fabrizio noticed and smiled broadly too, knowing he'd put his finger on it. Mercifully, he carried on with the menu. "For dessert we have a chocolate fondant and double-cream vanilla gelato or exotic fruits with mango and lychee sorbet."

"Or both," Jamie interrupted.

Fabrizio shook his finger at him. "No, no, no. Only rucola salad and a leetle piece-a meat for you tonight, Jamie. Guy says you're getting too *grande* for the horses."

More chuckles in the room, especially since a more accurate description of Jamie would have been "athletic Greek god." I was thrilled to see things warming up.

He concluded with, "From the kitchen, you will finish off with a wonderful selection of cheeses, crackers, chutney, glazed kumquats, and fig preserve, which you should pair with French port wine."

I preferred Gigi's serving of Madeira port. I thought of mentioning it to my father, but then decided I would rather keep that in Shrewsbury.

Fabrizio ended with, "And I'm terribly sorry, but at Rockwell Manor, anybody needing balsamic glaze, vinegar, or olive oil will have to do their own dreezzzling."

I couldn't help giggling, and neither could my mum, even if she was having the mickey taken out of her.

"Chefs aren't allowed to use flowery language in this household," I said to Gigi in reply to her smiling but confused look. Thanks to Fabrizio, I saw she was starting to relax.

Just as he was about to leave, he referenced the breadbasket. He had no qualms in leaning over the table between my father and Gigi to pick one up. "*Mi scusi*, make sure to enjoy my bread rolls? They are freshly baked out of the pizza oven. Still warm, and just need a leetle butter, even if it is *Francese*."

I had to admit, looking at the bread rolls—the dusting of flour on the crust, and the thought of the butter melting as you spread it—had me looking forward to eating one. I loved Fabrizio's bread rolls.

On this occasion, I didn't think seven would be enough. I say this pointedly because I knew how many bread rolls were in that basket. Not because I had counted them, but because there were six people having dinner. English etiquette dictated there should always be just one bread roll more than the number of people at the dining table. When as a young boy I had asked my mother why, she had explained it was so that the last person to take a bread roll would not feel embarrassed about taking the last one. It didn't make sense to me because someone may have already taken two bread rolls. "No, Sunbeam. It would be impolite to eat two bread rolls at a prepared dinner. It would be ill-mannered to the chef to fill yourself up on bread when he has gone to such lengths to prepare a nice meal."

What a contrast between my first dinner with the Blackwoods in Shrewsbury and now, their first evening with the Featherstones. There would be no Charlotte and Gigi dancing, making me feel so comfortable and relaxed.

That gave me an idea. "Charlotte, would you mind helping me put on some music? We don't have the collection that you have in Shrewsbury, but I'm sure we can work something out," I said, smiling. "Plus, no one will ask me to switch it off if it's your selection."

Now everyone was smiling.

I was amused by how nonchalant my parents were acting about Charlotte's music selection until I realised it was nothing like what she normally listened to. Far more toned down but still far better than the background classical music playing over the entire downstairs sound system that I was used to.

The formal dinner that had me cringing earlier was turning into the most wonderful occasion as Eros Ramazzotti and Vaya Con Dios—replacing Richard Clayderman, Chopin, and Rachmaninoff—played in the background.

It could have been worse still, our own pianist. Everybody was chatting in vibrant fashion, the wine was flowing, and a few cocktails were being sampled.

Jamie decided he hated anything made with Guinness stout, the bitterness giving him an excuse to have both desserts. "Black velvet, my backside," he said, and my mother barely noticed as she carried on smiling. I knew I'd better not try it though.

And all seven bread rolls had been eaten. Jamie was the offender, having broken off pieces to dip into the melted baked brie cheese with nuts and glazed figs.

Watching him do this, I had an idea. In a hushed tone I asked Fabrizio to bring me a bottle of The King's Ginger and around of Camembert cheese.

The momentary flash of his teeth told me he knew exactly what little treat I was going to make, so I did not carry on with the list of ingredients. In no time, he was back with the squat black bottle of The King's Ginger liqueur, a platter carrying six sourdough crackers, a bowl of stem ginger pieces in sweet syrup, and the round of cheese.

I smiled up at Fabrizio as he leant down and whispered, "You are going to introduce your guests to your Nono?"

I was about eight years old when Fabrizio joined our household staff as our chef. He was thirty-five years old then, "unusually young," as my granddad had said. That would have put him at forty-eight by this time. In my mind, I was thinking about his retirement age and how sorry I would be when that day arrived.

I began setting out the crackers, immediately garnering Charlotte's attention.

"What are you making, Charles?" she asked.

"Help me. Please cut six pieces of Camembert cheese, about half an inch thick," I replied, thinking she could help me speed up the process.

This little production attracted everybody else's attention too. My parents knew what was coming next, but the Blackwoods didn't.

While Charlotte cut the cheese, I swiped a little French butter across the crackers before placing the Camembert segments on top. Then I said,

"Charlotte, please will you also cut six slices of ginger about the same size as the cheese but only half the thickness."

With the rounded back of the cheese knife, I pressed in the soft centre of each piece of cheese to make a basin. Then, just as I had done with my granddad, I filled each tiny basin with The King's Ginger. Steady as you like, I covered each piece of cheese with the ginger pieces.

I took one and led the way by placing it on my side plate. Charlotte did likewise before Fabrizio went around the table to serve each guest one of the creations. When everyone had theirs, I held up my cracker of cheese, ginger, and liqueur as if it were a glass.

Everyone replicated my actions, and my dad gave a pointer, saying, "Must eat it whole, folks."

I followed with, "To the gods of indulgence. Let's indulge. I miss you, Granddad."

Even though it was quite a mouthful, and I was very busy chewing away, I couldn't help the smile on my face at thinking of Granddad. It was for that reason I was caught totally off guard as Charlotte grabbed my cheeks with both her hands and gave me an exuberant kiss.

Gigi grinned at my shocked expression after Charlotte's spontaneous gesture. My parents loved it. And without admitting it, I loved it too.

Then, breaking tradition, etiquette flew out the window as Fabrizio brought the flambé trolley to the dining room and started making Crepes Suzette for everyone. My father joined in the preparation, having great fun "dreezzzling" Grand Marnier over the pan so that the flame climbed the trickle of alcohol up to the bottle. Fabrizio then made a show of placing them before each of us.

Unquestionably though, my highlight of the evening was when a track titled "What's a Woman" by Vaya Con Dios started playing.

"What's a Woman" – Vaya Con Dios

| YouTube | Spotify | Apple |

My Rude Awakening

As the mellow tubular sound of the saxophone wafted into the room, I watched in amazement as my father got up, threw his napkin onto his place setting, walked the length of the table to my mother, reached out his hand, and simply said, "Fran, dance with me."

My mum, even though she was looking slightly shocked and a little shy, didn't hesitate to take my father's hand.

Was this the start of dancing at Rockwell Manor?

Watching my parents as they began swaying back and forth to the methodical rhythm and eerie vocals of this lovely song was a beautiful sight, even though the lyrics didn't seem to relate to them. The opening line asks, "What's a woman when a man don't stand by her side, when he has secrets to hide and doesn't play by the rules? Will she be weak or have to be strong, struggle hard, or be made to feel like a fool?" *All wrong,* I thought, until I looked at my mother's face. The softness in her eyes, acknowledging my father for being the stalwart he was, secure in the knowledge he would always be by her side, no secrets to hide, always going by the rules. There would be no right turning to wrong there. That little moment showed me how big a part my father played in my mother's power.

With music and the soothing sound of conversation drifting through the Rockwell hallways, everyone still sipping after-dinner liqueurs and dessert wine, the evening slowly drew to a close. I was feeling a mixture of elation and contentment, not least because unexpectedly, it had been such a lovely evening.

After dinner and all the festivities, we were all more than ready for bed. I offered to walk Gigi to the cottage, hoping Charlotte would come for the walk. She did, and in jovial sarcasm said, "I'll come along to see where you are holed up, Mum," followed by a cute little giggle.

The three of us walked down to the cottage, and I waited patiently for Charlotte to ooh and aah over the place before escorting her back up the path, this time hand in hand. Just before reaching the floodlit area, Charlotte led me into the shadows and we kissed. It was my first truly romantic kiss that I didn't want to end. A most unforgettable moment.

We then continued back up to the hall leading to the east wing and her room. With my head still swirling, I headed to the north wing and my own room for some much-needed sleep.

CHAPTER 16
THE BARRETT CUP

THE NEXT DAY'S schedule had been finalised. Rockwell Manor Polo were playing against Balthazar in a semifinal match of the twenty-goal Barrett Cup, down to the last four of the top teams and players that had entered the tournament. Jamie was playing in his first mini tournament, a four-goal event over four chukkas. We were all invited to the Guards Polo Club for a dinner dance in the evening, after the match. After last night's kiss, the dance had taken on a whole new meaning. Gone were any reservations about whether Charlotte was with me, for me, or the concerns about how she would interpret Rockwell Manor and its 'stately country club' presence. I had liked Charlotte for a long time now, but it was as if last night's kiss had torn down a barrier and opened me up to the thrill of romantic nirvana.

Jamie and I were up early for breakfast, the next most important meal at Rockwell Manor. We finished our bowl of bran, berries, chia, and sunflower seeds and then headed out to Guards, less than a twenty-minute drive away.

As we walked out of the door, my father called out that he would follow shortly to watch our game, adding, "I will bring Charlotte and Georgina with me."

Once Jamie and I arrived at the polo field, it was full focus on the game ahead. Well, that's what was meant to happen. Being perfectly honest, my head was somewhere between where Charlotte was and what we'd be doing that evening. The thought bombarding my mind was, *Charlotte is now my girlfriend.*

Jamie still had a few minutes before the start of his match, so I took him to our gazebo, complete with our team's colours and emblem, standing

My Rude Awakening

at the end of the field. In addition, there were around a dozen fold-out chairs with Rockwell Manor Polo Team and insignia on the backrest and three tables had been set up with an assortment of snacks, water, energy drinks, and the like. This was where the players and their close connections would be stationed and invariably watch the entire game from. Then, about thirty yards farther back, behind this gazebo, were the full complement of our team's forty odd horses.

Jamie headed off, excited to be playing in his first tournament, even if it was only at the four-goal level. It was a modest start, but he had to begin somewhere.

The preparation was always the same. Horses were all properly tacked up with specialty saddles, bridles, and especially good leg protection, and their tails are tied up properly. A loose tail could obstruct one's shot. Next, players go about making sure their sticks, or polo mallets, are in good order. Ours were from Villamil, pronounced *Vije Mi-l,* from Argentina. One typically has at least ten in their bag, of generally three lengths—fifty-one, fifty-two, and fifty-three inches—catering for the different heights of the horses. The players need so many mallets because it is common to break a stick or two during play, considering they are made of just a wooden head and a cane shaft. Last, the players put on their knee guards, helmets, riding gloves, and sometimes, eye protection.

I had a quick warm-up, took my first chukka horse for a gentle canter and a little stick and ball, and I was ready for the start of our match at 1100 hours.

I had a quick look around for Charlotte but was disappointed that there was no sign of her yet.

Rockwell Manor was fielding a team that had been tried and tested in our mango strip, except for me, having been sidetracked by the Royal Air Force. We were very balanced. Our team captain was Llewellyn "Lew" Tomkinson, who was also the current English polo team captain when he was playing for his country. Our secret Argentinian weapon was Nicolas Aroldin, who was the proverbial seven-goal player going on nine-goals. He was playing for us for the first time and had already given a very good account of himself. And then came Guy Watkins, our polo manager, and a key player in our team. I was on a three-goal handicap—pushing four, people were saying—but perhaps they were just being flattering. There was no question that playing off a four-goal handicap, Guy was punching way above his weight. Hopefully today I would be able to match him, a tall order considering I had not been able to practise as often as I used to. I was secretly hoping that having Charlotte there would give me extra motivation. Rockwell Manor had gotten this far through using our reserve, George "Georgie" Graham, who had been playing exceptionally well. I was acutely aware of the pressure to not let the team down now that I was stepping in.

Our opposing team was good, with their own secret weapon, not that you could call an Argentinian ten-goal player a secret. Alberto "Beto" Cambiano was a consummate professional in his late twenties with mouth-watering skills. He would be playing in the number three position, generally where you would find the best player of the team. Think of him as the quarterback in American football. He was backed up by two solid players, an up-and-coming American teenager, Sebastian "Seb" Brentwood, on four goals and playing in the number two position. At number four, the six-goal Malcolm "Malcs" Barwick, who also played in the back position for England, always recognisable on the field because of his red helmet and square shoulders. And if you saw a ball sailing more than half the length of the field, chances were it came off Malcs's mallet.

The team's sponsor, Jerry Kapper, was a zero-goal player, and he would be wearing the number one on his shirt, indicating he was ostensibly the striker, or primary goal scorer. We didn't need to hold our breath though, as it was unlikely he would influence the game. Not because he was a zero handicap—a young, up-and-coming zero-goal player could be a real handful on the polo field—but because he was an ageing zero-goaler on the way down. Jerry Kapper was the typical "monied sponsor" or *Patrón*, as the Argentinians would say. And he liked to flaunt it, making sure his pilot chose an approach path that took his helicopter in view of the main grandstand on its way to the helicopter landing area. Had he seen himself on the polo field the way others did, he may have been inclined to be a bit more discreet. It just wasn't very English, and he wasn't.

"Monied sponsor, or mounted spectator?" I can hear my young reserve teammate Georgie saying. Cheeky, but accurate.

My Rude Awakening

In fairness though, sponsors played an important role in the modern game. Running a top team cost millions of pounds per year with zero return! The thing that irked me was when the sponsor's involvement was more about his image and showboating than the game. Our family were sponsors too, and it is fair to say that every team has an element of sponsorship. For us there was no embarrassment. We had played the game for generations and were significantly involved in thoroughbred horses and breeding, and it was all about the game. Jerry Kapper would have done far better exercising his body, improving his horsemanship and polo skills so that he could make a real contribution to his team, instead of spending two million dollars a year for a top-ten goaler just so he could put silverware in his boardroom. He was their weakness. They were a three-man, twenty-goal team. We were not.

Our simple strategy today was that all four of our players had to be a handful. Four players making an effective contribution meant we should always have an overlap. I hoped these weren't famous last thoughts. Playing against the world's best ten-goal player was never going to be easy. I knew we would have our work cut out for us.

After the customary presentation of the competing teams to the spectators, one of the umpires got the first chukka underway by throwing the ball between the two lines of players.

We got off to a bad start and almost immediately were two goals down, having not even finished the first chukka. Beto, their ten-goaler, had caught us all off guard, weaving his magic and scoring two impressive individual goals. My contribution was nowhere near my three-goal rating, let alone "going on four."

Another duffed backhand by me resulted in a glare from Llewellyn Tomkinson, our captain. "Featherstone, wake up," came his sharp censure.

I may have been the son of our team's sponsor, but on this field I was rightfully treated as the junior. I knew I had to focus, but still I found myself looking to the sidelines, trying to catch a glimpse of Charlotte.

The second chukka was underway, but no sooner had we begun than I heard the shrill blast of the umpire's whistle. Seb had tried to ride-off Nic, but instead of meeting him shoulder to shoulder, he had caught Hurricane,

Nic's horse, across the neck, and Seb had come dangerously close to bringing him down.

My concern turned to suppressed rage when I heard Jerry Kapper shouting, "No blood, no foul."

There was no place for this attitude in polo, arguably the most dangerous sport in the world. My anger was no doubt also exacerbated by the fact that we were down by four goals at the end of the chukka.

Chukka three improved only marginally, thanks to the increased contributions of the players around me, resulting in Lew's scoring one, even though he was in the number four back position. Guy was also linking well with Nic, which helped him score a goal.

We were trailing badly. I think the score was six to three. *We can't be beaten by Jerry Kapper,* was my overwhelming thought, even if it all came down to the phenomenal skills of his ten-goaler, Beto Cambiano.

With the end of the third chukka came the interval, the official halftime that lasted fifteen minutes. While most of the spectators took to the field to tread in the divots, the teams withdrew to their seating areas to discuss tactics, changes in approach, which horses they would be bringing on, and so forth.

Lew had only one thing to say. "I don't know where your head is, Featherstone, but you're missing a good game."

I looked at him ruefully, realising how sorely my game was lacking.

Was my play all down to my being distracted by Charlotte and these "first-time" feelings? Or has my lack of match fitness played a bigger role than I thought? Now that I am in the RAF, will I even get to four-goals? I wondered despondently.

I couldn't make up for the lack of practise just then, but somehow, I had to try to push thoughts of Charlotte aside and get my head back in this game.

With just seven minutes of the interval remaining, we started readying ourselves to take to the field for the second part of the match.

Just then I spotted my parents, my Aunt Edwina and Uncle Alexander—who I hadn't realised were coming—and Jamie, but my eyes were immediately drawn to Charlotte. Realising the interval was coming to

My Rude Awakening

an end, they hurriedly began making their way across to our gazebo, where we were all sitting.

When they were still thirty or forty yards away, I heard Charlotte say, "Come on, Mum, let's run to them before they go back onto the field."

"Go along," my mother encouraged.

Charlotte and Gigi bent down and removed their shoes.

"Race," I heard Charlotte say.

The sight of them running towards us, barefoot on the soft green grass, hair and dresses billowing as they ran, transfixed me.

They both came straight to me and kissed my rather sweaty cheeks, seemingly oblivious of the other three players whom they had not yet met.

"Ooh la la, *hermosa*," Nic exclaimed.

My Spanish was rubbish, but I knew enough to know *hermosa* meant *gorgeous* or *beautiful*. Nic, the bloody charmer.

Charlotte was wearing a very sporty-looking navy-blue-and-white-striped shirt. A loose navy-blue skirt reached down to her midcalf, wafting with the occasional gust of wind. Loosely draped over her shoulders was a navy-blue silk shawl. From her wide-brimmed straw hat and Jackie O sunglasses, down to her slip-on JP Tod's shoes, just like my mum—still in her hands, which had me glancing down at her feet—she was perfectly attired for polo. She looked beautiful. In contrast, I barely noticed what anyone else was wearing, such was my focus on Charlotte.

They milled around for only a moment before a groom hurriedly rustled up a few more director's chairs with Rockwell Manor on the backrest. As I watched Charlotte settling in to spectate the second half, not from the stands but as a part of our team, I felt a little excited tightening of my belly. Suddenly, I wanted the world to know she was there for me.

My mother came across to join them. Unusual for her, but I was pleased, nonetheless. I knew she didn't enjoy watching me play and that it would be followed by her usual "you must be more careful" speech.

As we took to the field for the fourth chukka, the start of the second half of the match, I was feeling a hundred times better.

Lew brought his horse alongside mine and asked, "Have I just seen the reason for your less than wonderful display earlier?"

I knew he was referring to Charlotte, so I allowed myself to smile sheepishly.

As we began to canter to the centre of the pitch for the throw in, a familiar voice called out, "Come on, chum. I haven't come here to watch my best mate lose." Jamie had clearly finished his match and hightailed it across to where we were.

I wouldn't easily admit it, but that was extra motivation too.

Shifting my full focus to the game, I asked "What's the score, Lew?"

For a reply, all I got was, "Oh, God, we both know where your head has been."

We just had to rescue this match. I was not going to have Charlotte watch her first game of Rockwell Manor Polo with us losing.

I began playing like a demon, which in turn rubbed off on my teammates, as everyone upped their game. And the second half miraculously improved. Our opposition responded to our increased tempo with no intention of letting their three-goal advantage slip, but I was all over it, playing like a man possessed.

"Now that's more like it," came Lew's encouragement.

We ended the penultimate chukka nine to eight down, but we had the momentum and one more chukka to score two more than them. We could do it!

We got onto our sixth-chukka horses, which normally are your best. Warbird was ready for me, and she was up for it, as always. I had another top horse, Mufti's Dream, in reserve in case I needed to switch her just before the end. Both mares would give me everything.

I had to monitor Warbird carefully, as she gave so much effort that she often drove herself to exhaustion. I loved that about her but was wary she might hurt herself through her unselfish commitment. Once, after she'd finished a chukka with me and I'd removed her saddle and bridle, I started untying her tail, and she threw herself onto the ground. This would normally be an ominous sign for a horse and could portend the start of heart failure. As it transpired, she was just exhausted and that was how she wanted to rest. Most unusual, but extremely endearing. Both Warbird and Mufti's Dream were from the Tom Fool line, a descendant of the notable

Buckpasser. They were racehorse thoroughbreds, my favourite. The horses, and especially the mares with this heritage, always have elegant, swanlike necks, dished snouts quite typical in Arabian breeds, bold eyes, and beautiful balance and symmetry in their gait.

We took to the field, everyone ready to fight for the win in this important knockout match. Alberto Cambiano and Malcs Barwick combined well to score the next goal. Pity they were the opposition. The pressure was on, with us being back to two goals down, ten to eight, and with time running out.

Next, I galloped down the left flank of the field and, with a perfectly timed cut shot, hit the ball to centre field, flawlessly placing it for Lew to pick up and score. Now it was ten to nine.

Better. We still need two.

Not wanting to tire Warbird too much in case I needed her for an additional period of play, I waited for the right moment and then shot off the field for a quick swap. I did this because I had a feeling that we could get another goal in this chukka and have to come back for a golden goal and what would then be the final chukka. As was typically done, I rode alongside Mufti's Dream and hopped from one saddle to the next without touching the ground.

Back on the field, I glanced at the big seven-minute countdown clock. Three minutes to go.

Soon, with seconds remaining, we got a well-orchestrated team goal, and I finished off with a perfectly executed neck shot and the equaliser, bringing the score to ten to ten. The clock counted down, and because we were drawn, the chukka would end with the next infringement.

Lew wanted to regroup and didn't want the opposition to sneak in a goal, a big possibility when you had a ten-goaler like Cambiano against you. Lew purposely hit the ball onto the boards. His cool calculation in the heat of the moment was exactly why he was England's captain.

The neck shot needs to be perfectly timed with the gait of the horse so as not to strike their front legs. When holding a polo stick and testing it for whip, there is barely any flex. With the momentum of the mallet head in a full-powered shot, you get a very different result, as captured in this photograph.

The bell rang for the end of the sixth, and because we were drawn, we would play a seventh "golden goal" chukka. The game would end when a team scored the winning goal.

We went off the field to ready ourselves for this last period of play, heads swirling with how to prepare for the crucial sudden-death conclusion of the game.

"Right, chaps, the next goal is ours and then we are through," said Lew pointedly. "Charles, more of the same!" He wasn't one for going into raptures.

Nothing more needed to be said, and no instructions to my seasoned groom were necessary either. Warbird was ready and waiting for me to take her back onto the field. This is customary in high-goal polo, to go back to your best horse for as long as she has something in the tank. I sprang onto her back, immediately feeling the calmness that always came over me when she was under me. My teammates knew I felt this way too.

"If you had nine of those, you would be on six-goals," they would say.

The seventh chukka was relentless, full gallops up and down the field as each team tried to get that golden goal. At three minutes, thirty-five seconds in, still nothing. I knew the horses would soon be starting to noticeably tire. There was no way you could play a whole chukka on your top horse and still expect to have much left for an unexpected extra period of play. I also knew that this was when Warbird was at an advantage because she had, and gave, so much more. The pressure was mounting.

The next moment, Seb was heading down towards our goal. I had to get to him quickly, and using all of Warbird's blistering speed, I caught up. As he was about to strike the ball for goal, I leant fully out of my saddle—perilously close to unseating myself—and straining every sinew of my body, reached under Warbird's neck for the under-neck hook, obstructing Seb's shot at the crucial moment. He could not complete his play as we both now harmlessly galloped over the ball.

Both our best players were free, and it was quite the procession as they galloped into our opponent's half. Lew passed the ball up field to Nic on Chance, the best horse in our yard. Watching him pick up the bouncing ball at a full gallop, bring it under control, and then hit it out of the air to split the wicker goal posts was a thing of beauty. Nic had an unbelievable eye for the ball. *Will I one day be able to do that?* I asked myself.

That was it. We had the golden goal. We were through.

Without dismounting, we rode up alongside our teammates and gave each other big hugs before we circled around to our competitors to shake their hands.

Relieved at having saved face with Charlotte, I looked around to find her. There she was, still at our gazebo with Gigi, my parents, Jamie, Aunt Edwina, Uncle Alexander, and Georgie—who was beaming from ear to ear for his team's success, even though he hadn't played. I could relax, knowing that I'd redeemed myself by playing well in the second half.

"Thanks to you we won that game, Carlo. That was an incredible hook, right under your horse's neck. Bet Seb did not like it though." Nic grinned broadly.

I smiled at the Italian version of my name, and quite liked the praise too. I thought about that for a moment, and as much as I enjoyed the recognition, he had misattributed a large amount of the commendation.

I had been able to pull off that hook for just one reason alone. Even though I had been hanging out of my saddle at a ridiculous angle, Warbird had maintained perfect balance and position at a full gallop, giving me a stable, reliable platform to confidently put myself out on a limb. Contrary to what most people thought, a horse responds to the rider's legs more than any other aide. The positioning of my legs would have told Warbird to do something completely different to what I needed at that moment. She was seemingly reading the game and what was required of her in that crucial period of play and had remained unswerving and perfectly balanced…*at a full gallop*. Horses are not credited with nearly as much intelligence as they should be.

Still on Warbird's back, I leant forward, my chin resting on the top of her clipped mane, and with both my arms outstretched, I rubbed her sweaty neck. As we walked back to the horse lines, I continued my adulation of her, wiping her face and sweat-frothed sides, letting her know that I knew very well who had really saved the game.

The gazebo was where everyone migrated after a match, so it was always very festive. Horses swilling about in the background. Beaming grooms.

The Featherstone/Blackwood group was joined by a few other well-wishers. Most importantly, Grace, our vet, was there to give our horses a once-over and a vitamin B-12 injection if they needed it, a powerful supplement to aid their recovery.

As we walked over to our waiting entourage, I saw other players leaning back, loosening their horse's tail whilst still sitting in the saddle. Some loosened the girth strap as well so their horse could begin to relax. I often thought of this as being similar to when one leaves a dance ball and immediately removes their bow tie, jacket, and pleated cummerbund.

As we got closer, Lew looked towards Charlotte and, picking up from the interval, asked, "So who is the blonde over there?"

"Oh, that's Jamie Blackwood's sister. You know, my Air Force friend," I said.

"Ah, I get it," came his reply. "Now I *really* understand your first three chukkas." He chuckled.

My Rude Awakening

As I approached the horse lines, Mum, Dad, Uncle Alexander, Aunt Edwina, Jamie, Gigi, and, most importantly, Charlotte met me there. I gave Warbird a final pat and swung off the saddle in a way that was akin to how a gymnast dismounts from a pommel horse, landing effortlessly on my feet. It wasn't entirely necessary, though it was a typical dismount after the adrenaline rush of a game.

Pablo, my Argentinian groom, walked towards me to collect Warbird, and I could see the relieved look on his face.

I walked over to Charlotte, who was quick to congratulate me. "Ooh, that was so exciting," She effused as she touched my arm. "Wow, what a brilliant, you know, that *thing* you did to block that goal." She was doing her best to describe my under-neck hook that someone else must have mentioned, which I appreciated anyway.

Charlotte then drifted off to find her mother and I went over to the gazebo to sit down. Others were milling around, chatting happily and we spent the next twenty to thirty minutes reminiscing about the game and going over some of the highlights. Shots made, hooks missed, nearly this or that. You would hear things like, "Jeez, did you see how Abacus turned inside Malcolm Barwick's best horse in the fifth?" or "What about how Lightning galloped past Jerry Kapper?" Perhaps it was trivial, but we all enjoyed it.

I noticed Jamie listening intently, affected by the post-match excitement, and knew then he was properly bitten.

As exciting as it was, I wanted to go across to where Charlotte and Gigi were chatting.

Then Jamie turned to speak to me about something that really interested him. "Tell me about Nic, chum?" he asked candidly.

Was it Nic's good looks, charm and natural charisma, or his flashy polo skills that intrigued Jamie so, drawing him like a moth to a flame? I had an inkling it was the latter, since he had the other in abundance.

"What do you want to know, Jamie?" I asked, but then I carried on anyway. "I really don't know him well, but you can see he is a good-looking, amazing polo player. Really should be an eight or even a nine."

I looked across the area as if to confirm what I had said. He was pretty tall at around six foot, a thick mop of jet-black hair that fell onto his forehead and swept away to the sides; deep, soulful brown eyes with thick eyebrows and long eyelashes; an athletic body; olive-coloured skin.

"Yes, what else?" Jamie pressed.

"Actually, he's a good, fun chap with a naughty sense of humour," I said while trying to figure out Nic's other virtues. "We should get to know him, Jamie, considering my dad's view is that he may well end up spending a few seasons with us, so he can develop with our team," I suggested, with a little chuckle. "Because I missed the first few games of the Barrett Cup due to our RAF commitments, hence Georgie Graham having stood in for me, I haven't had the opportunity to get to know him. My dad reckons Nic is heading straight to the top, a certain ten-goaler."

I had a sense that Jamie would just love to be just like Nic Aroldin.

We walked over to where he was sitting, listening to Lew chatting to Guy. "Hi again, Nic," I greeted, beginning the conversation.

"Ciao, Carlo," he answered warmly, wanting to stand up.

I put a hand on his shoulder as I took a seat opposite him.

"Well played today," we said to each other at precisely the same moment, which made us both chuckle.

"No, no, you played really well, especially off a three," he remarked. "You'll be going up soon, no question."

I said a polite thank you but took it from whence it came—a polo professional wanting to be sure of keeping his place in the team. It made me feel good, nonetheless. "Has Guy been looking after you over at Rockwell Manor, and are you happy with the horses?" I asked, even though I knew the answers to both.

Guy was a top polo manager with an easy manner. The question about horses I knew was completely superfluous. With my dad having slowed down a bit and his original string of some of the best horses in England being mostly available, we were able to mount players to the highest standard. The first choice of horses would always be given to the top overseas player of our team, which was now Nic. There would invariably be other of our horses available to bolster the strings of the local players we used. Rockwell Manor's horses were quite simply the best.

"Guy is amazing," Nic replied without hesitation. "And the horses? Well, nowhere in the world am I better mounted. These horses are incredible." He really drew out "incredible" in his American-Spanish accent. "And Chance." He shook his head as if speechless. "She should get Champion Pony for the tournament. One of the best I've ever ridden. Maybe *the* best." He made the ring gesture with fingertip to thumb, showing his appreciation.

I knew what he was saying was true and he wasn't just saying the right things. "So how are you enjoying England?" I asked.

"I love it here. More than anywhere else—Palm Beach, Long Island, Sotogrande. You can call me anytime. I like England the most, after Argentina," he replied.

"What is the big attraction in England?" I genuinely wanted to get a sense of why Argentinians so enjoyed coming to our country.

Nic answered, "Fantastic competitive tournaments. Great level of polo, great countryside, and oh, the girls. So many girls, so little time."

He said it with such a mischievous face that I had to smile. He may have picked this up as an expression, but I got the impression that it really resonated with him. I thought then that Nic's reputation, which had followed him across the Atlantic Ocean, was in all likelihood very well founded.

Deciding to bring our conversation to an end, I asked, "Are you going to the dinner dance this evening, Nic?"

"Of course," he replied in a slow drawl.

"Wonderful, see you there. Ciao, Nic. Very well played today," I said again, before standing and turning on my heels.

As I walked away, leaving Jamie to carry on socialising, I couldn't help thinking he was either going to love Nic or hate him! Nic would be difficult not to like.

After playing any polo match, I always felt more invigorated than normal, especially after a victory when we were competing for a cup, as was the case that day. This was the first time ever that I had someone with whom I was romantically linked watching me play. It gave me feelings of elation I had never experienced before. At that moment, I felt especially close to Charlotte and found myself looking around for her.

I walked towards where she was standing with some of our guests, casually chatting. Nic had joined the group, and by the looks of things, he was teasing and charming her. And I didn't like it. I felt a pang of jealousy I couldn't explain. Seeing her with Nic was not sitting comfortably with me.

Edward Charles Featherstone

My negative thoughts had me thinking she looked very much like a polo groupie right then. That would change. And would she mature into something like her mother? It was an interesting thought just as a well-timed old song, "Girl, You'll Be a Woman Soon" by Neil Diamond started playing.

"Girl, You'll be a Woman Soon" – Neil Diamond

| YouTube | Spotify | Apple |

She was certainly going to be a woman soon, was well on her way and already grabbing a lot of attention. *How will I feel about that?*

Some hurried steps later and I was standing in front of Charlotte, desperately wanting to take her in my arms but resisting because of it not being appropriate behaviour. Instead, I simply said, "Hello."

"Hello," she echoed. "And very well done again for getting into the final. I had better not miss that," she said with a twinkle in her eye. "Not even the first half."

I smiled. She must have overheard the interaction between Lew and me, looked at the scoreboard, and worked it all out. *Nothing lost on her.*

Just then, my parents walked up. Whilst everyone had congratulated me about the daring under-neck hook that had saved the day, my mother saw it quite differently.

"Well done, Sunbeam, but I was not happy with that last play of yours." I should have expected this reprimand. And she wasn't finished there. "You know how dangerous that was? If your horse were to lose her footing for one moment, with you leaning out at such a perilous angle, you would certainly have come down with no way of protecting yourself. That's how necks are broken!" she said tersely. "Please, Sunbeam, do not play like that. It is only a game."

After so many years of watching her father—my grandfather—and her uncles playing polo, she understood the game perfectly. She easily recognised all the intricacies and that what I had done was not unusual. Even if it was a natural part of the game, especially at the high-goal level, my mother did not like my putting myself out on a limb, both literally and figuratively.

My father grimaced slightly and then gave me a little wink. "Well played," he mouthed to me.

There were many more well-wishers, but I couldn't wait to have a moment alone with Charlotte. When we were not in earshot of anybody, I suggested to her, "Charlotte, would you like to come and look over the horses before we load them up to go back to Rockwell?"

"I would love to," she said without hesitation.

With that, we drifted away to where the horses were being prepared for the trip back home.

Walking close together, we began chatting amiably.

"Please explain how players of different levels, like Jamie as a beginner, are able to play polo together?"

Charlotte's question was a good one. How different levels of players were all able to compete against each other was often confusing to the uninitiated. I had to think of a simple way of explaining it.

"You know the handicaps start at zero goals, for absolute beginners, who must still be competent riders and fair strikers of the ball?"

Her nod had me carry on.

"And all the way up to ten goals for the top players."

"Yes," she replied without hesitation.

"And don't be confused by the use of the word *goals* in ten goals or ten-goaler. It doesn't mean he routinely scores ten goals in a match, because that isn't right either. There are ten-goalers who play in the number four, the back position, who may score just one or two goals in a match. Just think handicap when you hear *goal* in that context."

"Okay," Charlotte replied thoughtfully, still processing what I had just told her.

"Well, when a player first starts playing, he will be put into low-goal tournaments, like the mini four-goal tournament that Jamie is playing in." I knew I hadn't fully answered the question, so I carried on. "So, what that means is the sum of the handicaps of the four players in the team must not exceed four. You could have two zeros, a one-goaler, and a three-goaler to guide them all. Or a balanced team of four one-goalers."

Charlotte nodded her head signifying her understanding as she took my hand and gave it a squeeze.

As we continued our way towards the pantechnicon, I noticed my mother approvingly watching us.

My attention was diverted when I overheard one of the tournament directors saying, "Warbird and Chance from Rockwell must be contenders for Champion Pony for the tournament." I loved the sound of that.

As we approached our horse rig, my hand brushed against Charlotte's, which I playfully took a hold of. Thirty yards farther on, and finally we were alone. While the grooms were busy booting the horses up with leg protectors for the drive home, Charlotte and I sneaked into one of the eighteen birth-horse rigs and stole a quick but passionate kiss.

"I can't wait for the dinner dance at the club tonight, as your girlfriend," Charlotte blurted.

She had just answered the question that had been swirling around my head since that passionate kiss in the shadows. But before I could respond, I saw the entire team making their way over to the rigs, with my mum and dad, Gigi, and Jamie in tow. They were all looking forward to the evening ahead, so it hadn't been too difficult dragging them away from the gazebo.

As they got to where we were, my mum came up to me and said, "Well done today, Sunbeam. Granddad would have enjoyed that." This was my mother's way of balancing her earlier reprimand.

With that, Charlotte, Gigi, and my parents left for the car park and the short drive back to Rockwell Manor. Jamie and I followed, and with the early autumn darkness encroaching, we were soon on our way.

Because of the glitz and glamour of polo, an aspect that is not often understood is that it is undoubtedly one of the most dangerous games in the world. Whilst I am unsure of the actual statistics, I understand polo is responsible for more life-changing injuries and deaths per the number of people who play this exclusive sport than any other sport in the world, including motor racing. At the time of writing, years after this chapter I had lost three friends to polo accidents that resulted in spinal cord or neurological injuries. Two of those friends died in the 2000s, soon after being admitted to hospital, which quite naturally seemed the most tragic outcome.

I was closest to the third victim, Nick R, brother to one of my very good friends, JP. Also in the 2000s, Nick suffered a brain stem injury that not only left him quadriplegic—paralysed from the neck down—but also locked-in, which meant he could not speak among other things. He was one of five brothers and from the most incredibly close family whose bond was simply extraordinary.

Watching from the sidelines was devastating for me. I can't even begin to imagine how it was for his young family and JP, all of whom were also there when his accident happened. Nick was the husband to a wonderful wife, father to two lovely daughters. A wife who then dedicated her own life to her injured husband's care. Two daughters who lost forever the hero he was to them.

Nick's injury was the epitome of what is sometimes referred to as a "Hero to Zero" spinal cord or neurological injury. Simply put, once all powerful, more than just capable, at the top of their game, until in the blink of an eye they find themselves fighting death…and winning, only to be rewarded with a life sentence of dependency on others, in a prison of immobility. This then can be nothing other than a tragedy compounded by tragedy. Nick could communicate, but only those closest to him understood what he was saying. One of his wishes was to see his daughters finish school. He got his wish, and then he gave up the fight on 21 December 2016. The end of twelve years of locked-in immobility for Nick and the end of twelve years of loving care for his wife. Nick was a big loss to all of us, but with that loss, there was also relief.

You will never be forgotten, my friend.

CHAPTER 17
GUARDS DINNER AND DANCE

WE ARRIVED AT the club, everyone thrilled to be there, especially Charlotte.

The first event of the evening was a little prize giving. Commensurate of it only being the semifinal, we received what would be better described as a token to recognise our participation. The coveted Barrett Cup would only come after the finals.

As I looked across at our opponents, I couldn't help but marvel at the lineup of the eight players from the two teams. The group included handicaps from the lowest, Jerry Kapper on zero, to the highest, Alberto Cambiano, the best player in the world on a ten. The ages ranged from sixteen to sixty. It would've also been possible for a female player to have been in the lineup, as polo was not gender specific. As far as nationalities were concerned, there were three Englishmen, a Scotsman, an American, two Argentinians, and an Australian. A snapshot not dissimilar to most professional polo teams in England.

With the prize giving over, we were able to drift across to our tables.

Looking at the name cards at each of the place settings on our team's round table, I could immediately see my mother's influence. Starting with my father, Gigi was next, and then me, unsurprisingly next to Charlotte. *A sure sign my parents like her.* Nic, Lew and his fiancé Leah, then Guy and his partner for the evening, none other than our vet, Grace Brayers. No surprise that Jamie was next to my mother. *I love how she loves him.* She had managed a boy-girl-boy arrangement that placed everyone who had a partner next to their partner, except my parents who were opposite each other. *Perfect, couldn't be better.*

Looking around the room, I saw in attendance most of the players from all the teams that had been involved in the tournament, including the team we'd be meeting in the finals the following Sunday. One of the things I really enjoyed about polo was no matter how competitive it was, once the game was over, the winners and losers would intersperse quite happily together. I felt then, and still do today, that it should always be that way, in all sports.

As the evening began, I felt very comfortable sitting next to Charlotte and found being attentive towards her came quite naturally. I knew my mother would notice, which she did, and I could see it was meeting with her approval. I had a smug feeling of satisfaction that even though Charlotte was sitting next to Nic on her other side, she hardly paid him any attention. And for his part, I was pleased he did not impose himself on her. It is safe to say that he may have considered it career limiting at Rockwell Manor. It suddenly suited me that I was the son of the *patrón,* and I couldn't help my wry smile.

Dinner progressed smoothly enough, with everybody going to and from the buffet tables, as was always the approach at Guards Polo Club. It was quite normal for everyone except Charlotte and me. For the first time ever, we were out as boyfriend and girlfriend. Sitting next to each other. I helped her at the buffet and poured her drink. Lots of friends and acquaintances came over to say hello and have a quick catch-up with us. Our table was very merry, and we all mixed and chatted happily. The more we did these simple things, the more relaxed we became, and the more we enjoyed ourselves.

There were moments when I held Charlotte's hand and was caught up in how wonderful it felt. Or when she was popping something into my mouth at the buffet tables, to see if I liked it before serving it onto my plate. She'd laugh and grab my arm when I pulled a face, showing my distaste for something. The more we carried on, the more oblivious we became to everyone around us and the more it felt just like the countless dinners I had enjoyed in Shrewsbury. They hardly noticed us. Our behaviour was only unusual for me, not anyone around us.

Dinner was ending, and already people had started to dance. That was enough to draw in the merrymakers. Soon the temperature was rising to the heaving pulse of the party revellers.

Jamie had already left the table and was having a whale of a time chatting and mixing with various groups, and I could see how he was really getting into the swing of the evening. I wasn't the only one who noticed, as Nic got up to go and join him.

The two of them started dancing with some of the polo groupies, and watching Jamie and Nic moving to the music had me engrossed and mildly jealous. *Bloody hell, that Nic can dance too.*

With Jamie and Nic together, it would be fair to expect the worst, or best, depending on where you sat. Two good-looking young men, tall, dark, and handsome and as roguish as each other! *Jilly Cooper, do I have a novel for you.* Had Jamie been a polo player rather than an Air Force pilot, that book idea would have been a definite possibility.

With more and more people moving onto the dance floor, the time came for me to have a dance with Charlotte, even though dancing was not my favourite pastime. I would wait for the right song and ask her onto the floor.

A Whitney Houston song started playing, and I knew Charlotte would want to dance to this, as it was her favourite artist.

"I Have Nothing" – Whitney Houston

YouTube Spotify Apple

In contrast to my normal shyness, I stood up without a second thought, turned to Charlotte, and beckoned her to dance with me.

Once again, I noticed my parents' approving looks before they turned back to the people they were speaking to at the next table.

I was about to dance with Charlotte at Guards, and the thought of it caused a little tightening in my stomach.

Charlotte slipped her hand into mine as she rose from her chair, and we made our way onto the dance floor. Having found the most secluded spot, we folded into each other's arms, Charlotte's hands on my shoulder and my waist and my hands around her back. The feeling of her body against mine sent a quiver of excitement through me as we gently started moving to the rhythm of the music. Taking in the words of the Whitney Houston song, we held each other a little tighter.

Then Charlotte brought her mouth up to my ear to say something I didn't catch, so I pushed my ear harder against her mouth.

Her lips pressed against me, she continued, "Take my love…"

I realised then that she was going along with the words of the song, making them her own words to me.

"I won't ask for too much. Just all that you are. And everything you do. Stay in my arms if you dare. Do you dare, Charles?" she asked.

We let the song play out, and this time, I made some of the words mine. "There's nowhere I want to hide," I whispered as the song was coming to an end. *What's happening to me?*

Were we ready to open the floodgates of our feelings for each other? As if in response, I put my arm around her waist as we moved to leave the dance floor.

Charlotte brought her lips up to my right ear and whispered, "Let's get out of this stuffy place." And then she gently kissed my ear, which sent a shiver down into my tummy.

I couldn't believe how much she stirred up my insides and how much I enjoyed that strange feeling.

I glanced over to see the function room doors were fully opened, making me wonder why she felt the room was stuffy.

The wicked grin that lit up Charlotte's face told me that I was being naive.

"Oh yes, so stuffy," I said, a little unimaginatively.

"Let's go and have some alone time," she suggested, her forthright approach undoubtedly a result of her being more experienced than me in the dating department.

The perhaps over-exuberant nod of my head was all Charlotte needed to grab me by the hand and lead me off the dance floor.

No one seemed to have noticed our demonstrative behaviour as we arrived back to an empty table. Jamie, Nic, Guy, Grace, and even Gigi were on the dancefloor, and my parents were now sitting at another table with my aunt and uncle and other of their friends.

Charlotte got her handbag and shawl as I picked up my jacket, and we looked around to see who we could at least wave goodbye to. She caught Jamie's and Gigi's eye and indicated her tiredness by resting her head against her hand, then she gave them a little wave. I did likewise. They all waved back, quite unperturbed by our departure. I managed to catch my mother's eye and used Charlotte's sleepy gesture, then pointed to her, indicating that she was tired. My mother blew us two kisses. She really was changing. My father just beamed. Something made me imagine he was thinking, *A chip off the old block,* in that I may have a way with women after all!

It had been that simple, and we calmly walked out of the clubhouse.

I grabbed Charlotte's hand, and we ran to my car. I bundled her into the passenger seat and assumed my place behind the wheel, then leant over, desperately wanting to kiss her.

"Later, babe. Let's get home," Charlotte said.

It was the first time she had called me babe, and I liked it.

The quickest way home was the back roads, endless twists and turns winding through the English countryside. Foxes, rabbits, badgers, and on occasion even deer would pop out of the bushes. These roads had sections through which only one car could pass at a time, the second car needing to drive almost into the thick foliage to allow the other to get by. It was not safe to drive fast, but I put my foot down every now and then to speed up the trip.

Charlotte's hand was on my thigh and, every now and then, squeezed me, making me realise she was nervous, and so I slowed down.

"Thanks, babe," she murmured.

We rounded the bend that brought us to Rockwell Manor, the sight of the gates catching Charlotte by surprise. Recognising the entrance, she squealed excitedly, "We're home," as she dug her fingers into my thigh.

I couldn't help reflecting that right then there was nothing I wanted more than for us to be alone together, no matter how auspicious the event was at Guards Polo Club.

CHAPTER 18
TWO WORLDS MEET

THE NEXT MORNING, Jamie and I met in the breakfast room at around eight o'clock. Even though Charlotte had said she would only be joining us a little later, I looked around for her anyway, hoping she had changed her mind. Jamie looked worse for wear. Next came my mother and father with Gigi in tow. Not long after, Charlotte arrived. Our family was complete.

My dad seemed to be feeling very jovial as he enquired about our evening. Everyone enthused about how wonderful it had been, including Charlotte and me.

My mother gave Gigi and Charlotte an outline of what she had planned for their day. First, a visit to the organic farm nearby and then to London. Lunch at either The Brasserie or Bibendum before heading off to Harrods.

After breakfast, Gigi and Charlotte left to prepare themselves for their excursion. Having spent a wonderful romantic evening together, I was going to miss not being with Charlotte today. I would have loved to take her somewhere myself, just the two of us.

I turned to my friend and suggested, "Jamie, let's go and have a light stick and ball session."

Not needing a second invitation, he headed off to put on a pair of jeans.

"See you at the stables," I called after him before excusing myself to go up and get ready. On the way through the drawing room, I was distracted by the latest edition of *POLO Magazine* on the coffee table and sat down to quickly glance through it.

Thinking they were alone, my mum and dad started discussing

Charlotte and me, and then also Gigi. "Now that we have seen Charlotte and Charles together, what are your thoughts?" she asked.

"I think they would make a lovely couple. Just give them time," proffered my father.

"Charles has had such a very sheltered upbringing when it comes to the opposite sex. It is wonderful to see him with such a lovely young lady," my mother mused. Not yet finished, she added, "She's a bit older than him, but I don't think it will matter. Charles is very mature for his age."

"I think Jamie will be a good influence on him in that department," my dad suggested playfully. Jamie's ease around girls had not gone unnoticed by my father. Was it a case of birds of a feather? "And Charlotte can teach him a thing or two," he chuckled suggestively.

"Let's hope so," my mother agreed with a straight face, not rising to my father's mischief. "They have become such good friends, and neither of them look like the military type to me," she said, pointing out how similar she thought Jamie and I were. "Arthur, do you honestly believe Charles is cut out to be in the RAF? It doesn't make sense to me now. It won't make sense to either of us when he is deployed into one of those godforsaken places."

My father's silence had me wondering if he too was having second thoughts about my RAF career.

Not being able to see them from where I sat, I could only imagine that my mother's face would be showing worry and concern.

"And what about Georgina?" my mum continued.

"What an attractive and youthful mother she is," my father replied, a typical observation for him.

"And she and Charles have such a lovely little connection. Our families would fit perfectly together. I can't believe that she's on her own," said my mother, showing she was as observant as I suspected.

"Yes, don't forget Charles has spent a lot of time with the Blackwoods. She is almost his second mother. I think she is lovely and would really fit in perfectly in these circles," my dad suggested.

"Let's see if we can introduce her to someone. There are many eligible men around here who would be perfect for her," my mother concluded.

My Rude Awakening

They fell quiet just long enough that I decided to go up before they came through and found me eavesdropping.

The rest of the day was quite uneventful, with the only interesting part being a call from a friend, Humphrey Throgmorton. He offered me two pegs for the first shoot of the season at their estate, which meant of the eight-gun lineup of shooters, there were two vacancies for this coming Friday and Saturday. It so transpired that our fortnight leave coincided with the end of the polo season and the Glorious Twelfth, the start of the game-bird shooting season in the United Kingdom. The latter was something I hadn't even thought of when we were planning the trip to Rockwell Manor.

Even though they came at a hefty price—five thousand pounds per day, per gun—I jumped at the opportunity. The cost was not something I paid much attention to. I knew Jamie would love to shoot driven grouse or pheasant, and there were going to be six drives per day over two days. English law prohibited the shooting of game birds—or any quarry, for that matter—on Sundays, which worked perfectly for us, as we would be playing the final of the Barrett Cup then.

Of course, I also had an ulterior motive for accepting Humphrey's offer so readily. The guests would all stay at Bovey Castle, built on the edge of Dartmoor National Park in Devon, a county in the South West of England. It was a very convenient stone's throw from the Throgmorton estate, not very far from West Buckland School. By English standards, it was a new establishment, especially in Devon, which comprised numerous medieval towns. It was built as a lavish Neo-Elizabethan manor home on five thousand acres for William Henry Smith (1825–1891), later to become WH Smith and Viscount Hambleden. He was an English bookseller who expanded his business by selling books and newspapers at railway stations. What I found interesting was that WHSmith was my mother's favourite bookstore, to which she dragged me from time to time. After going through a number of changes and developments, by 1980 Bovey Castle had become well known as a very special five-star destination hotel.

The normal form for this shoot was that there would be dinners arranged for both evenings with the other members of the eight-gun lineup and their partners, plus other invited guests. These were often quite festive affairs. Six drives per day split on either side of a leisurely but sumptuous lunch. Then, after Saturday's afternoon shoot, we would head home in time to do evening stables for the big match the following day.

My mind began to race at the thought of this being an opportunity for Charlotte and me to spend two nights together in a country hotel. I needed to work out a way of ensuring she would come with us and discover more of my world.

My mum, Charlotte, and Gigi arrived home from London late that evening, in particularly good spirits. They had enjoyed a wonderful day, cutting short the trip to the organic farm, having a lovely lunch, and then spending the afternoon at their favourite store, Harrods—frequented by the rich and famous, which made no difference to me. I found it thoroughly boring.

I helped Gigi take her shopping to the cottage and then went up to the main house in search of Charlotte, anxious to speak to her. I found her with her feet up in the TV area. I could tell she was settling into Rockwell Manor very comfortably, and I liked it. She did seem to fit in very well.

"Darling," I said, the affection rolling easily off my tongue, "at dinner I'm going to invite you away this weekend. It may not be your idea of fun, but it really will be. Just say you would love to go, and we can chat about it later."

Jamie walked in and announced, "Dinner is at eight, and your dad asked that we meet in the game room for drinks first."

I gave him a nod and then returned my attention to Charlotte, who gave me a wink, letting me know she'd go along with my plan.

Elated, I went up to my suite to get ready for dinner. After a quick shower, I arrived at the game room first and was greeted by our butler.

"Hi, Hamilton. Kir Royale, please." French champagne and Crème de Cassis liqueur would slide down nicely.

I saw a reflection of myself and instantly understood why I was ahead of the others. I had thrown on a powder-blue silk shirt, untucked and with several buttons undone, white polo jeans that were at least clean, and tan slip-on driving shoes with no socks.

Just then my mum and dad arrived. My mother came over and ran her fingers through my hair, shaking her head. "Oh, Sunbeam, you haven't even dried or brushed that mane of yours."

Our attention turned to Gigi, Charlotte, and Jamie as they arrived together. As Gigi walked past me, she made a remark about my having lost my brush or something. Then she ran her fingers through my head of thick wet hair, literally mimicking what my mother had just done.

I looked at my mum, wondering what she made of it. Her expression was unchanged, finding it completely normal that Gigi, having become so close to me, was just doing a bit of mothering of her own. Not even a thought of feeling any competition with someone else behaving that way toward her only son.

Charlotte looked simply stunning with her tousled hair and the radiant glow of her skin. She wore open-toed leather sandals, and I had a sneaky feeling it was so I could see her feet, with her perfectly pedicured toes.

After our aperitif, it was time for dinner. As we went through to the family dining room, I couldn't help reflecting how unusual it was for us not to have other guests. As we sat down, I remarked. "Just the six of us, Mum?"

"Yes, Sunbeam, just a casual family dinner."

I beamed, as I shot a sideways glance at a smiling Charlotte.

After hearing about the ladies' trip to London, recounted with a lot of enthusiasm and excitement, I had an opportunity to tell the table, but more specifically Jamie and Charlotte, about the game-bird shoot. "Jamie, I have wonderful news."

He looked at me enquiringly.

"I have two places for the Throgmorton driven shoot this weekend. Since my dad is busy, I was wondering if you would like to do that?"

The expression on Jamie's face was priceless. "Would I *like* that? Are you crazy? I would *love* that," he blurted.

Out of the corner of my eye, I saw a look of dread on Charlotte's face. Because of what I had said earlier, she was expecting me to invite her to go somewhere, but shooting? That was another story altogether. I knew I would be hard-pressed to convince her.

"So, the plan will be for us to leave on Thursday afternoon. There will be a lovely dinner with the other guests and their partners, and usually some other friends of the Throgmortons. We will shoot on Friday, four drives in the morning, break for lunch, and continue in the afternoon with another two drives. Another dinner on Friday night, a bit more relaxed, and then a similar programme for Saturday's shoot, but of course, on six different drives. We will come home on Saturday evening in time to check the horses for Sunday."

Jamie looked thrilled, having been sold at just the mention of a game-bird shoot. Charlotte's expression told me she was still not convinced.

I continued, "We will stay at Bovey Castle, which has been turned into a lovely destination hotel. Mum, your favourite booksellers' old home," I added. "While we are on our shoots, the ladies have a few options. A lot of fun can be had truffle hunting. On the other shooting day, spending time at the health and beauty spa and shopping normally ranks high."

Charlotte's face lit up. Realising she was not expected to traipse through the woods while we shot game birds had totally changed her mind.

My moment had arrived. "Charlotte, would you like to join us and experience this aspect of country life?" I hadn't even thought to ask Gigi, assuming she would almost certainly prefer to be around Berkshire.

My mother then chipped in, "Oh, Charlotte, you will love it. Just be sure to find some lovely burgundy truffles for us. We can make truffle oil and some truffle shavings for a wonderful tagliolini with taleggio. You'll have such fun." Trust my mother to say the right thing at precisely the right time.

"Yes, umm, that sounds lovely. Thank you," Charlotte said.

I felt as pleased as punch with how well I had orchestrated all this.

Gigi, liking the sound of it, said, "If it is not an inconvenience, I'd love to also come along. Charlotte and I could just share a room."

"Of course, Georgina, you shouldn't miss it for the world," my mother enthused, as my dad nodded his agreement.

We retired to the study and a tired-looking Hamilton did his best to be sprightly, offering us after-dinner ports and liqueurs.

"Hamilton, I've got this," I said. Glancing at my parents and seeing their approving looks, I continued, "I'm sure you've finished your chores for the night, and I will be happy to deputise for you."

"Thank you, sir," Hamilton replied with a genuine smile, and without looking at my parents for approval, which was interesting.

The next day, Jamie and I had another stick and ball session that lasted the afternoon. As we were finishing off, Charlotte and her mum arrived at the stables, identically dressed in white blouses much like men's shirts, blue jeans, and below the knee black riding boots. I was impressed that they had the foresight to have packed them, which would save me trying to sort something out from our tack room if they wanted to go for a ride.

God, they look good, were my testosterone-driven thoughts. I imagined that Charlotte would someday be a similar version of her mother, which made me all the more excited about my feelings for her. *Was I already thinking about us long term?*

I looked at their boots and saw they were quite well worn, a clear sign they were experienced riders. "Let's all go for a ride in the country," I suggested.

Jamie excused himself from joining us, no doubt feeling there were more interesting things to engage himself with at the polo club. I had never seen either of the women ride before, and even though they said they had some experience, I quietly instructed the groom on which horses to saddle up for them anyway, wanting to be certain they didn't end up with two of our more highly spirited horses.

"Let's do a forest ride, ladies, and I can show you where I spent many happy years rough shooting with Osric." I looked skyward and saw an ominous build-up of cloud. *It had better not storm.*

We started slowly, going along the twisting path through the forest at a trot. Then the landscape ahead of us opened, and we moved up a gear, into a strong canter. Much to my relief, I could see they were both more than competent riders. I could just imagine the fun Charlotte and I would be able to have going on rides…unaccompanied.

There was an open field ahead of us, and being in the open air, on beautiful thoroughbred horses, we soon broke into a gallop. When we got to the other side, we gently pulled up our horses as the girls enthused about our exhilarating ride. Charlotte and Gigi were both red-faced and out of breath, laughing at the excitement and pure enjoyment of the exercise. The two of them looked beautiful, one an older version of the other.

I rode up alongside Charlotte, and she instinctively took hold of my hand and affectionately gave it a squeeze. "Oh, Charles, babe, that was so, so lovely," she exclaimed.

Then I felt the raindrops on my face. "Bloody hell, we are about to be rained on." I had been so preoccupied that I did not notice the further build-up of weather.

As the heavens opened and let loose a deluge of rain, Charlotte and Gigi were unperturbed. Just as well, because it would not have been a good idea to race back to the stables, overly exciting the horses. I suggested we take a slow trot to Rockwell Manor, and we made our way back.

By the time we returned to the stables, we were soaked. I couldn't help noticing my two riding companions had sodden white cotton shirts and wet, bedraggled hair, though they hadn't yet realised how exposed they were.

Then Charlotte looked at her mother and blurted out, "Mum, your… your…" Looking down at her own chest, she quickly covered herself with cupped hands, giggling.

Quite unperturbed, Gigi replied, "Goodness! Nothing like the two of us giving Charles a wet T-shirt competition."

Speechless, and a bit like a gawking teenager standing there dripping wet, I was not sure what to do next. Then, remembering my manners, I went into the changing room to get them each a towel. Still laughing and quite uninhibited, they began drying themselves.

I'd realised all along that Gigi was quite carefree and relaxed about things my mother might have called rude, but in this moment, I began to see how this had influenced Charlotte. Where I'd sometimes thought she behaved a little too much like a polo groupie, I had to realise that she too would be more relaxed about such things than my sheltered upbringing had taught me to be. I decided then to embrace that about her, to welcome the possibility of her helping me navigate the path from my naiveté, to emerge a bit wiser.

The rain subsided, so we walked across the polo field and back to the house. It was early evening, and we agreed to meet in the kitchen after a quick shower and freshening up.

Dry and cosy in a tracksuit bottom and long-sleeved T-shirt, I headed to the kitchen. Not long after, I was joined by Charlotte and Gigi, both looking radiant in their casual attire. Charlotte wore designer yoga tights and a relaxed half-sleeve, navy-blue top with flip-flops. Gigi was dressed in her typical below-the-knee length skirt, with a loose top and leather thong sandals.

My Rude Awakening

My parents came through next, my mum checking on kitchen arrangements while my father attended to bar matters. We all stood around the warm pizza oven, chatting about our day. They were thrilled to hear we had gone out on a ride, and the glance between my parents told me exactly what they were thinking.

My mother had arranged a pizza evening and invited our polo team and several of our other polo friends, among others. Our pizza evenings were always festive occasions in our oversized kitchen, the traditional wood-burning pizza oven being the focal point, and I was looking forward to this more relaxed dinner setting with Charlotte. My mother also said that Jamie had invited a couple of the Balthazar players, Seb Brentwood and Beto Cambiano. I was pleased he felt so at home at Rockwell Manor that he was comfortable inviting guests. This was how I felt at his home.

As our team members began arriving, Nic stopped to chat with Charlotte standing next to the oven. Strangely, I did not feel the jealousy that had beset me before. Had our relationship progressed to where I no longer felt insecure? Lew and Georgie were there too. Then my Uncle Alexander and Aunt Edwina arrived with some other friends of my parents. Having walked up from his manager's cottage was Guy and none other than Grace Brayers. My bet was that Guy would soon be recommending Rockwell Manor have a full-time vet and nutritionist, and Grace would undoubtedly be the one.

Fabrizio had prepared a perfect light and airy dough and arranged a dozen or so large bowls of assorted ingredients: ham, salami, olives, artichokes, prawns, anchovies, peppers, chillies, bacon, banana, brie cheese, cranberry jelly, sweet chilli sauce, pesto, and, of course, his special recipe of tomato sauce and mounds of grated mozzarella cheese. Much to his disgruntlement, he also put out a bowl of pineapple pieces for anyone who wanted to make the unmentionable Hawaiian pizza. Fabrizio always reminded everyone that pineapple had no place in an Italian pizza kitchen. Nearly everyone would join in the pizza making, with us all sharing each other's creations. At the end of the evening, the winner of the best pizza would receive a bottle of champagne, whilst anyone responsible for a substandard result had to down shots of grappa.

Jamie then arrived with Seb and Beto, along with Sandra Rawling and a girlfriend of hers who I had not met. Trust Jamie to bring along some female company.

A short while later, Malcs, having been invited by my mum, walked into the kitchen with a very attractive blonde English rose on his arm. It was familiar territory for him, a regular at Rockwell Manor, having often played on the home polo field. It was after matches that we would regularly attend our pizza evenings, so he was more than familiar with these occasions. His impeccable manners had him first seek out my mum and dad to say hello and introduce his English rose.

"Hello, Arthur. Hello, Fran," he greeted them, shaking my father's hand and placing a kiss on my mother's cheek. "This is Alex, my girlfriend."

"How lovely to meet you," enthused my mother.

Whilst I listened to Fabrizio giving Malcs some guidance on making the perfect pizza, I noticed Alex, or Ale as Malcs called her, in animated conversation with Beto, *in fluent Spanish*. It turned out she was in fact Spanish, probably Malc's motivation for having learned the language.

I looked around the room. There were probably around twenty-eight of us. It was also quite likely that others would drift in during the evening. It promised to be another typical, if not boisterous, night in the Rockwell Manor kitchen. This was what I'd wanted Charlotte and Gigi to experience. The side of Rockwell Manor that I enjoyed the most. The closest thing to their relaxed Shrewsbury home.

Soon the wine was flowing, dough was being rolled, and Eros Ramazzotti was playing over the sound system. The evening was going along wonderfully, drinks at the ready, people vying to make the best pizza, the occasional grappa shot for anyone who produced a substandard pizza—or any other offence, mind you—and the sound of generally animated conversation mixed in with a background of Italian music. Rockwell Manor's kitchen could best be described as "rocking."

I went over to where Charlotte was kneading a ball of dough for the base of her attempt at a perfect pizza creation. She began rolling out the dough in that rhythmical, rocking motion, then she made her selection of toppings and arranged them on the base before placing it in the oven using the pizza paddle.

Then the unthinkable happened.

Without giving any conscious consideration to what I was about to do, I rubbed my hands on the floury countertop and, as Charlotte turned around, in a moment of absolute madness, I placed both my palms on her breasts, leaving perfect handprints on her navy-blue top.

"Charles," Charlotte shrieked as she looked down at the confirmation of what I had done. Two perfect white handprints showing clearly on her dark top. We now had everyone's attention, and they all broke into rapturous laughter.

Seemingly coming to my senses, I quickly tried to remove the evidence by brushing the flour from Charlotte's breasts with my hands.

The look on her face was one of utter disbelief, which only made everyone laugh even louder.

"Oh, that's working out well, isn't it? Floured hands trying to remove flour," Charlotte remarked with jovial sarcasm as she regained her composure.

Above the commotion of everyone's laughter and chatter, I heard my mother's lighthearted reprimand. "God's truth, Edward Charles, is that what they teach you in the Air Force?"

By the end of the evening, all the ladies, barring my mother, had flour handprints on their breasts.

As the evening was coming to an end, my father stood up and commanded everyone's attention, then in a very formal tone, he announced, "And the winner of this evening's competition is Charlotte, unquestionably the very *breast* pizza."

My mother gave him a playful slap and, smiling broadly, apologised to Charlotte and Gigi. "Sorry, my dears. The Featherstone men have forgotten they are meant to be *gentlemen*."

Charlotte blushed shyly as everyone chuckled.

With the evening slowing down, my parents and the older guests went through to the drawing room for some port and tranquillity. My father half-heartedly gestured to Gigi, asking if she would like to join them.

My mother interjected, "Come along, Arthur. Gigi is having a good time here."

Even though she was closer to their age group and the mother of my friend and girlfriend, it was quite obvious where she best fit in. I guess Gigi was just used to being with twenty-something company.

It would be another hour or more before the kitchen emptied. The ambience with the pizza oven exuding its warmth made it one of the most comfortable places at Rockwell Manor. Jamie, Nic, Seb and Beto had the attentions of both Sandra and her friend, and they were all looking very content. Fabrizio was tempting the remaining guests with small dessert pizzas with fillings of Nutella chocolate spread and raspberries added after the oven process. This was also when further grappa or tequila shooters, served with salt and lemon, would make their appearance, or perhaps Disaronno Amaretto or even The King's Ginger, sipped as an after-dinner liqueur, a less damaging approach.

Charlotte and I would have liked to have left then, but instead we joined Jamie and his group and shared a little of The King's Ginger with them. A short while later, after chatting with some of the remaining guests and a few interesting looks from Sandra Rawling, I was ready to leave. It was still early, and I felt like a little fresh air. I often walked across the polo field to check on the horses at the end of an evening, and that was exactly what I felt like doing then with Charlotte.

I turned to her and asked, "Why not come with me to the stables to see how the horses are getting on?"

"As long as that Sandra Rawling isn't coming along, I might be tempted," Charlotte replied in a sarcastic voice. She clearly hadn't missed Sandra's glances towards me.

Ooh, she's jealous, I thought, feeling quite pleased with myself.

Brushing it aside, Charlotte looked at me and asked, "Will I be safe?"

"Three hundred and fifty yards from the house." I held my chin, feigning giving the idea some thought as I teased about how remote it was. "Not sure, but I'll look after you," I replied.

"And be my knight in shining armour?" Charlotte purred.

I grinned back at her like a Cheshire cat.

We said our goodnights to the last few remaining people, telling them I was going to check on the horses, and we left.

The moment we got onto the field, with the soft, dewy grass underfoot, I bent down and took off Charlotte's sandals and my JP Tod slip-ons. I turned to her and in a hushed voice said, "You do realise that by the time we are in the middle of the field, we will be in complete darkness. After all the teasing you have subjected me to today, you are likely to be in a very dangerous place on the halfway line. This is your last chance to turn back."

Charlotte looked up at me and replied, "Race you to the middle." She had no way of knowing what a special place the middle of this field was for me.

After sprinting the 150 yards, we reached the centre, out of breath, and immediately embraced each other.

"So, what now? Will you protect me from the dark?" Charlotte teased.

My reply was to lovingly kiss her.

Once in the horse barn, we slowly made our way around the stables with me telling Charlotte each horse's virtues, how good it was, how many times it won Champion Pony, and perhaps where it came from, Argentina, Australia, and South Africa, all being popular supply routes.

"I can see why you love coming here," Charlotte said, taking my hand.

Before we knew it, it was past midnight and time to go to bed.

We said very little as we walked back across the polo field, probably because I was still digesting all of what had happened that day.

When we finally reached the house, instead of going straight up to our rooms, we elected to stay on the edge of the moonlit field. I was aware of everything around me, and whilst I was taking it all in, a bare-footed Charlotte stepped onto my feet and reached up and kissed me. We stayed like that, holding and kissing each other for a long while.

The feeling in my stomach reminded me that I was still getting used to this new experience. I wondered, *Is this what love feels like?*

After some time, we eventually walked hand in hand up to the east wing, where I showed Charlotte to her bedroom door, before making my way to my North Wing suite.

Lying alone in my bed, I couldn't help thinking how quickly things had progressed between Charlotte and me since coming to Rockwell Manor. Was this because of changes in me, perhaps because we were now in my home? I secretly hoped it wasn't for that most dreaded reason—Rockwell Manor and all its trappings. Being very aware of this, I didn't think so.

I turned over and drifted off into a peaceful sleep. I just loved that we had kissed in my favourite place at Rockwell Manor, in the middle of our polo field, the resting place of my grandfather's ashes.

*I wonder what Granddad thinks? That w*as my last thought as I drifted off to sleep.

CHAPTER 19
THROGMORTON SHOOT

T HE NEXT MORNING, I was up early and decided to go across to the stables to check on the horses…again. My favourite pastime. On the way there, I couldn't help thinking about the upcoming Throgmorton shoot Friday and Saturday. The anticipation was killing me. As I walked through the barn, thoughts of the previous night flooded back.

Attempting to clear my head, I painstakingly tended to the horses until breakfast. We had organised a practise match, our last opportunity to prepare ourselves for the finals on Sunday.

At eight o'clock, I strolled back across the field to the house for breakfast and was surprised to find everyone had already arrived.

"Good morning, Sunbeam," my mother greeted me. "Where have you been, my love?"

"To the horses, Mum."

"Goodness, you can't leave them alone," she replied.

As I served myself bran and berries, Gigi turned to my mother. "I really can't wait for this weekend at the Throgmortons. I haven't had a good spa day in ages, and your suggestions of what we can do with the truffles sound wonderful."

I was so pleased to hear how everyone was now looking forward to doing some of the things I loved.

The day went by in a flash. Jamie and I enjoyed a great practise match, and I felt ready for the upcoming Barrett Cup final. The timing was perfect. We would exercise the horses the next day before we set off for Throgmortons in the early afternoon. The grooms would give them light work on Friday and Saturday, and they would be razor sharp for Sunday's big match.

My mother kept Gigi and Charlotte busy all day, taking them shopping and making sure they had all the appropriate attire for the weekend. Then they went over to Wentworth Club, where my mother had once been the ladies captain, I proudly told them. Charlotte had expressed an interest in starting to play golf, and my telling her what a wonderful coach my mother was may have been the trigger. Next, they lunched at Guards Polo Club.

I heard later that Gigi had "coincidentally" been introduced to a couple of nice men who were unsurprisingly both single. I loved the thought of Gigi, one of my favourite people, finding love in Berkshire.

The next day we set off after lunch to Devon and Bovey Castle, with Jamie and I having decided to take both our cars to give us a second vehicle for our time there. Gigi jumped in with Jamie, taking for granted Charlotte would come with me. We had over a three-hour drive ahead of us, which I was thoroughly looking forward to.

We soon slipped into a space of complete comfort. Charlotte held my thigh, affectionately squeezing me from time to time as we chatted amiably about all sorts of things. She made our song choices, fed me the occasional snack, and handed me something to drink, and we just talked and laughed.

I couldn't help remembering one of my granddad's lessons. *"If you're going somewhere special, start by enjoying the journey."* It didn't end there. He had another point on the matter when he asked me, "Which is more important, the journey or the destination?" I shrugged. "It's the company," he said. I was enjoying this journey, looking forward to the destination, and loving the company.

As we drove through the gates and approached the imposing Bovey Castle, Charlotte remarked, grinning broadly, "Upstaging the Featherstones, I see." She was happy and relaxed, which was exactly how she made me feel.

Unusually, I was driving some way behind Jamie, just enjoying the trip with Charlotte instead of racing ahead to our destination. We arrived in the car park just a few minutes behind them.

Walking into the entrance of the hotel, I watched Charlotte taking in her surroundings. The main building was in Jacobean style, and the interior was high quality, with wood-panelled rooms and elaborately carved features. Some of the rooms were in neo-Elizabethan style.

"Mmm, very interesting," she said, which meant she quite liked it.

We checked in at a separate desk with a sign that announced Throgmorton Estate Shoot.

Once settled in our separate rooms, I was wondering what to do when my bedside phone rang.

"Charles, are you going to show us around this place?" came Jamie's enthusiastic request.

"Good idea. Let me call Charlotte and you call your mum. I'm sure they would also like to stretch their legs," I said, taking responsibility.

He agreed, and soon we all met downstairs for a quick tour before dinner.

The early evening autumn sky was clear, contributing to the air being more than just a little fresh. A brisk walk, with me pointing out some of the features of Bovey Castle would be the perfect entrée to the dinner ahead. It was an exhilarating feeling, taking charge and showing the Blackwoods around the establishment.

Bovey Castle had lots to offer within its 275-acre estate, including gin making, off-road driving, fly fishing, clay-pigeon shooting, archery, an impressive championship golf course, and lovely long walkways in the park and surrounds. It was also home to a luxury spa and its renowned treatments, with its own Gentlemen's Quarter. Gigi wasted no time in arranging massages and manicures for her and Charlotte, even though their hands looked as beautiful as ever to me.

Dinner required gentlemen to wear a jacket, and most would don ties, as I chose to do, not feeling it appropriate to take a casual approach. I wore a dark green Ralph Lauren cashmere jacket, with a very faintly checked cream shirt and a tie that featured flying ducks, over dark khaki chino-type trousers, and brown Oxford shoes.

My mother had made sure I would be presentable for Charlotte and bought me her favourite aftershave and cologne sprays, which she'd slipped into my toiletry bag.

When I'd asked my father if he agreed with my mum's choice, his simple reply had been, "How would I know? Your mother has been buying my fragrances forever."

I applied both but not lavishly, remembering her words, *"Less is more, Sunbeam."*

For the final touch I put my tie-matching silk handkerchief in my breast pocket, with just the right amount showing, and adjusted my shirt cuffs so only about half an inch protruded from my jacket sleeve. Hands and nails looked neat and trim. Frances Featherstone would be happy. All set, I left the room, excited about the evening that lay ahead.

Jamie arrived in the private dining room, wearing a jacket sans a tie and feeling no qualms about his open neck.

He and I stood on the far side of the room at the bar, enjoying an unobstructed view of the area as we watched the other guests arrive, most of whom were more elderly than us. For this reason, I was very pleased when I saw a friend of mine, Edward Dashwood, walk into the banquet hall. He was well named as he certainly cut a 'dashing' figure while striding through the room. And what made him even more so was that he was the only son of Sir Frances Dashwood, the 11th Baronet of Great Britain, which meant Edward was destined to become the 12th Baronet on his father's passing. Along with his father, they had begun establishing what was almost certainly going to become one of the country's leading shooting estates. This included the continuation of the manufacture of bespoke English guns under the E. J. Churchill brand. I would be sure to spend some time with him over the course of the weekend and hopefully arrange some grouse shooting, his favourite. Right then though, I was more preoccupied with looking out for Charlotte, of course.

The place settings indicated there would be about forty guests. It was a grand room, with a large chandelier flanked by two smaller ones, centred over the long Georgian dining table. Various paintings, mostly of hunting scenes, were spaced between ornate glass and crystal wall lights. The waiters wore black tie, and the waitresses wore matching attire with a French-maid feel. Light classical music wafted out from concealed speakers. It all presented a salubrious setting, promising another memorable pre-shoot dinner.

Taking it all in, Jamie turned to me and asked, "Should I have worn a tie?"

My Rude Awakening

"Oh, don't worry, Jamie. A few of the men will be open necked," I replied.

When Charlotte and Gigi arrived, they were immediately noticed. Looking like a Renaissance beauty, Charlotte wore a midcalf, ruffled, stone-coloured skirt, a cream blouse with puffed sleeves, cuffs with at least eight buttons on each, and brown knee-high boots that laced up to the top. But it was a beige-and-green-piped underbust corset bodice over her blouse that completed her outfit. Coincidentally, the fabric was a similar duck-shooting scene as the one on my tie. The way the corset laced up on her back gave the effect of creating a very pronounced hourglass figure, while the push-up corset accentuated the fullness of her chest. She had completed the ensemble with a dark green French beret, which she had set to one side of her blonde head of hair. She had draped a mahogany-brown and gold-trimmed silk pashmina loosely over her shoulders. Anyone would have thought we had colour coded our dress that evening. My eyes never left her, and I couldn't wait to have her on my arm. As she got a little closer to us, I could see the result of her interlude at the beauty salon. Her nails were always on the short side, and once again, she had decided on her favourite dark burgundy varnish. I couldn't wait to feel those hands in mine.

Gigi looked less country chic but equally as beautiful. She wore a blue-and-brown-checked tweed skirt that landed below the knee, with matching short jacket and quite a low-cut peach silk blouse. She looked younger, much more like Charlotte's sister, with no more than ten years between them. The single men in the room were definitely noticing them both.

Jamie and I were joined by Humphrey, the son of our host, Alistair Throgmorton. There was a certain air of intrigue around us, having just earned our RAF wings. Jamie revelled in it. I didn't. It was nothing compared to the attention Charlotte and Gigi were getting.

From the moment they arrived, it seemed that nearly every man in the room wanted to engage with them, and this continued through the entire evening. My mother had clearly managed to get a message to the Throgmortons that one of our guests was the lovely Georgina Blackwood. She could hardly finish one drink before there was another eager man offering her a replacement, always inclined to touch her arm or hand. Goodness, I hoped Gigi was not feeling ambushed. As nice as it was for my mum to pave the way for her to meet someone, I could plainly see she didn't need any help from my parents.

We finally sat down to dinner. It was always mixed placings on the first evening, so everyone could get to know each other. I had already seen my name card but had not yet been able to see where Charlotte had been seated. I was pleased to see that whilst she was on the other side of the table, it was just four places down, diagonally across from me.

It was a lavish affair. Duck liver pate and fig preserve with toasted baguettes, salmon mouse with caviar, or crab legs, still half in their shell with various dips, were the starter options. The main courses were aged rib-eye roast, baked Scottish salmon, or rock lobster, all served with an array of accompaniments. The dessert trolley would come later.

The dinner progressed at a steady pace. After the starters, Humphrey's dad, Alistair, stood up and welcomed the guests to the shoot, followed by a short, comical speech. He felt it necessary to let everyone know what a shotgun shell cost. He was correct in assuming that most of the guests were a bit hazy on that point. He went on to estimate how many rounds would be fired, especially if you were a bad shot, which he suspected most of the guests were. He did a brief calculation of the cost of staying at Bovey Castle and then, of course, the cost of being on the shoot itself. He did a hilarious little animated exercise of adding it all up, coming up with the total cost per guest. He then estimated how many game birds would be shot, divided the total monetary value by the number of birds, and came up with a cost per bird, which turned out to be just under £1,000 if you were to bag say twenty grouse or pheasant. No one was particularly concerned and broke into further spirited laughter when Mr. Throgmorton suggested to everyone that, at £1,000 per pheasant, we ought not shoot too many birds. Befuddled logic indeed, which made everyone laugh even more.

Dinner finally ended. The normal form was that everyone would continue mingling and chatting. The music was usually changed to something a little more upbeat, encouraging the guests to have a little dance. I had no interest in being drawn into the remainder of the evening.

Much to the disappointment of at least three hopeful men, Gigi announced that she was a little tired and would be going to bed. She turned towards the door, waving good night to Jamie, Charlotte, and me as she left the room.

I looked across at Charlotte chatting merrily enough with two men, who were speaking in an animated fashion. But knowing her as I did, I realised she wasn't responding in the way I knew she would've had she been even half interested. It made me feel even more that she was mine.

I was just about to say good night to Jamie and go rescue Charlotte when one of the waitresses, Candy, came over and asked if we would like another drink. Over the past two hours, she had become awfully attentive towards Jamie. I hadn't given it a second thought because he just had that way with women, especially nubile ones like Candy. I thought it would be peculiar if I said no, so we both ordered something.

There was a little more chitchat, Candy telling us that she was a second or third cousin to Humphrey. "The poor cousin," she pointed out.

From what I could tell, not too poor for Jamie. She more than made up for it with a bubbly personality and pretty face, by the look on his face.

Candy said she was finishing off shortly and, if we liked, she could come and have a goodnight drink with us. Both Jamie and I agreed but for two different reasons. Jamie would be very pleased to engage with her, and she would be the reason for my escape.

Pleased with our responses, she declared. "Wonderful. Let me go and get your order and then I am *all* yours."

That was an invitation Jamie would undoubtedly accept.

With Candy having left to get our drinks, I told Jamie that when she returned, three would certainly be a crowd and I would slip away. His broad grin was unequivocal agreement.

I finally managed to get across to where Charlotte was, and in no time at all, the naturally demonstrative interactions between us made clear to the hopeful men who had been speaking to her that we were an item. Ooh, that made me feel good.

We chatted for a while before we both decided that an earlyish night would be a good idea ahead of the forthcoming exciting day. I walked Charlotte to her door, and instead of me just kissing her goodnight, we stood there and continued kissing each other affectionately. Then as if she had just thought of something, she pulled back and said in a matter-of-fact tone. "Edward Charles Featherstone, I think there's something you ought to know."

"Yes," I replied, wondering what that something was.

"I love you, that's all." And she kissed me squarely on the lips before turning on her heels, leaving me at the door as she went into her room.

I hadn't even had the chance to reciprocate, or say goodnight, but it made no difference to my instant elation or the excited feeling in my stomach.

In something of a dreamy state, I headed down the hallway to my room. How my world had changed, all because of a girl!

CHAPTER 20
COMING OF AGE

I WENT DOWN TO breakfast, and my timing could not have been better. I caught up to a very bright and cheerful Charlotte at the bottom of the stairs and got to walk into the bustling dining area with her at my side. I felt very vitalised, and probably quite in love, which may have been the reason Jamie gave me an enquiring, frowned look as we approached our table.

I couldn't help remembering a conversation we'd had when Jamie expressed his concern that Charlotte and me being together may affect our relationship. This must have been what he was thinking now. I made a mental note to speak to him about it and do things with him that would allay his fears. The two of us going on his first driven game-bird shoot was a good start.

Gigi arrived minutes later and sat down next to her daughter at the breakfast table.

"You look gorgeous and radiant this morning, Mum. As if you've just stepped out of the pages of *Horse & Hound*," Charlotte remarked.

Idle chitchat about the previous night ensued, but it was the shooting and truffle hunt that was foremost on our minds.

Once outside, Jamie and I walked towards the Land Rovers designated for the game-bird shoot party. Charlotte and Gigi went over to where three Range Rovers and a pickup truck waited to transport their group and a handful of dogs to a nearby forest known for burgundy truffles. In the past, it had been traditional to use pigs for seeking out these delicacies, but pigs were difficult to train and would often devour what they unearthed from the shallow roots of the trees. The hounds had a keen sense of smell, were easily trained, and had no interest in eating the truffles. Instead, they were thrilled to be rewarded with a sausage for their efforts. I enjoyed watching the Blackwood ladies enthusiastically preparing for their outing.

The Throgmorton weekend was a bespoke shoot, eight guns, all of whom were men on this occasion, dressed in the proper attire and careful to observe shooting etiquette. Because of the abundance of game bird that would be driven overhead, we each had a matched pair of shotguns.

One of my discomforts was that the loaders were often retired gentlemen who loved the outdoors and being involved in country shooting. In addition to loading, they were responsible for carrying your guns, various items of clothing, and your rather weighty cartridge case, and at the end of the day, they cleaned your gun. Having these seniors looking after me in this way did not sit well with me, so I was very quick to share the burden. Giving them a generous gratuity and as many grouse or pheasant as they desired, at the end of the day made me feel better. And I always cleaned my own gun, something I enjoyed.

As arranged, we did four drives between ten in the morning and one in the afternoon, with plenty of time to move from one location to the next, have a snack, and partake of a little sloe gin, the drink of choice on a shoot. I was sure Charlotte and Gigi would also be warming themselves with sloe gin during their truffle hunt.

It was wonderful being in the countryside again, working with the retriever dogs, moving from drive-to-drive and experiencing some of the best driven game bird in the country. I couldn't help but notice how Jamie had progressed. The delight on his face was a looking glass into how he was feeling, and he bagged six pheasant on the first drive.

Four drives later, we returned to Bovey Castle, first changing from our shooting gear into lounge attire. We then met our partners for a sumptuous lunch. I was more than tickled by the thought of lunching with Charlotte. *My partner.*

As we drifted into the collecting room outside the dining area, I couldn't wait to hear what she had been up to. She enthusiastically told me about her haul of truffles and that they were having a thoroughly good time.

After a jovial lunch, as we were preparing to go our separate ways again,

Charlotte came up to me and gave me a somewhat lingering kiss goodbye. What was unusual was how she no longer had any concern about her mother and brother witnessing it. I loved how she quite happily openly demonstrated that I was her boyfriend.

As Jamie and I set off together, I decided it would be a good time to say something. Being sure to give it a positive perspective, I came straight out with, "Jamie, wouldn't it be wonderful if we could always do these things, you know, shooting, polo, and perhaps one day even flying privately together?"

His face lit up with me having mentioned the two new pastimes in his life that he had become quite passionate about. "Yeah, so cool. As long as it doesn't change if you and Charlotte don't work out."

His one sentence spoke volumes. He'd already accepted that Charlotte and I were an item. And he had not hesitated in spelling out his concerns of how we could affect my relationship with him.

"That's not going to happen, Jamie. I mean, we will still want to do all of these things together even if Charlotte and I didn't work out," I assured him.

The day's shoot was an enormous success. Jamie did well, contributing around sixteen pheasant to the day's bag of 165 birds. I did fine, my contribution being about forty pheasant, after having left the easier pickings to the guns on either side of me. The other guns had noticed that I seldom missed my quarry, often getting two in quick succession, one with each barrel. The loaders would sometimes wager with each other on their respective shooters, which often led to the comical situation of a loader trying to win a bet by coaching his shooter in an attempt to improve his yield.

My favourite part of the shoot was the dogs and how they would retrieve the stricken quarry and bring them to your feet. When I saw an English springer spaniel, I couldn't help thinking nostalgically of my beloved Osric.

We got back to the hotel in the early evening, changed back into our jackets and shoes, and went to the quaint bar for drinks. I watched for Charlotte, who eventually arrived along with the other ladies, all rosy-cheeked and looking incredibly pleased with themselves. She was holding a medium-sized wicker basket with a linen cloth lining.

Charlotte walked up to us, gave me a kiss on the lips, and opened the cloth covering the basket to reveal their truffle haul. It was impressive by any standards. Charlotte began excitedly telling us about their day with Gigi interjecting every now and then. They clearly loved the outdoors and the lighthearted competitiveness of truffle hunting. It had been special for them to spend that time together.

"Ooh, and I must tell you about the most delightful bitch that I was working with. Daisy," Charlotte enthused. "She was an English springer spaniel, just like Osric I imagine, my babe."

I quickly looked at Jamie and Gigi to see how they reacted to this very forthright term of endearment Charlotte had just used for me. They didn't bat an eyelash.

She carried on, unconcerned. "She's only three years old and so beautifully trained. And guess what else, she will one day be a gundog. And, babe, for a moment while I was working with Daisy, I got an inkling of you and Osric." She then looked at me very tenderly and said, "You lost a good friend."

I was seeing a most unusual side of Charlotte, and it spurred all sorts of emotions.

"I just love it here. I would love to live in Berkshire, and we could get a springer spaniel," she went on, seemingly quite comfortable making these plans for the future.

There was no objection from me. Thinking about getting older and having a family was not something that had really crossed my mind before then.

"So, what is on the cards tomorrow?" I asked. "More truffle hunting?"

"Oh no, tomorrow we are going to have a lovely spa and beauty day together," Gigi said.

I was thrilled they were having such an enjoyable time. It meant I wouldn't have to do any convincing the next time there was a shoot.

We went to our rooms to freshen up for dinner. I dressed in light beige chino trousers, a white shirt, and a navy-blue Ralph Lauren cashmere blazer. Instead of a tie, I donned a light turquoise paisley silk cravat with a colour-matching pocket handkerchief, no pattern. As I was about to walk out, I remembered my aftershave and cologne spray, courtesy of my mother.

My Rude Awakening

Jamie and Charlotte were already in the bar when I got downstairs. "I told Mum we'd meet here," Charlotte said, glowing in an above-the-knee floral dress and high heels. The country air agreed with her. Jamie was now wearing a tie and looked a bit smarter than the previous evening.

Gigi arrived a short time later, looking gorgeous in a flowing cream coloured dress with tan leather trimming around the hem, cuffs, and neckline. Combined with her peep-toe leather platform wedges, the ensemble gave her a definite younger, edgier look. Once again she looked more like Charlotte's sister than her mother, and I think she secretly enjoyed dressing like that.

Once in the dining room, we were greeted warmly by the rest of the team, but it was Gigi who everyone made a special effort with. My mother had certainly done a good job in promoting her.

The evening was a lot more relaxed than the previous night. We'd all gotten to know one another and shared stories of our day's activities. Our maître d' announced that dinner would be served, so we moved in the direction of our long dining table. As was the norm on the second night, there were no place settings. While I wondered what we should do, I felt Charlotte's hand on my arm.

She asked me with a doe-eyed, hangdog expression, "Would you mind terribly taking me to my seat…next to yours?"

"Oh, as terrible as that is, I will accede, ma'am," I said with a little bow.

We had another lovely dinner, though we had to be mindful to speak to the people around us and not become totally engrossed with just each other. When it finally ended, Gigi was the first to leave, the fresh air and forest walk the reason for her tiredness. In fairness, the day had taken it out of all of us and so it wasn't long before we were all ready to retire. As had become our habit recently, one that I was happy to adopt, I took Charlotte to her room, gave her a warm kiss, and then went to my room.

The next morning as I donned my jacket, I thought Charlotte and Gigi having a health and beauty spa day together was a wonderful way to end a most enjoyable time in the countryside. I wondered what the Blackwood ladies might talk about while relaxing and being so pampered.

The agenda for the guns was more straightforward. We would continue as we had the day before, the only difference being that we would be going to six distinct parts of the estate. Consistent with trying to save the best for last, the drives arranged for the second day were all quite exceptional. Once again, we did four in the morning, then had another particularly good lunch, albeit a little shorter than the day before because everyone was inclined to leave a little earlier.

The two afternoon drives were unparalleled, with the Throgmortons having placed a far greater number of pheasant at those two locations so that the beaters, responsible for flushing the game birds, were able to put up far more quarry, making sure everyone had a good final afternoon. This was no doubt a little marketing ploy to make sure all the participants came back for more the following season. It worked on me. I think I added no fewer than thirty-five birds to the bag and made a mental note to return next year.

At the end of a day or weekend shoot, the participants are at liberty to take as many birds as they desire. This most often amounted to just one to three braces, two to six birds. At a good shoot weekend, if everyone did this, the estate owner would still be left with several hundred birds to send to the town's butchers for gratuitous distribution to the townsfolk.

We returned to the main house and, with lots of hugs and kisses, said our goodbyes. I thanked Mr. and Mrs. Alistair Throgmorton, who made sure I would pass on their best wishes to my parents.

Charlotte took up what now seemed her rightful place, next to me, for the trip back home.

Once we were out of the gates of Bovey Castle, I looked at her and patted my lap.

She knew exactly what I wanted and slipped off her shoes. After making sure she was still securely in her seat belt, she put her bare feet on my lap.

I had selected some music for the drive home, which I put into the CD changer. The first song, "(I've Had) The Time of My Life" from a recent favourite movie, *Dirty Dancing*, aptly described exactly how I felt as we drove along the winding roads. I listened to Charlotte half singing and half humming along to the song, with her feet on my lap and a hand on my thigh. Every now and then, she gave my leg a little rub or a squeeze, but not because I was speeding. I was in no rush to get back to Rockwell Manor.

My Rude Awakening

"(I've Had) The Time of My Life" – Bill Medley, Jennifer Warnes

| YouTube | Spotify | Apple |

I really hadn't ever felt like this before, and I had really *had the time of my life*. Consumed by the fantasy of the moment, I ignored the realities of our circumstances. Each verse seemed to describe us perfectly. Did I now have *someone to stand by me*?

CHAPTER 21
GOODBYE, ROCKWELL MANOR

O UR DRIVE BACK to my home was a most enjoyable one. Charlotte and I chatted about all sorts of things, giving us insight into each other's views and opinions about life in general, as well as the past two days, of course. The only time our conversation slowed was when a good song made Charlotte spontaneously sing or hum along.

En route, we stopped at the petrol station, and she ran into the convenience store to get us water and a snack. When I noticed that she drew the attention of two fellows, now, instead of feeling pangs of jealousy, I felt proud. *She's* my *girl.*

Back on the road, we played a game of guessing each other's likes or dislikes, naming something and guessing if the other would like or dislike it, agree or disagree. We discovered we were aligned on most things and even managed to accurately guess things like favourite colour for an evening dress and so forth.

We got back to Rockwell Manor in the early evening, both feeling disappointed that we would no longer be alone. We were greeted warmly by my mum, but my dad was not yet back from his business trip to London. She assured me that he would not miss the Barrett Cup final the following day.

Being reminded of this, I began getting my head into the next day's game. I was anxious to go across to the stables and check that everything was in order with the horses, even though I didn't have to worry about it with Guy.

Charlotte volunteered to come with me, obviously. I would have gotten that question right in our "how well do you know me" game.

My Rude Awakening

We walked across the field, clasping hands in the darkness until we got to the stables. Once we were in the dimly lit barn, we wandered around as the horses munched and snorted away. Every now and then, Charlotte gave one a rub on its snout or a scratch under its chin. Making conversation as we walked, I pointed out one or another horse, how good it was, how many times it won Champion Pony, and perhaps where it came from, Australia, South Africa, and Argentina all being popular supply routes.

"I can see why you love coming here," Charlotte said, taking my hand.

After spending a good three-quarters of an hour there, we then headed back to the main house and I walked Charlotte up to her room. We were both a bit sullen, all too aware our trip was coming to an end.

The next day, we arrived in good time at Guards for our afternoon Barrett Cup final. Charlotte and Gigi also got there with plenty of time to spare. Our team could not have been more ready.

Because it was a cup final, it was played on Smith's Lawn, the Guards Polo Club main field. It was much like any other polo field except for one inimitable feature. A first-time visitor would perhaps be surprised to discover that a wooden structure about the size of a large house of two stories, each level with slightly oversized balconies, was in fact a building of some significant importance and impossible to duplicate. That it had been built overlooking the centre line of the field would potentially give an inkling of its importance. It was none other than the Royal Box. I knew our match was unlikely to attract the attention of any of the well-known royalty, let alone the attention of our queen, Elizabeth II, or our club's president, Prince Philip. That of course did not concern me one iota. As was the tradition, one of the local regiment bands would lead the two teams out onto the field to be introduced to whichever members of the Royal Family were in attendance and other dignitaries in the royal box, and then to the other guests seated in the stands on either side of this structure. There was always a good turnout, the social world loving the opportunity of being able to put their glitz and glamour on full display. Another reason was that it was a bloody good picnic spot in bucolic surroundings.

After nearly losing our semifinal match with my head being in the clouds for half the game, there were no such scares this time. The entire team was in top form, and so were our horses. I played as well as I'd ever done, with a bit of déjà vu from the previous week's second half, when I'd played with great gusto. The difference could only have been Charlotte.

We ran out comfortable winners with a nine-to-five score line.

When we came off the field, my father was the first to shake my hand warmly and congratulate me as if I had won the match all on my own. Even my mother seemed pleased with the result, and I was spared her normal reproach after a match, singling out various incidents over the six chukkas where I had put myself in harm's way. Charlotte gave me a big hug and warm kisses on the mouth. My mother and father looked quietly pleased with her affections towards me. Jamie stood dutifully by, waiting for prize giving.

Sandra Rawling was there too, catching me unawares and giving me a big kiss right in front of Charlotte. "Wow, well done, Charles. Your team was brilliant. You can give me more of that anytime," she said.

I was not sure what it was she wanted more of. The expression on Charlotte's face told me she would prefer Sandra Rawling keep all her desires entirely to herself.

As was customary, the teams lined up alongside each other for the presentation and speeches. Even though I was not the captain of our team, the trophy was handed to me. Once again, I was aware of the deference shown towards me, which always made me uncomfortable. Best pony was won by Chance, something that was becoming a regular occurrence.

With the sun disappearing from the autumn sky, we walked into what was usually the club's main dining room and found the winners table. With none of us in a celebratory mood, we had decided to keep the evening brief, just to show our faces and have a drink before we would leave to go home for our last supper together at Rockwell Manor.

As the evening progressed, Charlotte did a good job of steering me clear of Sandra Rawling. Sandra seemed to notice and duly kept her distance, until Charlotte went to the lady's cloakroom. No sooner had she left than someone came up behind my chair, covered my eyes with their feminine hands, and the immediately recognisable voice of Sandra Rawling asked, "Guess who?" With no effort to disguise her voice, this clearly wasn't intended to be a real guessing game.

"How could it be anyone other than darling Sandra?" I asked, meaning for it to sound sarcastic, but somehow it didn't.

No one seemed to notice except my parents, who found it amusing enough, unaware of anything unusual, given that Sandra and I had practically grown up together. Wary of Charlotte once again having to contend with more of Sandra, I was pleased she disengaged from her little flirtation before Charlotte returned.

Soon thereafter, we were all ready to leave. Driving in convoy, we arrived at Rockwell Manor together. After a quick shower, we assembled in the family dining room for dinner.

Having come to the end of our visit, we were trying to enjoy the last night together before we would leave after a light lunch the next day, Charlotte and Gigi to Shrewsbury, Jamie and me to RAF Shawbury. Without exception, everyone was long-faced.

The mood lifted noticeably when Gigi came through to the family dining room with our entrée, which of course just had to be tagliolini and taleggio with truffle shavings. In fact, she'd asked Fabrizio to step aside and produced the dish entirely on her own.

Everybody was suitably impressed, especially my father, who loved pasta and knew when it was perfectly prepared. He was not afraid to voice his appreciation and, on this occasion, took Gigi's hand and proffered in his best Italian, "*Mille grazie,*" and kissed her hand.

What a charmer, I thought.

The final seal of approval came from Fabrizio, who stepped into the dining room just to let everyone know that it was the best tagliolini with taleggio and truffle shavings he had ever tasted.

Dinner ended without the more drawn out cheese board, port or liqueurs, with Gigi and Charlotte wanting to finish their packing. Not so for Jamie and me as our packing would only be a matter of minutes the next morning before we were ready to leave.

After a quick breakfast on the downstairs patio, the time had come to bid our farewell. Nobody was enjoying the fact that we were leaving, my mother especially. I knew she was feeling pensive, knowing full well that I would be starting the next phase of my RAF instruction, the advanced-training segment, and then transferring to Joint Helicopter Command and, hopefully, the AH-64 Apache attack helicopter squadron. In conflict with how much I would miss spending time with Charlotte for a while, there was nothing that excited me more, and there was nothing that excited my mother less.

We threw our last bits of luggage into the boots of our respective cars, mine into the tiny space in the front of my Porsche. I took the water and snacks my mother had prepared for us and handed them around, feeling a little like my mother was still treating me as if I were at boarding school. In addition, there was a basket covered with a cloth, holding a few bottles of truffle oil and truffles, the riches from Charlotte's and Gigi's hunt. I hoped we would be tasting those again soon, but back in Shrewsbury.

It was now time for the matter of goodbyes. The three Blackwoods seemed to have imagined it would be a drawn-out affair, but not in the Featherstone household. Because my mother was always emotional at these times, in contrast to her normal more stoic manner, our goodbyes were unusually brief, with my father always on hand, ready to put a comforting arm around my mother's shoulders. We bid our brief farewells to my mum and dad, with Charlotte and Gigi promising to return.

Jamie went on ahead. I was in no rush to get back to our base camp. About ten minutes into my journey, I turned to my Walkman. It was not the rock playlist I selected but rather the one I had been creating during my time with Charlotte.

I found the track I was looking for. My head filled with thoughts of the girl who had become an important part of my life, I began listening to one of my favourite groups.

"I Want to Know What Love Is" – Foreigner

| YouTube | Spotify | Apple |

I couldn't help but think that Charlotte had made me feel what love was, and I was desperate not to let that go. I had found love, but would I be able to keep it?

The RAF posed such a formidable obstacle, especially with the new phase of my military career ahead. It was undoubtedly going to be the most demanding training syllabus of my time in the Air Force, followed by falling under the umbrella of Joint Helicopter Command and the inevitable postings into the field, there was a lot on our minds. My RAF future of what I would be doing was clear. I had to be successful, but the future was very unclear as to where it would leave Charlotte and me! We both knew it. We both felt it. We both hated it, and we both felt it was better not to speak about it. *Part of being in love,* I imagined.

CHAPTER 22
ADVANCED TRAINING

MY DRIVE BACK to RAF Shawbury was filled with anguish. I dreaded the thought of not knowing how often, or even when, Charlotte and I would see each other again. I would just have to be content with a nightly phone call for the time being, though I knew many relationships with military servicemen experienced complications from not seeing each other.

Our two-week pass had been the most amazing time with Charlotte and me really getting to know each other and becoming a couple. I couldn't help imagining all the possibilities, including if we could ever get married. That thought was certainly in the minds of my parents, but how realistic is that with your first serious relationship? This was then followed by a harsh jolt back to reality with the resumption of our Air Force training. It was quite upsetting, but on the flip side, I felt twinges of anticipation as I got closer to RAF Shawbury and the exciting times ahead.

I sped into the base, and looking at the clock in my car, I knew everyone would have been at lunch, including Jamie. I sought him out, and after seeing where he was, I got my own plate of food and sat down across from him.

"Hello, chum. So I beat you," Jamie said, smiling.

We chatted for a while and then Jamie brought up something as nonchalantly as he could but which I sensed had been playing on his mind.

"And, bud, you are still good with helping me on the flying and things?"

"No question, old chap. It helps me too," I said honestly.

"Thank you, chum. I really appreciate it," Jamie replied.

My mood lifted at the thought that I may soon be back in Shrewsbury.

My Rude Awakening

Over the next few weeks, I spent a lot of time with Jamie, and as I had told him, it was also good for me in equal measure. At the end of this fortnight, we had our most important ranking assessment. Now that we were at the business end of our training, the instructors made sure we knew exactly where we stood on the ladder, thereby creating a lot of competition between us. That did not hold true for Jamie, Will, and me. Our friendship and support of each other came ahead of the ladder system. This subtle change of approach was the first time the reality of the grouping system struck home. Three of the original eight Group A pilots were dropped down to Group B, and in turn, three Group B pilots moved up. Jamie and Will were unaffected, though I could see it caused Jamie quite some consternation. Once someone from Group B had been moved up, they would be determined to stay there. It was a fight to hold onto our Group A positions, creating a lot of competition. Whereas previously we had all been together, almost "against the system" so as not to be ejected, we were now firmly up against each other. Was this how the RAF made sure they were getting the best possible combat pilots?

After just a few more weeks of training and many hours of working with Jamie, we completed our first big formal evaluations and were both still in Group A. Once we had finished this appraisal, it was time to move on to more advanced training.

All sixteen of us, comprising all of Groups A and B, had been summoned to the Ops Room for a briefing. This was an unscheduled examination. And a few of the other instructors had come along to watch the morning's activities. As I scanned the faces in the room, it was obvious who was feeling confident and who was not. Jamie was looking decidedly fidgety.

"Right, chaps, less than six weeks before streaming assessments. Time to go dancing," said Captain Swales, enjoying himself.

We looked at each other with slightly bemused expressions.

"The first move is the swirling line dance, and the next will be the pirouette."

We were lost. Dancing? I saw the bemusement turn to concern—it had to involve a helicopter, and it had to be complicated…and testing. Why else would there be a room full of instructors? Whatever Captain Swales was talking about had to be serious.

"So, this is how it goes," said Captain Swales. "For the swirling line dance, you will fly a thousand yards down the centre of the runway at twenty knots, maintaining twelve feet AGL in ground effect."

This meant the helicopter would use the ground cushion created beneath its blades and be airborne just several feet above the ground, not technically flying, per se, but doing hovering exercises.

Can't be that simple, I thought.

"In the process, you will do recurring 360-degree rotations."

Okay…not that simple!

"You will be judged on maintaining height and speed, remaining on the runway centre line, your fluidity of motion and, most importantly, the number of 360-degree rotations you complete. You will be given one practise run and then it's a go."

This was the crux of it. This "simple" exercise tested our control and fluidity because we were having to combine all three in the ever-changing parameters as we synchronised our movements in perfect, coordinated harmony and "swirled" down the runway.

Fly down the centre line of the runway whilst your helicopter is spinning. At twenty knots! How will the instructor know our speed? No sooner had I asked myself the question than I had the answer. Stopwatch.

I completely got it, and I could not wait. I had quickly worked out the best way to manage the speed element. *20 knots = 33.75 feet per second.* I needed to fly the thousand yards in one minute and thirty seconds, or ninety seconds, and that would give me my twenty knots. That was easy enough, without even trying to look at the airspeed indicator, which would be rubbish anyway, because of the perpetual change in direction of the helicopter. That alone would catch out most of this bunch. I also sensed I would have to watch the engine parameters, as I did not want to stress or over temp the jet turbines. Doing so would not go down well on my assessment results.

Once I saw the exercise clearly, my excitement surged. I looked at Jamie, who was anything but excited. "Don't go first," I said out of the corner of my mouth. "You will be fine."

"Featherstone, no coaching now. This is an individual assessment," came Captain Swales's sharp rebuke. Then he asked, "Who's first?"

My hand shot up. I did not need to be so enthusiastic, because as it turned out there wasn't anyone else that wanted that dubious honour.

I got into the Bell Griffin, started up the two jet turbines without the need of the checklist, and within minutes was lifting off into a hover to position myself at the designated start point on the runway. As I leant the helicopter forward while applying power with my collective and making small adjustments on the pedals because of the change in torque effect, I got a reference for the halfway mark, which was the windsock. I would need to be there at forty-five seconds. I started the stopwatch of the digital chronometer and began my exercise.

I reached my midway marker in forty-three seconds, a tad too fast. Just then, I felt the tail begin to whip around. The fortuitously chosen windsock billowed, indicating a gusting wind. I had completed seven 360-degree rotations with perfect height and symmetry, always keeping the runway aligned with the middle of the helicopter. *Great,* I thought. I slowed the forward speed very slightly to get a few more rotations.

I got to the end of my practise run in eighty-eight seconds, with fifteen completed 360s. I was happy with that and knew I could improve on it.

Now for the one that counted. I checked my most important instrument, the chronometer, the humble watch, and began. It went perfectly. I arrived at the end of the thousand-yard mark in ninety-one seconds, with eighteen completed 360s.

Evidently one of the other instructors shared his opinion of my results. Jamie told me later that after I had completed my test, Captain Piper turned to one of the other instructors and said, "Bloody hell, and that's his first time. This student could embarrass us."

I knew I had flown well, and his crude remark confirmed it. More and more I was feeling that the helicopter was not something I was piloting, but rather that it was an extension of me. Yes, something like a dance partner, and as we got to know each other, so our ability to confound others increased.

Some of the officers could be heard using profanities every now and then. *So much for being an officer and a gentleman,* I thought. A limited vocabulary, my mother would say.

The next chap to fly, Terence Preston, had not worked out how to manage his speed and was just guessing. I waited for the instructors to watch the next exercise, and when they were fully focused on that effort, I took Jamie aside and gave him the important pointers.

"Jamie, listen carefully. Set up to do your 360-degree rotations in an anticlockwise direction. That way you will not run out of pedal for the tail rotor. The most important instrument is the clock."

He looked surprised.

I carried on, "Your airspeed indicator will not work because it requires a constant flow of air into the pitot tube to determine the helicopter's speed. Manage your speed by completing the exercise in ninety seconds. At the midway point, which is where the windsock is, you should be at forty-five seconds or as near as possible. That is the time to adjust for the second half, if you are behind or ahead. Do not worry too much about monitoring the engine. I found that because you are in ground effect and rotating counter-clockwise, you won't over torque or over temp the engines. Rather, use that time to check height and keep the runway centreline directly under you. The thing that is going to catch this lot out will be speed—don't make that mistake—and the wind."

I continued, "There is a gust coming from 270 degrees at around fifteen knots. It will catch you as you are facing rearward, downwind the runway, and coming around again to face forward. Be sharp on your pedals. Repeat what I said, Jamie."

We went through it one more time, and I was confident that he had the points. He just needed to bring his maximum coordination to the dance party. I finished his briefing just as Captain Swales looked at us and scowled.

Jamie's effort was absolutely fine. His speed was perfect, though he could have been a little more careful with height management and general fluidity. A bit stop-start you might say. The gust out of 270 degrees didn't catch him out; he was ready for it. Twelve rotations. I figured surely that was enough.

Once all sixteen pilots had finished the exercise, Captain Swales stood up to address us. "Since this was a preparation exercise, I am happy to give you some feedback," he said. "In terms of number of rotations in the required time, and direction and height management, Featherstone gets top spot, followed by Granger, White, Blackwood, Jameson…"

I didn't pay attention to the rest. The only thing on my mind was that Jamie and Will Granger had made it into the top eight. My two companions were doing fine. Jamie looked across at me and grinned broadly. Captain Swales saw Jamie's smile and frowned at me.

"Right, gentlemen, now for the next exercise," he said. "The pirouette is straightforward enough. You will see a clearly marked eight-foot-diameter circle on the grass apron, off the threshold of runway twenty-four. Whilst in the hover, you are to place the nose of your helicopter over the centre of this circle, then swing your tail around in a perfect 360-degree rotation. The only difference though, is that you must carry on doing this for one minute. We will count the number of rotations you complete, and if the nose of the helicopter, the pitot tube, leaves the area of the circle at any point during one of the rotations, that rotation does not count. There is an interesting twist to this exercise, gentlemen. We look forward to seeing if any of you get it. You can have one practise run of one minute, and then you must do your exercise. Featherstone, you will go last."

I gathered he didn't want me to pass on tips to Jamie. Theoretically, going lower down the pecking order was an advantage because one may pick up some tips from the pilots who go before. I guessed they didn't want the other pilots to see my effort either. A backhanded compliment if ever there was one.

I managed to give Jamie my take on it anyway. "Think of your helicopter as the second hand on a watch. The nose must be held over the centre point while you swing your tail around the dial. The trick is going to be increasing power so you can increase the rate of your rotation."

I explained to him that doing this would have a big torque effect on the helicopter, and he would need to compensate significantly with the tail-rotor pedals, keeping it all in balance with the cyclic. I understood now why I'd been instructed to go last. If I got it right, it would almost certainly give the others a good idea of how to do it, instead of them working it out for themselves.

I watched my good friend Will Granger go first. He took it slow and easy in the practise exercise, and the nose left the circle a few times, but he seemed to get it right when he did his final test. It looked as if he completed ten rotations and was in the middle of the eleventh when the clock ran out.

Nothing to learn there. A few more went with nothing learnt there either. Then came Jamie's turn.

I noticed the wind had picked up, so as he walked past me, I said, "Wind, 270 degrees, gusting. It will be a factor. Don't forget, counterclockwise."

Jamie also completed ten full rotations but lost one because his nose went out of the circle. Not great, but not too bad either.

Then I watched Patrick White, the last one before me, who had come in third in the previous exercise. He did by far the best, completing thirteen rotations with one deduction.

I worked out that I could quite easily do one every four seconds for potentially fifteen total. Then I looked at the faces of the other instructors, finding them all totally unimpressed by what they had seen thus far. That spoke volumes. I had just learnt more from their expressions than from any of the candidates who had already flown. *These chaps are clearly way off the pace. Their efforts were rubbish.*

The thing I had noticed with Andrews was that his tail had been a lot higher off the ground. The aircraft had been at an angle of around 25 or even 30 degrees, nose down. I thought I would try something with my practise run and see how it went.

Then it was my turn and one of the instructors quipped, "Let's see what you've got, Featherstone."

I put my helmet on as I walked towards the helicopter, and as always, I made sure my gloves were secure and comfortable. In no time at all, I was in the hover, my nose over the eight-foot-diameter circle, and I was very aware of the excitement sitting in my gut. I was going to make my one-minute practise count.

I pulled a little bit of power on the collective while I fed in right pedal. As my rotation began, keeping the nose over the centre point, I started pulling more power. The helicopter felt remarkably stable, so I continued, pulling even more power. My rate of rotation was considerable, and I realised that the nose was decidedly down, which meant the tail would be a long way off the ground, the helicopter was probably at an angle of more than 35 or even 40 degrees. Since it was my practise run, I carried on pulling even more power. My nose left the circle, but I didn't abort because I wanted to test how far I could carry on pulling power and feeding in right rudder, all the time accelerating my rate of rotation. I started reaching power and tail-rotor limits, with the aircraft tail spinning around a theoretically "fixed" nose, pointing down low to the ground, and the tail so elevated that the helicopter was at an angle of around 50 or even 55 degrees. I knew I had it. Now for my test.

I began my exercise with a very high-power setting, feeding in a lot of right rudder while focussing entirely on keeping my nose inside the circle. I did not even bother to count my rotations, but it felt like I was doing one every two-and-a-half or three seconds. I could hear the twin jet turbines screaming in my ear. I checked my engine parameters, finding them at the top of the green. I loved what I was doing.

I finished the exercise with twenty-two rotations completed and was certain I had worked out the "twist" to the exercise. The congratulations from all the instructors and the other chaps in Group A and Group B confirmed this.

Captain Piper walked up to me and said, "So you worked it out, Featherstone?"

"Yes, I think so, Captain," I replied.

"So…what was it then?"

"You shouldn't use finesse. I was pulling nearly full power and really attacking the exercise," was my reply.

Captain Piper just nodded his head, the faintest smile curling the corners of his mouth.

Captain Swales then stood up and said, "I don't need to tell you where you finished because you all know the number of 360-degree rotations you did. I can say though, overall, most of you did well, just a few less so." He paused, as if deciding whether he should elaborate.

Then he continued, "Pilots typically fly to the limit of their capability. Every now and then we come across a pilot who can fly to the limits of the *helicopter's* capability. I'm pleased to say that in this intake, we may just have one of those." He looked at me, as did some others in the group.

That evening after a refreshing shower, I went down to the Officers Rec Room to meet up with Jamie and Will. Jamie was typically late, and Will was sitting on his own in the corner, going over some notes. It was obvious he was not only a very competent pilot but a good gunner too. What was not obvious was what Will's aspirations were—where he would like to be posted and what he wanted out of his RAF career. It was often something that trainee pilots were cagey about, perhaps not wanting to show their hand in case they didn't get the posting of their choice. Will and I we're close enough for me to initiate the subject with him.

"Hi, Will, nicely flown today," I greeted him.

"And you…bloody hell, you were a standout," he replied.

Exactly what I didn't want to hear as it made my remark seem as if I were looking for a compliment. Shrugging it off, I carried on, "Well, you're a definite for Group A, so where would you like to be posted?"

Will did not immediately answer but gave me a measured look before saying quite simply, "Apaches, nothing else."

Speak about being a dark horse. Those three softly spoken words and the tone in which they were said shouted Will's determination of being posted to the top combat squadron.

We had been back at RAF Shawbury for over four weeks and hadn't yet been able to take a single night or weekend pass, but finally, unbeknown to me, that was about to change.

It was my university graduation ceremony and my mother had invited Gigi, Charlotte, and Jamie to attend with her and my father. I was secretly very pleased, never having been one to show how I felt about receiving any accolade, but especially because Charlotte could be involved in something that had been part of my life for as long as she had known me.

I imagined the graduation ceremony was much like any other. Once the formalities were dispensed with, I rejoined our group when my mother caught me off-guard and remarked, "So you're following in my footsteps, Sunbeam."

I looked at her enquiringly before it struck me. After my mother had finished studying English Literature at university, she had studied computing and learnt to programme mainframe computers, something I had completely forgotten about when I was studying economics and computer science.

A week later, Jamie and I were heading to Shrewsbury for the weekend. As we drove down the driveway, I felt the familiar tightening in my stomach.

Gigi gave us warm, welcoming hugs and kisses. "It is so nice to have my boys home," she said. "I want to hear everything that has happened."

As we were taking our overnight bags out of the car, Charlotte bounded out of nowhere and flung her arms around me, giving me the biggest kiss.

The Blackwood family was complete. Funny how I had become a part of it. *How am I going to keep it that way?* I wondered. Somehow, I just had to. The RAF was such a big obstacle.

We sat down early at the cosy annex dining table, already set for four. It felt so good to be home as we sipped wine and snacked on Suzie's warm homemade bread with balsamic vinegar and olive oil and two dips Gigi had prepared, one black olives and the other artichoke hearts, both having been turned into delicious, lumpy spreads.

As anxious as I was to have some time alone with Charlotte, so too, I enjoyed the drawn-out evening, sitting around the table and enjoying the four of us being together again. It was perfect.

The only time I felt a little uneasy was when Jamie effused about how I had been helping him and how good it was looking for him staying in Group A.

"Charles has been brilliant. I have been cracking the assessment exercises, furiously looking at my notes he gives me just before I take my turn…brilliant, brilliant. I don't know where I would be without you, brother," he said, looking at me. "I'm going to stay in Group A, and we will be well placed to request transfer to Number 673 Squadron, Army Air Corps Apache training. Combat zone, here we come."

That is when I saw a dark cloud come over Gigi's and Charlotte's faces and knew we would speak about it later. Hopefully I could allay some of their fears.

At the end of our evening, Jamie and I drifted off to our bedrooms. Just as I was about to switch off my bedside light and go to sleep, there was a knock at my door.

"Come in," I responded, not knowing who to expect. I was mildly surprised as Gigi stepped into my room.

"Sorry to worry you, but can we have a little chat?"

"Of course we can," I replied.

"Darling, I want to speak about Jamie and his determination to get into that combat helicopter squadron with you."

I could have almost guessed this was what Gigi wanted to speak to me about.

Gigi began in a soft, affectionate tone, "I want to ask you whether you feel Jamie is ready to join that elite RAF squadron. The thing is, Jamie is just not like you. He doesn't have what seems to be your natural flying skill, reflexes, and the conciseness of thought you demonstrate in so many ways. I'm really worried that he is just caught up in the romance of flying those machines with you. What are those helicopters, Apaches or something? I just don't think he's ready."

Gigi paused for a moment before carrying on. "Darling, he is only there because of how you have coached and pushed him," she said, now in a surprisingly brusque tone.

"Gigi, I really believe Jamie is there because he wants to be, and all I have done is help him achieve his goals. If he does get into the Apache squadron, it'll be entirely on his own merit, and his heart has been set on it," I said as gently as I could.

Gigi gave it a little thought and then replied, "Charles, you would hate it as much as any of us if something happened to Jamie. Just imagine." She shuddered. "You are the only one who can change this."

A moment of silence followed with me absorbing what she had just said.

Gigi seemed to reluctantly accept that there was nothing she could do to stop Jamie continuing on his path. In a very sombre tone, she ended the conversation by saying, "Promise me that you will do whatever you can to protect him. Look after him as you would your own brother."

Gigi's last words on the matter not only made a very clear point but also hit home in a way that made me realise the gravity of what lay ahead. In an instant, I was feeling a weight of responsibility for Jamie. And, I may only have been speaking to Gigi, but I knew full well that she was speaking for Charlotte as well. Unquestionably, this is what they had been speaking about when we had gone to bed.

The next morning, I woke up long before the bedside clock sounded its alarm. Almost immediately the previous night's discussion crept back into my consciousness.

Gigi's words would play on my mind for a long time into the future. Saying that it troubled me was a hopeless understatement.

After a quiet breakfast and burdened by the weight of the critical stage Jamie and I next faced, all four of us decided to go for a walk around Shrewsbury. Our moods lifted with fresh air filling our lungs as we strolled, Charlotte and I hand in hand, down the treed lanes and into the town. Surrounded by the River Severn, Shrewsbury had lots of riverbank walks and trails that were lovely to explore. After a good coffee at the local barista, we went on to the fresh produce market to get a few things for Gigi and Suzi to prepare for our dinner.

The next day, our Sunday departure, earlier than normal because of some preparation we needed to do was especially difficult. We said our goodbyes, and I whispered into Charlotte's ear as I kissed her lips, "Catch up later, darling."

Gigi looked at me and then Jamie, and I couldn't help noticing the affection, but also worry, etched into her face.

We threw our bags into the boot of my car and headed back to the air base. Jamie's sombreness soon gave way to his real mood, which he'd not shown in front of his fretting mother. No purpose was served in her thinking either of us was looking forward to what lay ahead.

Jamie was in particularly good spirits, feeling more confident about the upcoming streaming examinations, of which there would be a few. Captain Swales had recently reminded us that Group A pilots would be able to influence which squadron they would end up in, so I was pleased Jamie was feeling positive. I just hoped his confidence was not misplaced.

Unquestionably though, the weight of what Gigi had said to me had persisted, and I was not entirely sure how I felt about Jamie ending up in the Apache Attack Helicopter Squadron. Even so, I realised there was no going back now, which only made me more determined to continue with our programme of me helping him. That was the best approach to ensure his safety.

The next eight weeks of our advanced training was as intense as anything we had done thus far. Testimony to that was that during this time we only managed three more trips to Shrewsbury. Coming to the end of this segment meant just one thing, an all-important final assessment.

Everyone was competing for the same thing. For this reason alone, the upcoming final examination was very intense. I would do whatever I could to ensure Jamie did not lose his place in Group A.

Am I just being selfish? played on my mind.

With the significant amount of time I'd put in with Jamie, and doing some revision with Will, our little group of three was well prepared. I was acutely aware of my benefit from coaching Jamie, because of how much more I concentrated on every aspect of my own flying and lectures, for when we went through it later.

Before we knew it, examination day had arrived!

It was a bit of an anticlimax because Jamie, Will and I had anticipated almost exactly what we would be doing. The only difference, perhaps, was that there was a significant focus on ground-proximity flying techniques, called "nap-of-the-earth." The most challenging part of this examination was how our lead instructors gave us difficult manoeuvres on the periphery of dead man's curve. I enjoyed being tested in this way, and it was crucial if we were going to be doing a lot of flying close to the ground.

An especially important aspect of helicopter flying is the dead man's curve, or more formally, the height-velocity profile. In the event of total engine failure, a helicopter either needs height or speed to land safely. Simply put, a pilot should stay out of the dead man's curve, meaning that if he is going slowly, he needs height, and vice versa. If he does not have altitude, he should have maximum practicable speed. Easier said than done when one is in a stealthy approach, flying close to the ground and searching for targets. That means potentially flying more slowly and, therefore, putting oneself and one's crew at significant risk in the event of losing an engine either through malfunction or having attracted enemy fire.

I secretly loved being put on the very edge of this dead man's curve—low and slow, one might say—knowing that I had to do a perfect autorotation to pull it off successfully.

As intense as the whole assessment was, it ended up being unusually informal. In the end, there were no changes to Group A. The overall duration of how long we had been in the top group probably weighed in favour of the instructors keeping the status quo. All three of us were thrilled but only expressing it to each other in little ways.

Jamie, Will and I formally submitted our request for transfer to No. 673 Squadron, Army Air Corps Apache training.

CHAPTER 23

FOX HUNT

FOLLOWING THIS MOST arduous stage of our training, we were given a four-day pass. I would have loved to go to Shrewsbury, but I knew Jamie would have none of it. To his mind, there was nothing going on in those parts. I put a call through to my father to see what was going on in Berkshire the coming weekend. My spirits lifted a bit when he told me that Berkshire Downs was staging a fox hunt and would I like him to book me a place.

"Make that two places please, Dad. Jamie can cut his teeth on another of our pastimes."

"Yes, I'm sure he would enjoy a little hunting," my dad replied with a little chuckle.

I knew from whence that came. Jamie was in for a surprise.

A good bit of southern England leisure, and we could have two nights at Rockwell Manor and two in Shrewsbury, I thought, feeling quite pleased with myself.

In the United Kingdom, the term *hunting* generally refers to hunting with hounds and has nothing to do with rifles or shotguns. This is rather confusing for foreigners, as in most other countries, hunting is a pastime involving the stalking and shooting of various game with the use of a firearm. There was no confusion about this for Jamie. Indeed, from playing so much polo with me in Berkshire and Surrey, he had already heard a lot about it.

Even though Charlotte and I spoke every day, we missed not seeing each other. I really needed to make the two days with her materialise.

"Hey, Jamie, are you up for some hunting next weekend?" I blurted, sitting down in our usual spot in the officers' mess.

"Am I *up* for it?" he replied sarcastically. "Bloody right I'm up for it, Charles. I can't imagine anything I would rather do with our four days off."

"I thought we could go down to Rockwell Manor for the hunt and then spend a night or two in Shrewsbury," I shot back, hoping I had done a good enough job of sugar-coating our coming to his home with some time in Berkshire beforehand.

"Ah, okay, whatever," he replied, shrugging his shoulders as he looked away, acceding to my quid pro quo arrangements.

"I will speak to Gigi and just make sure she is happy with it all," I suggested, knowing Charlotte was back at university.

I phoned his mum a little later. "Hi, Gigi. Good news. We have a four-day pass because we have finished our advanced training. I'm going to take Jamie hunting in Berkshire for two nights and then we will head up to Shrewsbury for two nights…if you will have us," I said jokingly. Chuckling, I added, "Can you speak to Charlotte and make sure she will be home?"

"I'm sure your friend needed some arm twisting to spend even a night at home. Well, Charlotte will certainly be pleased," Gigi remarked, knowing Jamie would sooner have stayed at Rockwell Manor for the duration of the pass out. Then she added, "Hunting pheasant?" She had that wrong, not being familiar with the terminology. Hearing my hesitation, she remarked, "Oh, don't worry, you can tell us about it another time."

The Blackwood ladies tolerated game-bird shooting on the condition that no felled bird would ever go to waste. They did not like anything gruesome, and because of that I knew they would not appreciate fox hunting with hounds. It suited me to not try to clear it up there and then. I would need to try and explain some of the aspects, perhaps how traditional it was, and hopefully it would soften their stance. That would take a little time, and I didn't want to do it just then. One thing I knew for certain was that my mother would not be impressed with my approach. I could almost hear her short reprimand telling me not to compromise my integrity. I immediately felt guilty for not being more honest with Gigi and for as long as I didn't say anything, it would sit uncomfortably with me.

The next day, we headed off to Rockwell Manor, with Jamie especially excited about the weekend ahead. The drive to Berkshire was relaxing after having come through such a gruelling training programme. We were both aware that, after the break, we would go under the wing of the Operational Conversion Unit (OCU). Converting onto the Apache was the first step to our seeing active combat service. This would almost certainly be in the Middle East, unless some other hotspot developed in some other part of the world, where UK or NATO forces were required. We were ecstatic at finally reaching this juncture of our RAF careers.

I already knew a great deal about the AH 64 Apache, the world's most advanced attack helicopter, all of which just drove my enthusiasm for flying it even more. Immediately recognisable for its tandem cockpit for a crew of two and on-display weapons and missile systems. The aircraft is powered by two jet engines with a combined output of almost 4,000 Shaft Horsepower. For the layman, *an unfathomable amount of power.* This enabled the aircraft to fly with a full weapons load at around 200 knots or 230 miles per hour, at an altitude up to 20,000 feet. It can carry 16 Hellfire missiles and 70 Hydra rockets. Other aspects were equally as advanced. Take, for example, the nose-mounted sensors for target-acquisition that also allow the Apache to perform at night and in adverse weather conditions. This helicopter also had significant systems redundancy, with its critical components duplicated. This allowed the aircraft to still fly if it lost any one of these systems, all designed to improve the Apache's combat survivability. Then there were other little niceties, such as a self-sealing fuel system. This meant if you took a bullet to a fuel cell, your helicopter wouldn't immediately start discharging fuel onto its jet engines, which could surely lead to an inferno of disastrous consequences. Yes, a very nice *little nicety.*

We arrived at my home to a warm greeting from my parents, them having become totally accustomed to Jamie and me being inseparable for such visits.

Jamie went through to his normal room, and we later enjoyed a wonderful dinner with my parents. We did not stay up too late because we had an early start.

The polo horses were out for the offseason, being rested, and the stables were occupied by just a handful of hunter horses, four of which were for Jamie and me for the next day's hunt. Two each. I did not have the same affinity for our hunters as I did for our polo horses, so it was nothing more than a cursory glance that I gave them when I went across to the stables before going up to bed. *I should have brought Jamie,* was my idle thought.

When we arrived at the secret location the next morning, the first order of business was to check that our grooms had arrived safely and prepared our first horses for the day.

"Bloody hell," was Jamie's first response when he looked at Rambling Man, the hunter he would be using for the morning session.

Jamie was familiar with the polo horses, typically standing over fifteen hands. Rambling Man stood a good eight inches taller at around seventeen hands, with the proportionate increase in size all round. I just chuckled, knowing that Rambling Man was not going to be his biggest challenge of the day. In fact, Jamie would come to find both his horses to be wonderfully comfortable armchair rides. It would be the crashing through hedges and going up and down embankments, through little creeks and such, that would be his real challenge. But I also knew he was going to love this.

I then helped Jamie orient himself and get used to the other hunter horse he would be riding, all the while giving him tips about hunting. Once again, I found myself behaving as his instructor.

Tapping himself on the helmet, he looked at me and asked, "How do I look, Squire?"

"Spiffy," was my honest reply.

Jamie did indeed look very smart in his beige riding breeches, black jacket, tweed tie, heavy white cotton shirt, black riding hat, polished black riding boots, and riding crop. Even though his ensemble had been assembled from probably all of our wardrobes, he definitely looked the part. Jamie looked at a bit of a loss, not unlike just before he embarked on some of his advanced helicopter training exercises, I thought with some amusement. Wide-eyed but still enjoying this new pursuit. He was especially tickled by the hunt masters in red jackets assembling all the riders in preparation for the start. Enthusiastic horsemen, excited horses, and keen hounds all milling around, blowing off steam, anxious to get going, listening for the sound of the hunt master's bugle that would signal the start of the hunt proceedings on some remote farmland, on a late autumn morning in the South West of England. That's where it would start, likely going through the woods at times. Where it would end up was anyone's guess. I had to admit, I was excited as well.

With this being Jamie's first hunt ever, I had to be sure that he understood how it worked. He was already taking a big step-up in testing his horsemanship, because fox hunting involves a significant number of jumping obstacles through the English countryside.

What makes fox hunting such an exciting sport is that when the hounds pick up the scent of a fox, they immediately give chase. Given that the fox is fleeing from the hounds, there is no telling where it will go to try to escape from its adversary. The horsemen follow the hounds on whatever merry trail the fox takes them, be it through the woods, brush, hedges, or little creeks. This procession of a fox leading a pack of hounds, with the thunder of hooves from fifty or sixty following riders, made for an adrenaline rush like few others.

I had been hunting since about the age of sixteen or seventeen, and since then, had always made sure I would do at least one hunt every season. I enjoyed many aspects of it, especially riding a big hunter, striding and galloping through the countryside on a trail determined by a fleeing fox. But in that breath and as I got older, there were aspects that I enjoyed less and less.

Foxes may have been, and still are, vermin that cause farmers endless problems, but was it necessary to be so savage in the pursuit and killing of them? Of course not. It was sport. A *blood* sport written into the annals of our family's and British history. Was that a good enough reason for it to continue? Methinks not.

A good day's hunting would involve a morning session, the occasional break for a little sloe gin, a good lunch, and then a change of steed for the afternoon's hunt. For all intents and purposes it would continue in a similar fashion to the morning session, just over another part of the countryside.

Our day's hunting did not deviate from this agenda. Jamie, and me, to be fair, were consuming the adrenaline rushes coming fast and furious and found ourselves trying to recover our wind as much out of exertion as from the breathlessness of our excitement. Jamie loved the pomp and ceremony. *So like his sister. So unlike his mother.* On more than one occasion, I heard him shouting "tallyho" along with some others to spur on the hounds when the fox was sighted. Something I had never done.

We finished the day's hunt in high spirits. Jamie said it was something he could happily get used to, making me promise to include him in one or two hunts every year.

I gave Jamie a history lesson on the origin of fox hunting. According to what I had been taught by the fox-hunting club, it had started in England centuries ago, when farmers were simply trying to perform pest control. Foxes were known to be nuisances, killing small livestock and chickens, so the farmers would hunt them down with hounds. Packs of hounds were first trained specifically to hunt foxes in the late seventeenth century, with many organised packs later hunting both fox and hare. What first started as a necessary duty to keep farms running smoothly soon became an admired game of the rich and noble, who added specific rules and regulations about attire and vocabulary and created the sport we have come to know.

Since fox hunting was popular with the nobility of England, who often happened to be military officers, this activity quickly became a favourite among the cavalries. Based on endurance and stamina, hunting was a wonderful way to keep cavalry horses in shape when they were not training for battle.

Hunting with hounds in the traditional manner became unlawful in Scotland in 2002 and in England and Wales in 2005, but at the time of writing, it continues in Northern Ireland. Drag hunting, during which a pack of hounds follows a scent laid by a human rather than a trail left by a fox, is an accepted alternate approach and has subsequently grown in popularity in Great Britain.

There was just one problem though. The hounds were not always clear on this new legislation and animal instinct being what it is, they quite often became sidetracked by the scent of a real fox. Unbeknownst to the following field of horsemen and women, they were unwittingly breaking the law, only discovering this when catching up to the hounds once they had already caught the fox. *Not our fault,* was the collective stance of the field, accusingly looking at the hounds.

To most, hunting laws have been changed for the better in Great Britain, which includes the method for shooting birds. In 2005 it became unlawful to shoot game birds while they are not in flight, an action which has long been considered unsporting.

Participants in the hunt that came from farther afield would stay at the nominated boutique hotel. However, even those that lived local to the event would often stay there the night after the day's activities, in anticipation of what was invariably a very festive, celebratory dinner. Revelling for no other reason, perhaps, than finishing the day in one piece—an achievement in itself after more than six hours of navigating slippery slopes, inclines and declines, ominously large hedge jumps, and generally tearing around the English countryside on horseback.

On this occasion, the private dinner had been arranged in one of the banquet rooms, but unlike the more formal dinner at the shoot, this was a casual and fun affair. A room of burgundy velvet furniture, hunt scenes adorning the walls, dimmed lighting accentuating the glow from an over-sized log-burning fireplace. Typical English countryside decorating, not that anything in those parts was decorated. It was just *there*.

There was also the local brew and red wine flowing and a menu of stews and pies and desserts that could have come out of your grandmother's kitchen, like sticky toffee pudding and custard, bread-and-butter pudding, or trifle. We finished with an assortment of cheeses, sometimes baked pastry Camembert, preserves, ports, liqueurs, and cigars. Just like Shrewsbury and Rockwell Manor, except the cigars.

I really did not enjoy the day after a hunt because it seemed so drawn out, and as a result, I wasted little time in leaving the next day.

It was still midmorning when we got home to Rockwell Manor, so in time for a light snack lunch, a restful afternoon, and a very welcome early night sans the rich food, the alcohol, and the stench of cigar smoke.

After a good night's rest, we had a healthy Rockwell breakfast, my mother making sure we didn't want to stay another night, and we were ready to head off to Shrewsbury. Our goodbye had to be especially brief since my mother, ever mindful of what was coming next in our RAF programme, would have difficulty holding her tears at bay. My father, as always, put his arm around her shoulders in support.

The drive up to Shrewsbury was quick and uneventful. I sped most of the way, without a word from Jamie. *Or a squeeze on the leg,* I thought, grinning to myself. I could hardly contain my excitement at the thought of seeing Charlotte.

We finally drove through the Blackwood gates and were warmly greeted by both Charlotte and Gigi, Charlotte flinging her arms around me and kissing me with a loud smooching sound.

Once we were indoors and had put our bags in our respective rooms, we sat down to an almost instant examination of what we had been doing. It transpired that Gigi had taken a bit of time to research hunting and did not like what she had discovered. She and Charlotte let me know their disdain in no uncertain terms.

"Charles, I can't believe you would take Jamie away on such a barbaric excursion," she said.

After another few minutes of me and Jamie trying to defend our position, the conversation finally came to an end with Gigi's last word on the matter. "And what do you do with the dead fox? Send the skin to the pelters?" she asked sarcastically.

Fortunately, it was a rhetorical question. I did not think it was a suitable time to tell her that once the hounds got hold of the fox, there would be nothing left. It would be surprising if you could find a square inch of pelt. Yes, on further reflection, fox hunting with hounds was a gruesome blood sport that did not fit well in modern society no matter how steeped it was in old English tradition and culture. I would make my apologies to Charlotte and Gigi and somehow make it up to them.

The two nights and a day in Shrewsbury flew by but were some of the most enjoyable moments I had experienced at the Blackwood residence since having first visited there with Jamie nearly three years before. Then it was once again time for us to leave. As brief as farewells were at Rockwell Manor, they were conversely drawn out at the Blackwoods'. I wasn't too sure which I disliked more.

After the customary hugs and kisses all around, I went over to Charlotte for a last goodbye. As I kissed her lovingly, she seemed to sense my anguish and then whispered into my ear, "Don't worry. We will see each other soon, babe."

I would miss these little warm-breath whispers in my ear.

We left Jamie's house hoping that we would soon be transferred to No.

673 Squadron, Army Air Corps Apache training, and shortly thereafter, be seconded to Joint Helicopter Command, with a hot posting to follow. Once we received our posting, there would be many months that Charlotte and I would not see each other.

With the Blackwood residence receding behind us and my heart still in my mouth, I found myself fumbling around for a particular song on my Walkman, one that would lift my spirits and help me think about what lay ahead.

"Up Where We Belong" – Joe Cocker, Jennifer Warnes

| YouTube | Spotify | Apple |

These words had an eerie truth to them that did not give me any comfort. The road was almost certainly long, but I could not wait to begin the journey.

From the time we got into the car until we reached the end of the song, I hardly realised that Jamie was even with me. He had been sitting quietly, allowing me to deal with my feelings and not saying a word. He then gave me an affectionate pat on the shoulder, leaving his hand there for a moment. It was a clear indication that he understood my relationship with his sister and how important it was to me.

"Thanks, Jamie. Thank you," was all I said.

CHAPTER 24
PREPARING FOR COMBAT

THE NEXT FEW days were a whirlwind. The only thing that mattered was that Jamie, Will and I were transferred to the Operational Conversion Unit, OCU, Apache attack helicopters. We would first need to do a Conversion to Type, CTT, adapting our knowledge to the Apache AH-64. Then, because this versatile helicopter could operate in a wide range of operational war theatres, we would do a Conversion to Role, or CTR. This was a prelude to going into combat with this magnificent machine.

With just a few short months of training ahead, we were one step away from falling under Joint Helicopter Command and our first hot posting.

Our introduction to the Apache attack helicopter began with a short presentation, a lot of which I already knew, such was my interest in the helicopter. The part that stood out for me was the opening address of Lieutenant Colonel Berrycloth.

"Good morning, gentlemen. Welcome to Army Air Corps 673 Squadron," he said in a clear, crisp voice. The tone of his greeting matched his sharp facial features. "I hope none of you think you have come here to learn how to fly the Apache AH64," he said, his searching gaze scanning the room.

No one ventured a remark, taken off guard by what was contrary to all our expectations.

"You are here because you have already demonstrated that you know how to fly helicopters, and the Apache, whilst it may be the most advanced of them, is essentially no different. It's what they can do that really sets them apart." Again, he looked around the room before continuing.

"Yes, gentlemen, you're not here to learn how to fly this machine." He purposefully repeated himself in a very deliberate manner before saying, "You are here to learn how to *fight* this machine, the most formidable piece of aerial combat hardware ever developed," Lieutenant Colonel Berrycloth concluded, his steely blue eyes again taking in the faces before him.

My heart rate quickened. A moment of light-headedness. I couldn't wait.

Excited, we were led to a viewing deck to watch a flight demonstration of this extraordinary fighting machine. Studying it as it went through its paces, we couldn't help noticing the chain gun protruding ominously forward from under the nose. Rocket and missile pods on stubby winglets gave it a sinister, mechanical look that made the hair on my neck and arms stand on end. The Taliban called it the Mosquito, which was an apt description. The *coup de grâce* of the demonstration was watching the Apache flying inverted because of its rotor system that allowed it to perform loops and rolls.

When will I do that? I wanted it so badly.

This was the reason I was in the RAF, doing my own thing, on my own. Rockwell Manor and being a Featherstone was the furthest thing from my mind.

The Apache's tandem cockpits are organised so that the upper, rear position is the Pilot-in-Command station, with its array of flying controls and selectable video screens from which the pilot monitors all the helicopter systems, including weapons systems. One of the many distinguishing features of this helicopter is its Helmit Mounted Display, HMD, with an eyepiece positioned over the right eye, a bit like a small scope that shows flight and weapon systems information to help fly and fight the helicopter. This can also display imagery from the Pilot Night Vision System, allowing the helicopter to be flown at night and in all weathers. The Apache was formidable in the daytime, lethal at night. One of the other capabilities of the HMD is that the pilot or gunner can slave it to the helicopters 30mm chain gun. This meant wherever you looked, the chain gun jutting out from under the nose of the helicopter would point, following your gaze. *Menacing* was a good word to describe this capability. Part of the Pilot-in-Command's duty is to back up and follow up on target assaults that the copilot-gunner has engaged.

The copilot-gunner (CPG) sits in the front cockpit, which is very similar to the rear Pilot-in-Command station, but with an emphasis on weapons and target acquisition. In his cockpit, he has the systems to locate targets, day and night, and fire the Apache's supremely advanced weaponry systems. The most formidable of the weapons is the Hellfire missile, each one essentially a miniature aircraft with its own guidance and propulsion system. It inflicts fearsome destruction, with a high-explosive warhead powerful enough to burn through some of the heaviest armour in existence, giving the enemy no place to hide. The CPG is also a fully qualified pilot, and he too has all the flight controls and can take over from the pilot at any time and fly the helicopter single-handedly. But his primary job is firing the helicopter weapon systems. Don't for a moment think that copilot, the first two letters of the initialism CPG, means he is any less qualified. Quite the contrary, as he is not only capable of being Pilot-in-Command but is also a very competent weapons specialist.

Ordinarily, I would share all that excited me with Charlotte and Gigi. But not this. It was just impossible for them to embrace it with me. I would still speak to them about it, and hopefully they would understand a little bit more. Understand what? I was not sure.

The Apache AH-64 Attack Helicopter.
Forward Copilot-Gunner and aft Pilot-in-Command cockpits, forward chain gun, side-rocket, and missile stations. A thing of beauty. There are no words.

Pilot-in-Command Cockpit.

Apache AH-64 Helmet-Mounted Display (HMD)
Instrument flying and using an eye monocle require reprogramming your brain to work in two compartments.
(Image used under licence from Shutterstock.com)

The Apache was designed and built to be effective in a wide and varied range of combat missions. With all its essential systems duplicated, it had great survivability, giving the crew the confidence to take it into battle. The variety of weapon systems meant the crew could be inventive and tailor the way they fought the helicopter to a given situation. It also has multiple radios, giving the crew the ability to monitor and talk on several separate radio nets at once. It can move around the battle space quickly and stealthily, which gives it the advantage of being able to surprise the enemy.

Unlike jet fighters, helicopters are used in close-combat roles, near to the ground. In order to do this successfully and as safely as possible, it has a very different suite of equipment intended to keep the helicopter and crew safe in close ground proximity. This includes forward-looking infrared so that ground targets can be located at night and behind foliage during the day. It also has technology that enables the pilot to fly in the darkest locations with no external white light. Because the two systems work autonomously, the pilot can use his sensor to fly while the copilot-gunner works the target-acquisition systems to search for targets or to survey the route ahead.

Although it is primarily used as a weapons platform with a lethal array of munitions, it is also a great intelligence-finding asset. The multitude of sights and sensors allows the crew to gather a good deal of information on the battlefield and then relay this back to HQ over the secure radios. It is also used to escort more vulnerable support helicopters and prevent them from being targeted, like the big dual-rotor Chinook helicopters that carry the Medical Emergency Response Teams. This life-saving asset often picked up seriously wounded casualties from the battlefield while the firefight still went on around them, and it was our job to try to destroy attackers before our evac copters were targeted. The Chinooks were always a target for insurgents.

A squadron of Apaches can defeat whole brigades of armoured vehicles through selected targeting of the enemy assets. Another role is to support ground forces with precision weapons when they are engaged by the enemy and pinned down. With radio communications from the ground forces, the Apache is able to identify the enemy and single them out from the population and civilian areas before decisively engaging them.

Apaches normally work as a pair, referred to as a *flight*. During an engagement, one helicopter acts as the shooter and the other as the observer to look out wider for more targets. The observer also puts himself in a position to follow up on the first helicopter's assaults if necessary. If the squadron is fighting together, you may find two or more flights working in an engagement area to attack targets.

While the copilot-gunner is head down, looking in the sight for the enemy, the pilot is looking after the safety of the helicopter and often commanding the squadron. He is monitoring the systems and ensuring that all is in order, but more than that, he is watching for any nearby enemy trying to shoot them down.

Flying any helicopter means both hands and feet are doing different things at once. Your fingers also have to work independently as you speak on the radio on multiple channels and trim the helicopter flight inputs to create the most stable weapons launch platform, so your CPG can fire either your cannons, rockets, or missiles. Even your eyes have to learn how to work independently of each other. With the HMD monocle permanently over your right eye, your left eye is free to look outside the cockpit, saving valuable split seconds it would take you to look down at the instruments and then up again.

This small screen over your right iris can, at the flick of a button, display a dozen different instrument readings from around the cockpit. The slaving of your head position to the cannons means the CPG or pilot are only a couple of button presses away from firing the 30mm cannon or rockets. All he must do is pull the trigger to fire on a target.

In addition to everything else going on, we had to condition our bodies into doing things they had never done before. I remember explaining to a friend how, as an Apache helicopter pilot with an HMD, we had to somehow split our brains and our visual systems to be able to process two bits of information at once: aircraft controls and weapons systems. It was no wonder that we suffered daily headaches as we got used to this innovative approach to processing information.

Another of the Apache's many design features are its graphite-composite and titanium rotor-blade structure, which allows it to withstand brushes with trees and other minor obstacles when flying nap-of-the-earth at high speed. This is a mind-boggling concept for helicopter pilots, who normally do everything they can to protect their delicate rotor-blade systems. And of course, the helicopter was largely bulletproof. Very unusual.

The sensation of defying gravity and flying is one thing, but knowing you are going to war in a hugely capable machine gives you the confidence to take on anything.

The training on the Apache was extensive. It had to be. All the basic elements were the same as any other helicopter, but it is an attack helicopter designed to go and look for the fight, withdraw, and then look for the next one.

Lieutenant Colonel Berrycloth's view that the Apache was the single most lethal and effective piece of military hardware in the theatre of war was undeniable.

During my Air Force career, I flew many different helicopters, but undoubtedly Attack Helicopters were my passion. In addition to the Apache AH64, I flew the Westland Lynx AH7 and the Agusta A129 Mangusta. Although all three are amazing to fly and very manoeuvrable, nothing compares to being in an Apache. It is a battlefield helicopter in the truest sense, and the capability that it brings to a fight is quite phenomenal, unrivalled by any other combat helicopter.

I would not have given it up for the world, which wasn't something I could share with Charlotte and Gigi. I could not talk to them about any of this, and that fact coupled with the intensity of our training meant we missed the occasional evening telephone call, and I hated it.

I often thought back to the commitment I had made in helping Jamie. In doing my best to equip him in flying and fighting the helicopter to the limits of his ability, was the surest way for him to protect himself. He wasn't able to fly the Apache at the limits of *its* capability. Few pilots could do that. My sentiment never wavered, even though my own hands were full trying to absorb all the new information that was being imparted to us daily. This meant Jamie and I were spending a lot of time with each other, going through all we had learnt, me guiding him, and somehow, I was beginning to think that Jamie would be okay. Though I couldn't forget Gigi's sage words. *"Jamie's just not like you."* The time with him gave me an even greater sense of closeness to the Blackwoods, and I felt a level of comfort that I was doing my best at what they had hoped for—*help protect him.*

There was something else. I couldn't immediately put my finger on it, but then one evening while I was trying to get to sleep, it dawned on me. Was this taught behaviour, in a way replicating what my mother had so painstakingly done with me? And something she too had learned from her governess, Mrs. Kearns, the teacher.

Over the next twelve to eighteen months, so much happened at such a frenetic pace that it is difficult to put a timeline to it. It was as if we got sucked along in one of the most advanced Air Force programmes of all, and hopefully we would come out of it as Apache combat pilots. I put this timeline against my relationship with Charlotte, which by then was, unbelievably, going on over two years. I checked it against my age, nearly twenty-five years old. For someone who was agile with maths, I was really struggling with this one. Where had the time gone?

We could have done so much more together, I thought remorsefully.

The one constant during this time was that Jamie and I were able to go out on night and weekend passes to Shrewsbury about every ten to fourteen days. Charlotte and I were able to continue our relationship pretty much as before, though we knew it couldn't last forever. Each time we met, we became more aware that we would have to face an exceedingly difficult juncture that the Air Force, and indeed military life, generally put in the path of many young couples.

When we weren't at Shrewsbury, if I wasn't playing a round of golf with Will, you would often find us in the gym, making sure we were keeping fit.

During the early stages of our Air Force training, we were a lot more lighthearted about keeping fit, competing against our peers, generally having fun. Now that we were established in our squadrons, preparing for warfare, we did far more than the daily PT program. Knowing that being fit, ready, and poised could make the difference between life and death when going into a combat zone gave an entirely different motivation for the extra hours we would spend in the gym or on the treadmill each week. We wouldn't easily admit it, but as much as we may have been looking forward to going into a combat zone, there was another element that crept into our psyche. Fear.

Along the way, Major Gifford reiterated what we had heard from time to time since beginning our RAF careers, that as Pilots and Copilot-Gunners, we would be better served by not having relationships back home. "You know, not being sure about what a girlfriend sitting at home is getting up to can be somewhat distracting and counterproductive," he sneered, as a few of the men chuckled at his insinuation.

Well, it was obvious who the single ones in the room were. For me, no amount of lightheartedness could lessen the weight that this brought on my emotions. This was the contemplation I had to face, and the effect of his words on me was undeniable.

When that briefing session was over, Jamie and I walked over to the officers' mess together. He put a hand over my shoulder and simply asked, "You okay, bud?"

I didn't say anything, giving only an unconvincing nod of my head.

There were many things that continually brought Jamie and me closer together. Even the most unlikely of things, like this.

Just as I was wondering if I would ever see Charlotte again, almost as if it had sneaked up on us, we got a night pass, our last before being posted. This time it had been more than three weeks since I had seen Charlotte, both of us acutely aware that even these precious moments, now fewer and further apart, were a luxury we would soon lose altogether. I didn't even want to contemplate what that meant for our relationship. This time, I had no choice but to chase those thoughts from my mind with vehement determination before they swamped my emotions and then my actions.

Notwithstanding all the consternation about our relationship and its future, when I called Charlotte to tell her I would be seeing her in three days, she was similarly elated. It seemed she also had the same ability to drive the inevitable outcome of our relationship from her mind.

We arrived at Shrewsbury and bundled out of the car, and the four of us stood in the driveway, warmly greeting each other.

A little while later when we sat down to supper, although it was much the same as any other delightful dinner at home, with wonderful cuisine prepared by Suzie with Gigi's oversight, it was also different. Glaringly different. When the conversation got onto our being posted in the operational area for a series of tours of duty, the change in our moods was unmistakable.

It was Gigi who first brought it up. "So do you know where you're going and for how long?" she asked, looking from me and then to Jamie.

"Not sure, Mum, and not stuff that we really talk about," was Jamie's mumbled reply.

Not wanting to end the dinner on that sombre note, I cut everybody a wedge of brie cheese and gave them a good serving of port, then turned up the hi-fi system, which had just started playing the soundtracks from *Grease* and *Saturday Night Fever*. The mood immediately changed, and with the red wine, followed by the port, we all became more relaxed and indeed let our guards down, if not our hair, as everyone got up and started dancing.

"You're the One That I Want" – John Travolta, Olivia Newton-John

YouTube   Spotify   Apple

Having recently seen the movie *Grease*, we were all quite expert at these dance moves. Charlotte looked delectable as she danced to the beat of the music, not looking at me until it got to the part, "You're the one that I want," and then she playfully pointed to me.

I was so enthralled by her cute little moves and gestures that my expression was proverbially jaw-dropping. This was so obvious that Gigi, in an animated fashion, put a hand under my chin and pretended to close it, which brought loud laughter from all of us.

When the next track started playing, Jamie danced an amazing solo effort spurred on by the enthusiastic encouragement of his audience of three.

"Stayin' Alive" – Bee Gees

YouTube   Spotify   Apple

He was really enjoying himself, but it was no doubt me who chortled the loudest each time it got to the part, "You can tell by the way I use my walk, I'm a woman's man." *Is he a woman's man, or simply a womaniser?* I thought, smiling at his comical dance moves. So uninhibited and confident.

The Blackwoods certainly knew how to dance, and it was all going splendidly well until we got to the next track.

"Hopelessly Devoted to You" – Olivia Newton-John

| YouTube | Spotify | Apple |

Charlotte and I slipped into each other's arms, where we swayed and danced slowly together. Right then I truly felt hopelessly devoted to her. I felt her holding on to me as if she were physically not going to let me go. We were oblivious of anyone else in the room.

Then, when it got to the line, "I'm out of my head, hopelessly devoted to you," she drew away so we could rejoin Jamie and Gigi at the table. I could not help though, seeing the wistful look on Charlotte's face, a sadness that had more to do with her and me than the evening's mood.

All of us were now looking down into our glasses of port as the song played out, all feeling the gravitas of what lay ahead. It was not only the emotions of Charlotte and me that were laid bare, but those of Gigi and Jamie as well. We were going to miss these wonderfully jovial, impromptu occasions, of which there had been many. With a depressing thought I wondered if there would ever be another evening like this one. The likelihood of it not happening again was yet another thing I would have to vehemently drive from my mind.

Soon we were ready to go through to our bedrooms, and Gigi checked one last time to see if anyone needed anything.

As difficult as it was, especially after such a loving evening, I knew I had to speak to Charlotte. The weight of responsibility for Jamie, Gigi's expectation of me looking after him, and where we were now headed in our military careers had been weighing very heavily on me.

I went through to Charlotte's bedroom and gingerly knocked, then listened as her footsteps reached the door.

She opened it, then smiled broadly at my unexpected visit. "Charles, babe, what a lovely surprise."

I felt guilty that what I needed to talk to her about would not be a "lovely surprise." As I stepped into her room, I knew there was no other way but to get straight to the point. "We need to talk a bit, my gorgeous darling." My tone of voice did not disguise what I was feeling as a frown immediately showed on her forehead. Sitting on the side of her bed, I started hesitantly. "You have heard what Major Gifford said in his lecture and what others have said, and they are right, my darling."

"What? What part?" Charlotte demanded to know, even though I was sure she knew.

"That they don't think it is a good idea for pilots to be in a relationship going into an operational zone. That being single is for our own good. Concentrating on the job at hand is for our safety," I blurted out, not entirely coherently.

Charlotte could only look at me with her doe eyes as the real meaning of my words sank in.

Before she had a chance to protest, I added, "And you know that your mum is very nervous about Jamie and what lies ahead for him in the RAF. She is relying on me taking care of him." I didn't need to mention that Gigi's view was that I was largely the reason for Jamie being where he was. "She will know that I'm taking her seriously by what we decide now," I said, trying to make her part of the decision.

Shoulders sagging, she could barely look at me.

"My darling, we need to move on, you and I, from what has been the most wonderful time of my life," I said, unable to fully conceal the emotion welling up in my throat.

Charlotte was struggling to hold back the tears.

"I don't even know what dangers lie ahead for Jamie and me, but I know I owe it to everyone, especially you and your mum, to do whatever I can to protect him. I cannot be distracted. That could, God forbid, have far-reaching or even tragic consequences. Do you understand me, darling?" I was not entirely convinced of my own argument.

Charlotte took hold of my hands and looked into my eyes. No longer able to hold back her emotions, she began sobbing. I put my arms around her, drawing her close to me as her tears streamed down her cheeks. I felt exactly as she did but needed to be strong for both of us.

After a while, as if trying to make herself feel better about it, Charlotte mumbled through her sobbing, "And you need to be safe too, my babe. You'll be back, you *will* be back, and for those reasons, I will not protest too strongly."

The next morning, we sat down to the most sombre breakfast, none of us eating very much. Then it was time for us to leave, and we lethargically got our bags and headed for the door. I knew this would be the last goodbye. I kissed Charlotte lovingly and as I began to draw away, she whispered in my ear.

"We will never leave each other, babe. You will always be in my heart."

We slowly drove out of the gates of the Blackwood residence, and with Jamie sitting quietly next to me, lost and sad, absorbed in my thoughts of Charlotte and the sudden end to the first romantic relationship of my life, we headed back to base.

I was struggling to hold back the tears, feeling that in reality it was unlikely we would ever find a way back to each other. *Damn the Featherstone doctrine of being brutally honest with yourself.* I couldn't face the thought, dreading the empty space she would leave.

I had become so close to Charlotte I couldn't begin to contemplate my life without her, my first love, even if I could not see a road ahead for us.

I searched through my Walkman and found a song that didn't make me feel any better.

"Don't Cry" – Guns n' Roses

YouTube　　　　　Spotify　　　　　Apple

Just the opening bars had me struggling to contain my emotions. I couldn't bear the thought of her crying.

Don't you cry tonight, because there is a Heaven above us, my darling. But please just give us a whisper or just a sigh.

As the song ended, Jamie again gave me an affectionate pat on the shoulder, leaving his hand there even longer this time.

Yet again, I was grateful for this bit of understanding from my dear friend.

CHAPTER 25
THE MIDDLE EAST

NO AMOUNT OF training in England could have fully prepared us for the baptism of fire we faced when we landed in the Middle East for our first tour of duty. One of the first adjustments was acclimatising to the temperature range. When we arrived, it was sometimes below -4°C (or 20°F). Then in the summer it was regularly 40°C (104°F), and all the discomfort that came with it. *Everything is so sandy and dusty!* Never a great sleeper, these conditions played further havoc with that endeavour.

We were warned, I thought wryly. Then with a chuckle to myself, *Another meaning to 'hot posting,' I guess.*

Just looking at the lineup of Apache helicopters had my heart racing. Any challenge was worth it, just for this. This was what I had first dreamed of, then trained for, and now I was finally here. But so too came the reality of the situation as I played with the disc hanging around my neck.

Looking at one of my two dog tags, I read again the engraving. My service number, surname and initials, religion, blood type, and my military branch. "What are these identification tags for, and why do we have two?" I remembered an air cadet having once asked.

"In case you forget who you are," had been the sarcastic reply.

The airman may have preferred the instructor to have left it there, but instead he gave the real reason.

"In case you cop it, dear boy. They will put one around your big toe so they can identify you, because by then you certainly won't know who you are."

The chuckles around the room said it all. War discounted the value of human life to bargain basement levels.

Thank God my mother, Charlotte, or Gigi hadn't heard about that conversation.

Just a few days into this new way of life and the myriad of different things going on all around us, I received my first two letters from home. Well, from my real home and Shrewsbury. This was something new. I guess no longer being three or four hours from home and having no easy access to telephones, it was to be expected.

I felt a little guilty that I read Charlotte's letter first. A few times, in fact. I found myself trying to figure out if there was anything I could read between the lines. It seemed she had purposefully steered clear of writing anything that would make things more difficult for me. I hated the loss and emptiness I was feeling.

I then read the letter from my mother, with my father's contribution added onto the end. I smiled, not in the least bit surprised at this sensible approach. By the end of it I had a good idea of what was happening at home. It struck me my two letters were surprisingly similar. A catch-up with the goings-on, hoping I was doing well, taking care of myself, and thinking of you all the time.

Hang on. There was something. "Thinking of you all the time," in Charlotte's letter gave me an immediate lift. I wished I could tell her I felt the same.

I couldn't help my mind drifting off to the green fields and emerald forests of Berkshire. Cool. Moist. Sometimes a fresh gentle breeze. Even the days when it drizzled incessantly seemed appealing. Then, of course, I thought about Rockwell Manor and my parents. How was my mother taking me being in a combat zone? As close as we were, it was sometimes hard to tell how she was feeling because of her stoic manner. My father's contribution to the letter had been silent on what was happening with his own polo. Was he getting more involved during my absence or withdrawing even more? And I couldn't help but think about Fabrizio. I must have been missing his cooking. I loved how he was so eager to please us with his "famous" meals, which were all of them, of course. His secret herbs and spices. Never mind Fabrizio's lavish feasts, I would give almost anything for a slice of his roasted sourdough bread with French butter and his scrambled eggs. I would happily concede that they were indeed *famous*. I smiled as I thought about my breakfast that morning. Interestingly, it had been scrambled eggs on toast. Just like Fabrizio's. Well, sort of. Just a few small differences.

Eggs in a combat zone needed no scrambling. The reason was that eggs came in a large tin container, in the form of powder, as did the milk. No need for double cream either, just add water! *How convenient is that?* I smiled at my sarcastic thoughts. And when your eggs were plated—okay, slopped into one of the compartments of your stainless-steel plate—who needed finely chopped parsley and grated parmesan cheese sprinkled over the top, with homemade tomato sauce using Roma tomatoes, secret herbs, and a little honey splashed artistically on the side? That was completely superfluous. Oh yes, and toasting the bread was just a waste of time. Instead of toast, it was far more efficient to have pre-sliced white bread with no butter, let alone French *beurre*. What did the French know about cooking anyway? At this stage, I was quite openly chuckling as I experienced the cuisine of military dining. I found it interesting how a simple dish like scrambled eggs on toast could be so vastly different.

Fabrizio's scrambled eggs were to die for. In the operational frontline, you could die from those.

And I would be sure to tell Fabrizio about the secret seasoning we *did* have in the RAF and the Middle East. Salt and pepper.

And then my mind shifted to the highlight of my daydreaming, Shrewsbury. The food, the wine, the music, and the dancing. And in the middle of it all, Charlotte.

Just as I was getting lost in longing thoughts about Charlotte, so another oppressive wind drifted into our camp with its hot, dry, dusty character, doing nothing for my already parched skin and lips. Not to mention the tiny particles of sand that would cake in the corner of your eyes. Was this really for me? Was my mother right in questioning if I belonged in the RAF? Here? She was right about most things, but was this different? Her contention that I was not a military man may have had some validity to start with, but I certainly felt like a military man now. The greater my challenge meant just one thing—the greater my accomplishment. On my own, Serviceman M17112011. In a strange way, I was relishing every bit of it.

Born with a silver spoon in my mouth or not, no one I had come across from my basic training through to where we were now, had endured military life better. Was it because of *my* poem that I was able to shrug it off?

If neither foes nor loving friends can hurt [me]… [Mine] is the Earth and everything that's in it, And—which is more—[I'll] be a Man.

My *own* man!

Everything about the military and the RAF was deliberate. Not surprising. This being our first tour of duty, we began with routine patrols. Only later did we come to realise that it was not intended for us to experience a contact in the first several missions regardless of how eager we were to engage the enemy. A naivety that in time would change.

As the tally of our routine patrols increased, so too did we settle into our new base. Whilst the temperature differences compared to home may have been the reason for us losing sleep in the early stages, very soon this became the least of our concerns. The thing that caused most of our sleepless nights were shoulder-launched Stinger missiles or, more correctly, man-portable air-defence systems (MANPADS), deadly against most aircraft but especially helicopters. The Apache cockpit may have been protected by reinforced armour and bulletproof glass, able to survive 23mm rounds, but a Stinger missile was a different proposition altogether.

Thinking about them slowly gnawed its way into every part of your brain like a cancer, and there was little you could do about it. Ironically, these lethal weapons should never have been in the hands of our foes but were supplied to the insurgents by the USA. An example of the confusion of Western politics. The problem with this weapon was that they could simply be carried on the back of a combatant and very quickly brought forward and placed onto the shoulder, ready to launch a deadly missile. An insurgent with a Stinger missile launcher could easily conceal himself in any nook or cranny and strike when one least expected it.

My Rude Awakening

We were all very aware that Russian helicopter losses in the Soviet–Afghan War in the early eighties numbered more than 300 helicopter gunships and their crews. Stinger missiles from MANPADS were responsible for most of those. This constant threat was always in the back of our minds, knowing that at any moment you could be facing a lethal attack from seemingly nowhere, and this very seriously affected some flight crew members.

A case in point had been an incident just a few days earlier. I was in a flight of four Apaches, lined up and about to go on a routine patrol. We had been given start-up clearance, and as I was going through my sequence, bringing my engines and rotor system up to flight readiness, I noticed alongside me that the blades of Lieutenant Greg Andrews's helicopter were motionless. Only for a moment did I imagine he had a technical malfunction, because these machines had all been fully prepped just shortly beforehand.

The look on Greg's face and the slouch of his shoulders—with his CPG Lieutenant Harper Jameson craning his neck around, trying to work out what was going on with his Pilot-in-Command—made clear what I had begun to suspect.

As they climbed out of the Apache, Harper put an arm across Greg's shoulders, comforting him, while Greg's apologetic expression of despair confirmed the worst nightmare of every combat pilot—he'd lost his nerve. Greg couldn't do it that morning. He had surrendered to the deep-seated fear that stubbornly sat in the pits of all our bellies.

We had then sat at flight idle while the mission was reorganised to include just the three remaining helicopters. Just as well it was a low-key patrol and reconnaissance mission because we had all become distracted with what happened to Greg.

Was this also one of the RAF approaches, to do routine patrols and potentially sift out weak links? If so, then Greg's undoing was a victory for the system and probably the saving grace for a really good helicopter pilot, just not in a war zone. And that's to say nothing of his CPG. It didn't make me feel any better about Greg's departure.

We could all feel the escalating tension of the routine patrols, but it was perhaps an innocuous little notice that suggested things were about to step up a gear. The powers that be were upping the ante.

We had by then been in the Middle East a few weeks when our intake received the unexpected instruction to attend a black ops briefing to our veteran peers. We soon discovered it had to do with an imminent operation in the southern provinces. We were to attend in a listen-only capacity.

In contrast to the bright sunlit day, the low lighting inside the presentation room gave it an eerie feel. Will and Jamie were seated on each side of me, our close-knit trio. There was an air of tension as we sat waiting in anticipation for proceedings to begin. With the aid of an overhead projector and a white board on which was written the heading SITTING DUCK, Group Captain Ralph Dogwood began his presentation.

"Today we have some of our freshman Apache crew who will be sitting in on the initial part of the briefing," the operations group captain said, explaining the nine people seated in the back row of the presentation room. The missing tenth freshman was of course Greg. Including ourselves, there must have been around forty of us in attendance.

"In summary, the mission is to flush out a group of insurgents using a contrived engine failure and crash landing of a Puma HC2 helicopter as a decoy. The flight crews and SAS Operatives involved in the operation will be given preliminary details at today's briefing, with one follow-up meeting tomorrow," he said.

"This covert mission will involve two Puma gunships and two Apaches. The first Puma, designated Papa Alpha, will be fully armed, and in addition to the piloting crew, there will be twelve Special Air Service Operators. They are the main actors of this operation. The supporting roles will be the second Puma, designated Papa Bravo, and a flight of two Apaches, collectively designated Alpha Foxtrot. Papa Bravo will be unarmed and only have a pilot and copilot on board. We will need Papa Bravo's full payload capability for reasons that will become clear," Group Captain Dogwood added, before continuing.

"Papa Alpha will approach the target zone in the area of the insurgents at a height of two and a half thousand feet. It will then deploy a smoke trail to suggest an engine failure and fire. The helicopter will then enter autorotation and descend into the selected area. At the approximate point of ground contact, Papa Alpha crew will deploy a thunderflash and black smoke decoys to imply the helicopter crashed on impact. In our experience, this will bring the insurgence to the crash site out of curiosity or in the hope they can retrieve something from the wreckage. Or just to gloat," he added as an afterthought.

"Crucially, leading up to this moment, Papa Bravo and Alfa Foxtrot, the support group, must remain completely out of sight and out of earshot. This will mean being four and a half nautical miles downwind from the decoy zone. These three gunships should be on the ground, 'turning and burning' at flight idle. Anything else will compromise the mission. They will only be brought into the fray in the event of an unexpected resistance."

A wave of excitement rippled through us as we continued to listen intently. We had done a little work with thunderflashes, also known as flash grenades or sound bombs, which, as the names suggested, emitted a sound akin to an explosion.

Group Captain Dogwood continued, "Once Papa Alpha is on the ground, the two flight crew and the SAS operatives will vacate the helicopter. The SAS combatants will be placed in predetermined strategic points in relation to the helicopter. Call them the insurgent *welcoming party*, if you will."

The veteran SAS operatives in the room chuckled at the thought of this. The freshmen, of which I was one, sat there wide-eyed. *God, this is exciting.*

"When the insurgents expose themselves, it is important that our SAS friends act decisively. We don't want to lose a perfectly good Puma helicopter unnecessarily," Group Captain Dogwood said dryly. "In the unfortunate event that Papa Alpha is taken out by the insurgents and there is unexpected opposition, then the two Apaches, Alpha Foxtrot, will immediately be brought into the offensive. The Apache Flight will launch an aerial attack on the insurgents within two minutes, bearing in mind they will be some five miles away. When the threat has been eliminated, Papa Bravo will be on the ready to extract Papa Alpha flight crew and SAS operatives from the site."

That concluded the part of Group Captain Dogwood's presentation that we had been cleared for. We were then invited to leave.

I couldn't help but think of a term that I had often heard, *the theatre of war*. Well, this stage had certainly been set. And the title, SITTING DUCK. That could only have been a reference to the Puma helicopter.

Seasoned SAS could *never* be described as sitting ducks. Sitting duck my backside, as Jamie might have said.

I remember at the time being very preoccupied with the thought that this manoeuvre could very likely cost the Royal Air Force a Puma HC2 helicopter gunship. It only dawned on me years later that I had not for even a moment considered the lives being put at risk. The group captain too seemed to be making a bigger point about protecting the Puma ahead of the personnel's lives. Did discounting the value of human life simply go with the territory?

I reconciled that our invitation to this briefing was likely as premeditated as everything else. Had we been given a taste of things to come?

It seemed I got that right when just a few days later, Will and I, along with two other freshman Apache crew, were called into our own Ops meeting. The whiteboard was still blank except for the heading DEAD AHEAD.

In summary, this was a mission to launch an offensive on a convoy of enemy vehicles traversing between two of their strongholds.

Operational Command had received on the ground intelligence that this convoy would be using a route that our topographical information showed a section of road that ran for a little over a mile that would be the perfect kill zone. We were put on alert for a mission start at 0400 hours the next morning.

Will and I had already spent a lot of time flying routine patrol missions with each other, with him in the Copilot-Gunner cockpit and me as Pilot-in-Command. This would be the first time we would be flying a contact mission together. A first for both of us. I couldn't have been more pleased.

Already we were asking the question. Would MANPADS be a factor? Would the insurgence know this road section was a point of vulnerability and have shoulder-mounted stingers in place…just in case?

The following morning, the flight of two Apache helicopters, with Will and me in one of them, had departed the base to seek out this convoy of insurgent armoured vehicles. AH64 fodder, as the sardonic expression went.

The planned kill zone was a length of road bordered on one side by a steep embankment and an even steeper drop off on the other side. Once on this stretch there was only one place they could go. Dead ahead. *Dead* being the operative word.

My Rude Awakening

The insurgent armoured vehicles had simply been no match for the Apache's weaponry systems—rockets and Hellfire missiles. The speed at which we had tracked down and then engaged the enemy was only eclipsed by the swiftness of our fiery assault as we obliterated the entire convoy. We watched what had seemed like a menacing threat being reduced to a ramshackle of vehicles trying in vain to scurry for safety, leaving behind a cloud of dust. They had no chance.

As it turned out, they did have MANPADS, but not in the surrounding hills. They were on the back of two or three of the vehicles in the convoy. This didn't help them any as they scurried away at full speed to their early demise.

When Jamie, who had not been on the mission, asked me about it in a subdued tone, I went through how the mission had played out in a matter-of-fact manner. When he asked me how I felt about it, I could only describe it as "unbelievable." Jamie had been perceptive enough to leave it at that. I didn't even want to decipher those feelings. My first mission with a contact. I allowed myself to count the number of armoured vehicles that had been eliminated. Eight. When I reluctantly asked Will how many of the eight we had accounted for, he hesitantly mumbled, "Five or six." *Unsurprisingly, Will got more than his quota,* was my melancholic thought.

The thing is, for every vehicle, there was a given number of occupants—a tally of human lives. As much as I didn't want to do the simple arithmetic, I couldn't help myself.

That night I slept even worse than ever before.

More and more I was finding myself having to keep Rudyard Kipling's *IF* words top of my mind.

If you can force your heart and nerve and sinew… And so hold on when there is nothing in you, Except the Will which says to them: 'Hold on!'

CHAPTER 26
Mission zeero niner

IT WAS BECAUSE of some still classified and unique military circumstances that had us return to our Middle East posting after just a short break.

I had wanted to visit Charlotte during this time but knew it wouldn't have been the right thing to do, for either of us. We had reluctantly come to terms with our circumstances, and it would have been destabilising for both of us had I interfered with this delicate balance. Instead, I spent my fortnight at home in Berkshire, savouring all of those things that I had so missed since being posted to the Middle East, and what I had previously just taken for granted.

Now in our second tour of duty in frontline operational service, we had participated in countless missions. Whilst Jamie, Will, and me were beginning to feel like veterans, technically this was not yet true. Regardless, we were decidedly seasoned, and we felt it.

Notwithstanding my transformed world, Charlotte was never far from my mind and always firmly in my heart. Falling asleep at night was often delayed irrespective of how tired I was, because of the thoughts of her and the time we had shared together. I often tossed and turned until my tiredness overcame me, and I had to consciously shut down my thinking so I could finally doze off. I had occasional dreams about her and me that I loved, until I dreamt she was with another man, which was tortuous. I hated that I had no control over my dreams and far preferred my daydreaming.

For the most part, communication between us was near impossible and, at times, virtually nonexistent. Whenever I was in a location where I could make a phone call, I did. Not to my parents but to Charlotte. Despite having made the painful decision to go our separate ways, the love and passion we felt for each other simmered just beneath the surface, and neither one of us dared prod it, knowing it could so easily erupt. As a result, our conversations were often bland monologues, the weather being a regular topic. Even if we had wanted to speak about what was going on in our lives, it would have been impossible from my point of view, since I was not allowed to discuss where I was or what I was doing.

As if to convince myself that we had gone our separate ways, a particular song from my playlist became a regular for me. My attempt at defiance. Unfortunately, it was not that convincing, and sometimes it seemed that I played it just to torture myself.

"Separate Ways (Worlds Apart)" – Journey

| YouTube | Spotify | Apple |

I wished everything for her, but the thought of her loving someone else was more than I could bear. How could our lives go separate ways after having just touched so briefly? I still loved her and couldn't help holding out hope for the future.

When we were in training to become pilots, we used music to pump us up and get our adrenaline going. No more. We still listened to music, but often it was to settle our nerves. Or just a bit of calm before the storm. The subtle difference now was that things were for real.

After many months passed with scant communication between us, I finally accepted that there would be no going back to what had been my first romantic relationship.

My one irrefutable connection to her was Jamie, and as a result, my relationship with him flourished, as if my deprived soul fed off the connection to Charlotte. Jamie felt this. He would often ask how I was, and we both knew what he was asking.

Then, just as our time in the operational frontline seemed to become a little routine, there was a change. A dramatic change, as if to prove just how unpredictable life in the RAF and Army could be.

It was around 0650 hours on a Thursday, and I was making my way to breakfast when I received a sealed communication. It was a notice to attend a black ops meeting at 0800 hours the following day. A tingle ran down my spine.

I sat down next to Jamie, wondering if he had received the same communication. Because it was to do with a covert or secret mission, no communication of any description was permitted, even between your peers, including even our being summoned to a meeting. Then I noticed Jamie was reading something.

I thought for a moment and then said, "Jamie, any chance you can drop something off for me tomorrow at 0800 hours?"

"Negative," came his reply. "I'm tied up at that time."

We had our ways and means. Obviously, he'd been summoned to the same meeting.

The next morning, Jamie and I sat down for breakfast in the normal manner. When we were finished, we headed off in the same direction.

After three or four steps, Jamie quipped, "It looks like we are going to the same place. I could have guessed." He slowed his pace, letting me walk slightly ahead of him so we would not arrive together.

We met again in the black ops meeting room and sat together as we usually did.

The briefing was simple: A group of insurgents had established themselves in a well-protected area not far from our temporary air base, Delta-One-Fife. From this position, they had been able to launch shoulder-mounted MANPADS, which had put flight operations in and out of the temporary base at significant risk, especially for helicopters. It was to be a stealth mission, a flight of just two attack helicopters from our Apache squadron, executed by the four of us in attendance.

Watching me for a reaction, the officer briefing the meeting continued, "Your flight leader will be Lieutenant Charles Featherstone."

I didn't react. I was ready for this, and there was not anyone else in this flight of two helicopters, crew of four, who was better suited. I nodded my head assuredly in acknowledgment, even if this was my first mission as flight leader.

"I will not be speaking to you collectively again before the operation. Debrief is set for 1030 hours, once the last helicopter has landed, after a successful mission. Good luck, men, and Godspeed. Lieutenant Featherstone, you can remain for further ops briefing. The rest of you are dismissed."

I was then given all the critical information, including the most up-to-date intelligence on enemy positions. I went through the tactical attack plan, alternate routes, retrace considerations, mission-abort parameters, and the always ominous mission-failure and recovery plan.

Will—*who else?*—would be my CPG, the best in the squadron. Great-Shot Granger and I had become an inseparable team. A relationship built on a foundation of a solid friendship, Will and I were more than just regular partners flying our Apache. We had seldom taken to the skies without each other. This was something the RAF nurtured, realising the value of crewmen really getting to know each other.

In life you get many types of partnerships. An example, perhaps, would be tennis partners. If they misread each other, they lose a point, maybe a set, even the match. Afterwards, they kick themselves.

When you're in a combat helicopter, in a warzone, the word *partnership* takes on a whole new meaning. There, if you misread your partner, you may lose your life. No kicking yourself afterwards. Will was my partner, and I trusted him with my life as he trusted me with his. The bond between Will and me and the trust that had developed between us based on the primal human instinct of survival was difficult to describe. As close as Jamie and I were, Will was unquestionably the one I would always choose to go to war with.

The mission log showed that the second Apache would be crewed by Lieutenant James Blackwood, Pilot-in-Command, and CPG Lieutenant Patrick White. Our flight of two helicopters had flown several missions together, but the ante had been upped with this being a black ops mission.

I left the meeting still thinking about the details but comfortable that all the particulars were clearly understood. Notwithstanding my acute focus and attention to my first briefing as a flight leader, there was something else lingering in the back of my mind.

I headed straight for the officers' mess, where I knew I would find Jamie, and saw him sitting on the far side of the saloon area, on his own and deep in thought. I went over and sat opposite him.

"How do you feel about the mission?" I asked, getting straight to the point.

"Yeah, fine, cool," he said unconvincingly.

I thought there was no point not addressing the elephant in the room. "A bit of a downer that we are both on the same stealth mission," I said. The only small consolation was that we were not in the same helicopter.

Jamie looked up for the first time. "Yeah, I know," was all he said.

I put my hand on my friend's shoulder, "Jamie, careful how you manage it—black ops, et cetera—but give your mum a call."

Jamie again looked up at me and said, "Yeah, you should speak to her too."

He made the call to Gigi as I waited for him in the officers' mess, trying to use my time to go through some of the pointers for the next day's mission.

It was impossible to concentrate and not wonder what Charlotte and Gigi would feel with Jamie and I going on a stealth mission the next day, but in thinking about it further, I knew exactly how she would be feeling. The idle time while I waited for Jamie to finish his call made me realise just how much I hated the fact that I would be leading a flight on a mission into a very hostile environment, with Jamie under my command. What would I do if something happened to him? But I had to chase that thought from my mind. It was exactly that kind of thinking that could get us both killed.

He seemed to be taking a long time, but eventually he came back and assumed his seat opposite me. I looked up at him expectantly.

"My mum's very cut up," was Jamie's short summation of his phone call. "Be sure to phone her, Charles. I said you would."

I decided to wait before calling Gigi, thinking it would be better for her to have a little time to absorb and perhaps reconcile the situation. Just as well Charlotte was at university because that would have only given me more to contend with. It was a phone call I did not look forward to making. A couple of hours later, when I did finally make the call, there was not much I could say without breaching secret-mission protocols.

When she answered immediately, I realised she had been waiting by the phone. "Gigi," I said.

"Yes," came her reply.

"Hello, Gigi. Jamie called you?" I remarked, not really knowing what to say.

"Yes," was her short reply. Then as she inhaled slightly, I heard a quiver with her intake of breath that told me she had spent a lot of the past two hours sobbing.

"Please don't cry. Everything will be okay," I said.

"Promise me you will both be safe," she pressed.

"Gigi, everything will be fine."

She knew I could not make that promise.

I woke early the next morning, feeling twinges of excitement for what lay ahead. Flying these machines always brought a spring to my step, but today was a whole new ballgame.

The four of us involved in today's mission, all friends, walked amiably across to the apron of the air base, where our Apaches were standing. The weapons ground crew were already in attendance, readying the two attack helicopters with the required munitions.

Will and I began our own inspection, the engineering team having already completed a more thorough examination of the aircraft, and we circled the helicopter, going through all the preflight checks. Will's primary focus was the weapon systems, while I focused on flight controls, tail rotor, main rotor, and the like. We shared the responsibility of checking the Apache's twin jet engines, each from our opposite sides of the helicopter.

The weaponry ground crew finished prepping and checking the different armaments we would be using that day. In addition to the 30mm chain cannon, the helicopters had been armed with sixteen Hellfire missiles of around fifty kilograms each. We would also be using Hydra 70mm rockets.

Today was not an opportunity to use any fire-and-forget missiles. We would have eyes on target and be relying on the HMD and fire-control radar (FCR). Everything would be recorded by the cameras in the nose of the two Apaches. After every mission, if there was a kill, the videos would be carefully reviewed to look for culpable evidence. This had always puzzled me—kill them but follow the rules.

This mission would be close-combat fighting. No doubt the pungent smell of nitroglycerine would be more than evident after firing our weapons, even though we were sitting in our helicopters. *Hopefully keeping out of harm's way,* I thought grimly. In reality, this was the reason I was in a combat helicopter squadron, preferring to be *in the fight,* something you could not experience sitting in a jet fighter.

Preflight inspection done, Will and I came up alongside the helicopter before climbing into our respective cockpits.

"How are you feeling, Will?" I asked quietly, encouraging him to give me a truthful answer.

"Alive, excited, and as nervous as all hell."

That summed it up for me as well.

We climbed up into our respective cockpits. I pulled the safety harness and restraints over my shoulders, then around my waist and up between my legs, clipping them into the circular restraint housing. I took one last look around the cockpit, felt the free movement of my flight controls, then placed my flight helmet purposely onto my head. I did up the strap and plugged in the communications, instruments, and weapons systems.

My concentration belied the fact that I had done this hundreds of times before, because this time, it was different. I could not have been more tuned in to what had become a simple and somewhat-menial procedure.

I checked one last time that my gloves were comfortable and secure. You could call it my pet concern. In the event of an accident, and the helicopter catching fire, my hands would be better protected from the risk of burns. I pulled down my helmet visor, feeling the calm that always came over me just before I embarked on the start-up procedure. I was comfortable in this place, that old feeling of the aircraft being an extension of me.

"Base Delta WUN FIFE on TOO SEVEN AIT DECIMAL TREE, this is Mission ZEERO NINER requesting flight start-up clearance," I said into my microphone on the military-dedicated UHF-AM channel, using the strict pronunciation and procedures protocols that were standard Army and Air Force practise.

My Rude Awakening

"Mission ZEERO NINER, confirm TOO helicopter flight," came the reply from the air traffic controller.

"Mission ZEERO NINER, that's affirmative," I replied.

"Flight start-up approved," said the air traffic controller.

This authorised our two Apaches to start up our jet engines, advise when we were ready, and then prepare for liftoff for our departure from Base Delta One Five. Because this was a stealth mission, I knew the air traffic controller would not wait for me to request liftoff clearance.

I began the complicated start-up procedure without hesitation. The beautiful, logical pattern was now second nature, and I went through the steps with a fluidity that came from having done the same thing many times before. I heard each of the twin Rolls-Royce jet engines as they whined and then roared to life. *Bloody hell, I love this,* crept into my subconscious.

With the rotor system at full rotational speed, I again radioed air traffic control. "Delta WUN FIFE, we are *turning and burning.*" Excitement gripped my stomach.

"Mission ZEERO NINER, set mode FIFE, SQUARK SIX AIT ZEERO FIFE. Wind TOO TOO knots at WUN AIT FIFE degrees. When airborne, establish on outbound vector TOO SEVEN FOWER below TOO HUNDRED FEET AGL maintaining broad radio silence." This was air traffic control giving me our transponder setting so that we were recognisable on his radar, and he could keep track of our outbound track. This was also an instruction that there would only be communication between our helicopters.

I gave him the read-back, and once he was satisfied I had everything, he responded, "Mission ZEERO NINER, you have liftoff clearance at your own discretion."

Remaining below 200 feet AGL meant the two helicopters would engage the combat zone as close to the ground as we dared. We did this for a few reasons, not least of which was we would not easily be detected by enemy radar. Additionally, with helicopters being unavoidably noisy, if we were not close to the ground, the enemy would easily detect us if we were at say, 500 feet AGL. I knew I would lead our flight to less than half that height. We would generally be just fifty to sixty feet, or twenty yards, above the terrain. It also meant that when we came up on our target zone, they would be taken by complete surprise because it would be difficult for them to tell which direction the sound was coming from. They would likely only see us when it was too late for them to respond. By the time they did, we would have already begun our attack and deployed our missiles.

Flying missions in a combat zone was no longer cursory classroom information or training ground procedure. It was now a life-or-death situation, which gave it a vastly different complexion.

Was I ready? Yes, I was ready. I prayed Jamie felt the same way.

Our two helicopters became airborne a few moments later. We were not even through transition when the air traffic controller came back on the line. "Mission ZEERO NINER, QSY TOO NINER TREE DECIMAL FIFE. Maintain listening watch," came the curt order. This was the instruction to change our radios over to our mission frequency.

I took the command role, and the second helicopter slotted in behind me for our outbound flight into the combat zone. Mission Zero Nine was underway under my flight command. I felt confident we would successfully deliver our lethal, fiery blow, but there was one small problem.

With the insurgents in such a dangerous position, interfering with our flight operations at the base, it had been difficult to gather intelligence on this area. The screen in front of me showed a contour map that indicated the insurgents were roughly 80 nautical miles from the base, potentially behind a small hillock. We had decided that the best plan of attack was for one Apache to remain at low level and approach from around the side of the hillock, keeping close to the valley floor, while the second helicopter came over the hill at high speed and deployed its cannons and missiles from this elevated position.

A crucial element of the attack was that, even though we were coming from two different directions, we would arrive at the target at the same instant, so the insurgents had to divide their attention. I knew they would only hear us for a short while before we reached them, and with two helicopters coming from different directions, they would have even greater difficulty in discerning where we would be attacking from. As the two Apaches got closer to the target zone, they would likely be more aware of the low-flying helicopter coming up through the valley but be ill-equipped to easily attack it because of their own position relative to the flight of this helicopter. That would be enough of a distraction for the more exposed Apache approaching from over the hill to deploy its weaponry from its elevated position. As I was commanding the flight, it was appropriate that I assume this riskier situation in the attack plan.

With adrenaline pumping through my veins, causing my every sense to be heightened and on full alert, I made a very quick and informal radio call to the other three crew members. "Will, Pat, Jamie, we are sixty seconds out. Remember that our biggest threat is the MANPADS Stingers. Check that your Missile Approach Warning System (MAWS) is armed now, but don't rely on it. Keep your eyes peeled for smoke trails."

Unlike radar-guided missiles, infrared-guided missiles are difficult to detect when they are fired at a helicopter or plane. They do not emit detectable radar and are often fired from behind the helicopter, normally towards the engines. Whilst the MAWS does help, as it can automatically detect missile launches from the distinct thermal emissions of a missile's rocket motor, it is often more reliable for the flight crew to spot the missile's smoke trail and give the alert. For this to be effective, situational awareness becomes critical.

Once a Stinger infrared missile is detected, the crew of the aircraft releases flares in an attempt to decoy the projectile. The aim is to make the infrared-guided rocket seek out the heat signature from the flare rather than the aircraft's engines.

The other method of trying to avoid a missile strike is by breaking the line of sight (LOS) that the missile has of the heat emissions from the helicopter's engines and exhaust gases. This is not always possible, as you cannot simply duck behind a building or hillock without potentially endangering yourself and your crew further.

Great fun and games unless your life depended on it!

I came back onto the radio a moment later, calmly giving them the heads-up. "Thirty seconds out. Hard and sharp, chaps. Hard and sharp."

No amount of training or preparation ever fully equipped you for what comes in a situation like this, for one simple and obvious reason. On the range, it was similar in many respects, except you did not have people retaliating, knowing that the only possibility of them surviving was to kill you. *There is nothing quite like that to focus the mind,* I thought dryly.

We were both flying at top speed just above the treetops, Jamie up the valley whilst I was climbing the backside of the hillock, about to break cover as I crested the ridge.

"Ten seconds out. Are you on track?" I radioed to the other helicopter.

"Affirmative," came Jamie's terse reply as we closed in on our target at around 145 knots, or 165 miles per hour.

Our timing was perfect. As I levelled out at the top of the hill, I caught a glimpse of Jamie as I scanned ahead to pick up the target. My instrument panel told me that we both had eyes on target at almost the same time.

Our 30mm chain cannons each had 1,200 rounds of ammunition and fired at a rate of over 600 rounds a minute (ten per second). Multiply that by two. In addition, we both had sixteen Hellfire missiles, deadly by any measure. The attack that these two highly sophisticated combat aircraft could deliver was brutal and lethal.

Once we were certain it was a hostile enemy position, we used the forward-looking infrared (FLIR) system to be able to see our targets through any foliage or camouflaging. It made no difference that we could not actually see the target when deploying our armaments.

"Tree, two, one, fire," was all I said.

Both helicopters immediately and simultaneously began firing the highly explosive 30mm shells and a volley of Hellfire missiles and Hydra rockets, strafing the enemy position mercilessly. We obliterated our target in less than one minute. Their post went up in a mass of explosions, fire, and thick black smoke, without the enemy firing so much as a single shot in retaliation, such was our speed and decisiveness.

Almost immediately, I radioed the controller. "DELTA HOTEL," said it all—direct hit.

The only thing left to do was survey the scene, the nose cameras of the helicopters hoovering up a photographic record of the assault and consequences, for careful review later.

As I completed my last fly past, my primary radio channel came alive. "Mission ZEERO NINER, Base Delta WUN FIFE, do you copy?"

"Mission ZEERO NINER, go ahead."

"Return to base, track route Bravo. Your route Alpha has been compromised."

My Rude Awakening

This meant insurgents had positioned themselves on our return to base track, and because we did not have any intelligence on this, we could not take any chances. We certainly did not want them to spoil what had been an audacious attack and a remarkably successful mission. Route Bravo had already been planned and, once again, it required nap-of-the-earth flying, but this time it was in proximity to a nearby town.

I assumed the lead command position, and Patrick and Jamie fell in behind me a short distance back. It concerned me that our intelligence and topographical information for the region was limited. Notwithstanding this, we moved decisively so that we could exit the area as quickly as possible.

Then our radios crackled back to life. "Mission ZEERO NINER, QSY TOO FOWER TREE DECIMAL ZEERO." This was our instruction to change frequencies to the designated military emergency and guard channel. We were now being assisted by evac command, who were monitoring our activities from an Airborne Warning And Control System (AWACS) aircraft, complete with its sophisticated suite of radar technology. Flying overhead at somewhere around 35,000 feet.

We were about seven minutes into our extraction route but still deep in enemy territory. The change in tactic had us all razor sharp and alert. I was feeling extremely uncomfortable with the lack of intelligence and dependable terrestrial information, especially considering we were flying the contours of the earth.

Jamie was diagonally behind me, off to my right with about fifty yards between us, so I could still see him if I looked over my right shoulder. I was trying to calculate his best flight level, my inclination to tell him to take a little more height, but I didn't, knowing it would make him more exposed. I found myself paying as much attention to what lay in Jamie and Patrick's flight path as I did our own.

Mine and Will's cockpit activity was frenetic as we went into defence mode. He focused on interpreting flight and engine instrumentation and reviewed weapons status and our scant topographical information. At the same time, I was scanning the horizon, fervently checking the area ahead for enemy threats.

Less than ten nautical miles into our extraction plan, a gleam of reflection off metal tubing caught my attention. A feeling of dread immediately swamped me. I looked into the monocle over my right eye, set on target-acquisition mode. The infrared sight showed four red smudges indicating hotspots—probably two pairs of insurgents, each pair carrying a MANPADS. They were perfectly placed to launch their shoulder-mounted Stinger missiles at Jamie and Pat, putting my other crew members in mortal danger.

Focus, I screamed into my subconscious. Extreme urgency gripped me instantaneously. "Jamie! Johnny Jihads at your eleven o'clock low," I shouted into my microphone.

The feelings of horror were immediately set aside as my mind and body burst into action. Even though the activity in my cockpit was frenzied, a calmness came over me as I took control of the situation.

Almost instinctively, I banked hard right, and my helicopter came up alongside Jamie's. This would distract the insurgents. With them having to deal with two threatening targets halved the chances of them firing on Jamie alone. Most of all though, I could be more certain of taking evasive action. I felt better positioned to deal with this grave danger than what Jamie and Patrick were.

"Ready decoys," I shouted, making sure they were ready to deploy their missile defences. "Fire rockets, cannons, go, go, go," I shouted urgently.

I doubted we would get the insurgents before they fired their missiles, which was confirmed when almost immediately my MAWS squawked into my helmet as it detected the imminent mortal danger of the missiles. My "ready decoys" command could not have been a moment later.

I shouted my next order, "Fire decoys." As I was speaking, I saw the next volley of two Stingers heading towards me. "Jamie, break right," I barked, my headset squawking urgently back at me.

Once I felt Jamie was clear, I banked hard left, both of us moving away from the flares we had deployed. Ordinarily, we would have also reduced engine power to cool our thermal signature, but we didn't have that luxury because we were flying nap-of-the-earth.

As I watched the missiles heading towards us, I saw the result of our combined assault on the group of attackers. They had been eradicated in a flash by our Hellfire missiles and Hydra rockets.

Any comfort I got from that was short-lived, as I felt my controls begin shuddering violently. I had been hit with the glancing blow of a missile on my tail rotor, making this critical flight component inoperative. My Apache immediately yawed violently as I lost the counter torque effect my tail rotor provided against the powerful twin jet engines.

I immediately did the only thing I could do. I dropped the collective, eliminating the power completely, thereby preventing the helicopter from spinning out of control. The Apache began to drop as I initiated an autorotation. The problem was though, because we were so close to the ground, the instant we lost lift meant I was hurtling towards terra firma at an impossible rate of descent. I instinctively knew our ground impact would be way more than 10 Gs, the maximum survivable gravitational force on the body. My calm estimation was that our impact would be closer to 15 Gs and we would die instantly.

Everything had unfolded in fractions of a second, yet the whole sequence of events seemed to have played out in absolute slow motion. I was less than a hundred feet above the terrain, moments away from a fatal ground collision, and thinking, *It was worth it.*

That's when the unimaginable happened.

Instead of hitting the ground, I felt a massive deceleration of my already stricken helicopter. A split-second processing of what had happened made me realise it could only be high-tension wires. At around 75 feet AGL, I had flown into 60 KVA power lines. This unfortunately, offered no relief and statistically lowered any chances of our survival to less than 1 percent.

I remember waiting for what I imagined would be a burst of white light from the explosion, which I reckoned would be the last thing I would see before our lives ended.

It didn't happen!

The force at which we hit the power lines caused the cable to stretch and then snap, not at the point of impact but a little farther up the line. The next moment, the end of the cable was whipping back around us, getting caught in the main rotor mast. But still no explosion. Little comfort as we neared the collision point of the very unforgiving terrain. I was acutely conscious of somehow needing to reduce the force of the ground impact.

Somehow I managed to pitch the nose of the Apache up into a 50- to

60-degree angle so I could slam the tail boom into the ground first, reducing lethal energy before the fuselage and our cockpit crashed next.

With us angled in this way, I saw a burst of rockets as Will simultaneously fired all our remaining missiles. *Attaboy,* I thought, knowing that what he had done was crucial for us not having to contend with our own munitions exploding under us when we crashed.

As we struck the ground, we experienced the bone-jarring and organ-distorting symptoms of a high G-force impact, coupled with the deafening noise of hitting the terrain, and the screeching of tearing metal. I still had the presence of mind to think how well the cockpit shell held up, and even more, how effective my manoeuvre had been. This all went through my mind in the last split seconds of our crash.

We are still alive, I thought.

But it wasn't over yet.

In those few seconds, my next thought was the most sobering. We still faced the life-threatening danger that our highly flammable jet fuel would ignite and explode, something that was not an uncommon consequence, if not likely, when an aircraft is transformed into a mangled wreckage. It was an aftermath that airmen most feared because of it being the most painful and drawn-out demise.

I was consciously looking around in those split seconds, very fearful of seeing and then feeling the orange eruption of our jet fuel. Were the self-sealing fuel cells working?

Each second that passed had me hoping…and more hopeful. Fifteen seconds, and still nothing.

Thirty seconds…nothing.

I think we're going to be all right.

CHAPTER 27
THE EXTRACTION

THE MANIC CHAOS of just a few moments before gave way to an almost deathly silence and calm.

I pressed my transmit trigger to speak to Will in front of me in the forward cockpit, only to discover that we had no radios. I took off my helmet and immediately called out, "Will, are you okay?"

For a reply all I got was, "You are bloody amazing."

Will seemed to be okay.

I began to take further stock of our situation. Knowing we didn't have radios, I thought about activating our locator beacon and wondered if the insurgents had access to it or if it was even necessary. Jamie and Patrick would have seen where we went down and already radioed back to control.

Not necessary, I decided.

Then I thought, *Oh, damn! I didn't get permission from the controller to fire.* I thought about it for a moment and then remembered, *Oh yes, permission to fire was not necessary. We were in imminent danger.*

Then I remembered how the nose camera must have picked up the Stinger missile that got me. Now *that* was some footage I wanted to get hold of.

I smiled, realising I must have been a bit lightheaded.

While I was going through this, I became aware of excruciating pain in my legs. I looked down and saw a mess of flesh and blood, *a lot of blood,* which I just stared at for a while, wondering how bad it was. My back was also starting to ache. *Amazing what a strong anaesthetic adrenaline can be,* I thought as I felt the effects starting to wear off. Not being able to feel my feet and legs would portend spinal cord damage. I tried to move my toes and grimaced. My left leg was excruciatingly painful, but I was quite relieved that I could feel both of them. I could now smell the blood. *Not good*, I thought.

Will was very quiet, and I became more worried about him now that I had taken stock of my own injuries. Being in the lower, forward cockpit, he would have suffered a higher impact than me.

"Will, is everything okay?"

It took a while for him to say anything. Then came his uncertain reply, "I am fine," followed by another long pause. "I think my back got hammered though," he finally said.

I dared not ask him if he could move his toes, not wanting to hear the answer.

"Do you think we should try to get out of this thing?" he continued. "I wouldn't like it to pop on us after all we've been through."

He was also fearful of the possibility of an explosion, but by now I knew the risk was low and that he had sustained heavy injuries. Anyway, we would not be able to extract ourselves from the mangled wreckage on our own.

"Don't worry about that, Will. Just breathe, chum," I said calmly.

The best thing for both of us was to sit there quietly, knowing that a medical evacuation helicopter would come and get us soon. It was incredibly quiet and peaceful.

A typical injury sustained in high-impact accidents like this was to the neck and back, ranging from lower back spinal compression to something even more serious. Different levels of paralysis from spinal cord injuries were common.

My thoughts turned to Jamie. I knew he was safe because of our having killed the second lot of insurgents. *Thank God he is okay*, I thought. I also knew that he would immediately get backup, because maintaining our stealth on the mission was no longer necessary. Priority would be given to extracting Jamie and Patrick. It did strike me that they would be ordered to hold a rear-guard position while waiting for either the medevac helicopter or additional support for his extraction. What this meant was that while keeping clear of the actual crash site in order not to attract enemy attention to it, he would guard our stricken helicopter from a distance just in case there were other insurgents in the area who wanted to take a closer look.

I couldn't be certain how long we sat there, but because of the ever-increasing discomfort from my injuries and the possibility of us bleeding out, it was with some relief that I heard the unmistakable sound of the big twin-rotor Boeing Chinook helicopter with two Apaches providing aerial guard. The Chinook found a suitable landing place less than a hundred yards from our position while the two escort Apaches continued their aerial guard, now also joined by Jamie and Patrick.

The medical evac team moved with remarkable efficiency. Two jaws of life extrication tools were brought to the site, and in no time at all, they had opened the cockpit and were ready to transfer us to the Chinook. Two separate medics came to each of us, with others in attendance as well.

The medic attending to Will called out, "Oxygen. Syncope here," indicating to his colleague that Will had lost consciousness.

I had never been religious, but I said my own simple little prayer now anyway. *God, please don't take him now.*

This serious development made no difference to the medics' clearly well-versed emergency procedures. Before either of us was moved, they made sure we had not suffered cervical (neck) spinal cord injuries or head injuries. They could not be certain we did not have spinal injuries lower down the back, so our extraction from the helicopter was done in a way that indicated they assumed we may have.

We were both lifted out of the mangled helicopter and placed onto litter stretchers positioned alongside the cockpit. A minute or two later, we were in the Chinook and I could hear the two huge turbine engines spooling up from flight idle as we prepared for liftoff. That must have been just before I too lost consciousness.

We arrived at One ME Military Hospital and, with the same efficiency as before, were met by more medical staff already conversant with our conditions.

Will's injuries were far more serious than mine. His initial diagnosis was that he suffered a lower back transverse bone fracture and what was known as a burst fracture of the lower spine. This meant that one or two of his vertebrae had been crushed in all directions. Because there was a high probability that he had suffered a spinal cord injury, he was airlifted almost immediately to Defence Medical Services (DMS) back home in England.

I got off far lighter, with a spinal cord compression fracture to my lower back, which they decided not to operate on. My biggest injuries, however, were a smashed left ankle and multiple lacerations on both of my legs that would require surgery, which was scheduled and performed later that evening. It was amazing how efficient and effective medical treatment could be when medical professionals did not have to worry about bedside manner or the red tape that was typical in civilian medical practise.

Miraculously, I had not suffered any injury that a few weeks in hospital and six weeks of rest and recuperation leave (R&R) wouldn't cure. I couldn't say the same for Will. Even though what had happened was a normal consequence of war, it weighed heavily on my mind.

As I lay in my hospital bed, I couldn't help but relive the trauma of what we had been through.

There are certain light conditions that make it impossible for helicopter pilots to detect high-tension wires. This had been one of those occasions, as if I hadn't had enough to contend with at the time.

A wire strike, the term used by aviators to describe flying into power lines, nearly always results in catastrophic consequences from any one of three distinct possibilities, each almost certainly fatal. A combination of these factors decreases the likelihood of survival exponentially. The first possibility is that a 60 KVA high-tension wire acts as a lethal blade that can cut through the helicopter and its occupants much like a wire cheese cutter going through cheese. The next possibility is that the helicopter loses all or most of the flight controls as the cable rips through the control rods located on the rotor shaft, making it impossible for the helicopter to be flown at all, never mind during the critical phase of trying to land without an engine. The third, and perhaps the most dangerous likelihood, is that 60,000-volt-amps, 60 KVA, coming into contact with a helicopter carrying extremely flammable jet fuel is nothing less than an explosion waiting to happen. Any one of these possibilities, without even considering the complexity of being in a war zone, is enough to bring about one's early demise.

The extreme irony of our accident was that what should have killed Will and I had actually saved our lives. The speed at which I was approaching the ground would have resulted in an impact of about 15 Gs. Impossible to survive. Flying into the high-tension wires, which should have exacerbated our situation, had instead saved us. The powerlines had acted as arresting lines, like the type you find on aircraft carriers to arrest the forward speed of fighter jets when they land, which ultimately prevented us from the worst possible outcome. Our flight data recorder registered our impact at 10.1 Gs. The accepted survivable impact was supposedly under 10 Gs. Only because of our training, our level of fitness, and our bodies being used to experiencing elevated G-force conditions did we survive, but we had not been able to avoid serious back injuries.

While I was in the hospital, I had plenty of time to think intensely, not only about the mission, the near-fatal missile attack on Jamie and Patrick, and Will's and my near-miss, but also to ponder the experiences I'd had during the past six years of my service in the RAF. These thoughts bombarded my mind, and I was struggling to make sense of it all, eventually just shutting them out without any resolutions.

Then, on what I thought was the seventh or eighth morning, I woke up feeling decidedly better after a good night's rest. My mind was clearer, and I felt that I could start making sense of things again.

As a result of my improved health, I was able to make a phone call to my parents. My mother and father of course knew about my accident, and had been assured of my good health, even if that was not strictly true. My dad had been cheerful and upbeat, making sure I was in a good headspace, while my mother could not help but be very sombre about what had happened. My call ended with her saying, "It's enough now, Sunbeam. It's enough."

My parents couldn't reconcile me being in the RAF. Initially it had seemed fine, but since being posted into combat zones doing tours of duty, they'd felt that I'd been sucked into a system where I didn't belong.

"Why, Sunbeam? Why? When you have so much here at home and even more to look forward to." I could hear my mother's words.

Deep down I agreed with her. As I lay in my hospital bed, I couldn't help but think about the alternatives to the RAF, which unquestionably became extremely attractive. I knew there were all sorts of possibilities for my future. Going into business was a strong probability, and Rockwell

Manor Polo, with all its attractions, was also an option. These were the obvious ones.

Had I proven my point of doing something on my own? Would the RAF impact my life? And how would *Charlotte* influence it? Little did I realise how much those thoughts would shape my future.

Having survived such a traumatic accident also had me consider some of life's bigger questions.

Does risking your life bring you closer to death, or does it make you more alive than ever?

I thought long and hard about the RAF. I loved it. I always had. But not all aspects. Pilots were referred to as "glamour boys." I suppose it didn't help matters that we wore T-shirts with either a jet fighter or an attack helicopter on it, depending on what squadron you were in, with inscriptions like:

> "If you are not living on the edge,
>
> you are taking up too much space."

After spending time in the operational zone, the last thing one felt like was a glamour boy. And once pilots had flown combat missions, they stopped wearing those T-shirts. Perhaps actually being on the edge brought with it a reality that had no place for bravado, no matter how lighthearted.

Another aspect I found myself thinking about was the overall effect the RAF and being a combat pilot was having on me. Was it ultimately going to turn me into somebody I wanted to be or something I abhorred? The one thing I knew with absolute certainty was that Mission Zero Niner and the emotional pressures it had come with would have a long-lasting impact on my life.

Since Will had been airlifted back to England, I had heard nothing more of his condition. It gnawed away at me and had me saying my own prayer for him. *An unbearable feeling.* It brought into sharp focus my role as a combat pilot.

Post-traumatic stress disorder (PTSD) was not something typically associated with pilots. The truth is, the continual pressure and stresses of risking one's life, flying attack helicopters on combat missions, would ultimately bore deep into one's psyche. The more time one spent in the operational area, the more one would think about what it was they were doing.

I loved the flying, and I knew I was good at it. Particularly good. I had chosen not to be a Copilot-Gunner, even though as Pilot-in-Command I did almost as much target acquisition and weapons deployment as the CPG. The reason was that as a CPG, it was 'in your face' acquiring targets and gunning them down. But of course, they were seldom just targets. They were people whose lives we were taking.

Military service makes young men hard and strong, but fragile too. No matter how resilient you may be, it would eventually take its toll. All that remained to be seen was how well one could handle the aftereffects and how quickly one could overcome them. Many experienced some form of PTSD in the course of their lives.

We listened to rock music and showed lots of swagger to our peers, especially about girls. But behind the scenes, we felt very differently. I imagined all our letters to our families were of a similar vein, no bravado but rather filled with many truths about our fears. As much as I had loved rock music, I began enjoying love ballads equally, still not something I would readily reveal to the chaps.

At twenty-five, men are still boys. Psychologically I don't think they handle war well, even though they would never show it. I think women would probably do a better job of that. But only psychologically, as they generally lacked the recklessness that is inherent in men. Which is why men drive too fast and take risks that result in them breaking their necks around twenty-two times more often than women do, in military and sporting roles.

Is it ultimately being polar opposites that attract men and women to each other? And the more men are men, the more women love it but dislike it at the same time. John Gray, PhD, probably understands this better than most, as it was the basis of his book, *Men Are from Mars, Women Are from Venus*.

Then, of course, I thought about Charlotte. All the time. It was impossible not to. Even though I had not seen her for almost a year, I'd spent literally every day with her, through her brother, who had many of her mannerisms and facial features. This made her larger than life. And it had come so close to changing.

An unfortunate reality were the many nightmares I'd been having about how close Jamie had come to being brought down by Stinger missiles. Irreversible consequences, too hideous to contemplate. Charlotte, and especially Gigi, would have blamed me, and I would have blamed myself.

I knew that if I left the RAF, Jamie would too, and that was how I wanted it to be. My thoughts about my future were beginning to crystallise. If Jamie and I both left the RAF, the reason Charlotte and I had ended our relationship would have gone. I still had a tremendous amount of feeling for her, and she was often in my thoughts. Having not seen her in such a long time since we had agreed to go our separate ways, and as much as I felt I should not disturb that, I thought there wouldn't be any harm in me at least finding out if she had indeed moved on.

Then, late on the afternoon of my eighth day in hospital, I received my first and only visitor, none other than Jamie, of course. He had managed to get special permission to come and see me, which I was really pleased about.

I was sitting in a chair next to my hospital bed, nursing a very tender back and legs, when he came in. Without a thought for the other patients, he leant over me and hugged me, holding me for an appreciable amount of time.

"What's up, Jamie? Are you okay?" I asked.

"God, you nearly killed us," was his reply.

I didn't understand. Surely Jamie was not blaming me for the insurgent Stinger missile attack on his helicopter.

He saw the confusion on my face and quickly gave an explanation. "God, no, not like that. You saved my life. We thought *you* had been killed. I didn't know what I was scorching. Mum and Charlotte have been beside themselves. You have to speak to them if you can," he rambled.

My ears pricked up at the mention of Charlotte's name. "Jamie, Jamie, slow down. What are you talking about?" I asked.

He stopped for a moment and just shook his head while he continued looking at me. Then he cupped my cheeks in his hands. "I thought I had lost my best friend," he said, looking into my eyes.

Conscious of others around us and to lighten the moment, I joked, "Just don't kiss me."

With that, Jamie kissed me, fortunately only on the forehead. He then put his hands on my thighs and said, "You have to phone Mum. She will be able to speak to Charlotte."

"Jamie!" I said, stopping him again.

"Okay, okay, I will explain, but first tell me how you are?" he asked, taking a breath.

"I am fine, just need some R&R. I am very worried about Will though. He took a heavy blow. He was airlifted straight back home," I said. I was brief because I was anxious to hear what Jamie had been going on about. "I will tell you all later. First, tell me what is going on," I demanded.

Jamie calmed down a bit and went and got another chair, which he placed right in front of me. Speaking in a hushed tone, he began, "So let me tell you from the time you said to me that you had spotted the Johnnys. I looked out but still couldn't see them and just followed your instructions. The next minute, you were alongside me in that slightly low and forward position. I wasn't too sure what you were doing until you told me to fire my decoy flares. Only when the first Stinger was coming our way did I truly realise what was going on. I was a little slow in banking right and saw the second volley of missiles heading towards you. Just when I thought the decoy flares had done their job, I saw your tail rotor being struck. I didn't think you had a chance. It is just as well we had killed our attackers because I was focused completely on you. I saw you hit the power lines, but your ground impact was concealed from me. You went down so fast, I was convinced you had copped it." Jamie took a breath.

I replied in a matter-of-fact tone, "I managed to reduce a lot of the impact by slamming the tail rotor onto the ground first. It did an excellent job of absorbing a lot of the downward force that I guess would have killed us."

Jamie shuddered.

"What happened next?" I prompted, not wanting him to lose his train of thought.

"Do you know, had you not come up alongside me to help with the decoys, those Stingers would have got me?" Jamie continued, putting his hand on my knee.

I didn't say anything, knowing he was probably right. "Carry on, Jamie," I insisted.

"Once you went down, I immediately contacted Ops Control. They told me to stay clear of the crash site and to hold a rear-guard position, staying in the area until the medevac helicopter and backup arrived. I didn't know what had happened to you, and when I radioed you frantically but got no response, I realised you must have lost all electrics.

"I just wanted to go in and see if you and Will were okay, but of course I couldn't, and I wouldn't have been able to do anything anyway." Jamie paused for a moment and collected his thoughts.

"It seemed to take forever, but eventually the Chinook medevac helicopter arrived with two Apache escorts. All three Apaches were then engaged in holding a guard position around the crash site, making sure we distracted any would-be insurgents from attacking the soft target of the Chinook and you, if you, you know, were still okay. The problem was that I still had no idea what the crash site looked like and what the medevac team was doing. To be honest, I thought they were extracting yours and Will's bodies." Jamie stopped again, tears in his eyes.

He then continued in a quivering voice, "The Chinook lifted out, and we were ordered to scorch the crash site. For a crazy moment, I wondered to myself if they even managed to get the two of you out of there or I was about to incinerate you. Bloody hell, Charlie, the thought nearly killed me."[1]

I reached over and put my hand on his shoulder, truly appreciating in that moment that he had become a really special friend.

He wasn't finished yet. "We then escorted the Chinook until we were over friendlies, and they carried on to One ME Hospital with the other two escorts. I returned to base with dangerously low fuel, which was why I

---

[1] The Scorched Earth Policy was the destruction of any assets, including military equipment, transport vehicles, communication sites, industrial resources, food and water stores, or anything that may be useful to the enemy. Until surprisingly recently, even local people themselves could be destroyed under this policy, but thankfully this law was changed. The scorching of local people, along with food and water stores for civilians, was banned under the 1977 Geneva Convention.

couldn't continue as an escort for your Chinook. I still did not know what had happened to you and Will." Jamie then took another deep breath. After a while, he continued, "I got to the base, and I didn't know what to do. I knew I had to speak to Mum. She went crazy, bud. I couldn't console her, and I was in no state myself. We got no news for twenty-four hours, and it nearly killed her and Charlotte.

He answered my slightly surprised look with, "You and Charlotte may have ended things, but you are family, bud. We've all been together a long time."

In fairness, that did explain Gigi's and Charlotte's emotions.

Jamie carried on from there. "When we did hear something, it could hardly have been less informative. And then the day before yesterday, I heard you had been operated on and were okay. That is when I made a plan to get here. I heard about Will. You have to speak to Mum, bud. She needs to hear from you. I think she was close to a nervous breakdown. She doesn't know that I managed to get here." Jamie had begun rambling again.

"I would like to speak to Charlotte and Gigi," I said. "But how can I?"

"I don't know how easily you would be able to speak to Charlotte at uni, but wild horses won't stop her speaking to you. Mum will be at home so you could speak to her anytime," Jamie finished off thoughtfully. "Can you walk? On your own? I can help you," he asked, looking at the cast on my left leg.

I could tell he was busy hatching another plan. "I can. Slowly," I replied.

"Give me a moment," Jamie said, and with that, he dashed off. He left me contemplating whether I could actually walk, but then he returned before long, beaming. "All organised."

I gave him an enquiring look.

"I just sorted it out with one of the nurses," he replied to the question I didn't ask.

I guessed his disarming charm had its uses.

We went through to an admin section, and I was ushered into a small back office where the obliging Sally-Anne pointed to the phone. "Don't be long, Lieutenant. I really shouldn't be doing this," she said.

Quite surprisingly, I patched into the UK telephone network on the first attempt.

The Blackwood residence phone rang just twice, and Gigi answered in a very shaky voice, "Georgina Blackwood here."

"Gigi, it's me," was all I said.

She burst into tears. "Oh, God, my darling!" And then she carried on sobbing. Eventually she said, in a very quiet voice, "Thank God. I am so happy to hear your voice. God, I thought we had lost you. I didn't know what had happened. No one could tell me where you were…or if you were…you know… Thank God you're alive."

She slowly started pulling herself together as I told her a little bit about Will's and my injuries, which I understated just a little, even if it was not strictly true.

"How have you managed to phone me?" Gigi asked.

"Jamie's here, he organised it. You know how he can organise things?" I replied.

"Thank God. What happens next? What is going to happen to you?" Gigi asked in a concerned tone.

"I'm going to be transferred to Defence Medical Services in England, Birmingham, actually in the next week or so, for about six to ten days of treatment—traction and observation. Just up the road from you, not far from Charlotte's university."

"Yes, okay," Gigi replied a little hesitantly.

Her uncertain response was almost certain confirmation that Charlotte had indeed moved on.

"Then I should get six weeks R&R, you know, rest and recuperation," I finished off.

"Is that like leave?" Gigi shot back.

"It is," was my short reply.

"Call me when you are in Birmingham, and Charlotte and I will come and see you."

"I will. That will be nice. And, Gigi, please phone my parents as I have not been able to speak to them," I said.

"Of course. I have been keeping them in the picture as best I could all along," Gigi responded in a gentle voice.

We ended the call with me wondering if I was right about Charlotte having moved on, or was Gigi's hesitation because of my ordeal.

My Rude Awakening

I gingerly made my way back to the ward where Jamie was waiting for me.

Eventually it was time for him to go. Just as he was getting up to leave, the senior nurse told us that Lieutenant William Granger had come out of recovery a short while earlier, following his second operation to his lower back. On all accounts, it seemed to have been a success. She told us that his prognosis was good and he was expected to make a good recovery, but it would take many months. She had sounded a little guarded, but I was focused on the positive, hoping beyond hope that he would escape what seemed like certain paraplegia.

Jamie saw the concerned look on my face and put an arm around my shoulder, giving me a tight squeeze. "He will be okay, chum."

As he was about to leave, he turned and said, "Oh, damn, I nearly forgot." He handed me my Walkman. "I had a feeling you might want this."

Jamie had such an endearing side.

Two days after seeing him, I received the devastating news that Will's injuries had resulted in him suffering paraplegia, the loss of the use of the lower part of his body, and there was almost no chance of that changing.

The emotional part of my brain questioned, *Why do I still have the use of my legs and he doesn't? Was I sitting more upright when he may have been slouched?*

The analytical parts of my brain gave me the high probability reasons.

Will had been in the more forward, lower cockpit. When I had slammed the tail structure of the helicopter into the ground to reduce our G-force impact, it had created a whiplash effect on the tandem cockpit. Because of his more vulnerable position, and his cockpit having less protection from the two landing-gear assemblies and big wheels, with their significant shock-absorbing capabilities, even Will's powerful body was no match for those forces.

Had it not been for my actions, we would've both died. I'd saved our lives, but surely ruined the rest of his. This became my biggest conundrum. I hoped that time would provide some answers. We were much the same age, and that meant a lot of ruined years lay ahead of Will. This soon began to play on my mind, subliminally at times, then at others it was an unrelenting, persisting thought. *What could I have done differently?*

In the theatre of war, William Granger would make it into the record of statistics under the column "Life-Changing Injury." I couldn't really get my mind around that. *How life-changing?* I had a sense that those words were an understatement in the extreme.

Another four days passed, and I was being prepared for my discharge from One ME Hospital. During this time, I didn't manage to speak to Gigi again. It seemed I did not have Jamie's powers of persuasion.

After losing track of time, the day finally arrived and I was on my way back to England.

During my Air Force career, I flew numerous missions in several war zones. Many people have felt I should've included more of these encounters. My young son especially has been a strong advocate of me writing more chapters, especially my own SITTING DUCK mission. I have refrained from doing so, mindful of not wanting to turn this memoir into an Air Force war story. However, as declassification occurs with the passing of time, I may well write something more on the matter in the future.

I chose to write in detail about this mission because it encapsulated so many extraordinary aspects. Not only was it unusual and dramatic, but I had been extremely lucky. Added to that, not only did it affect my near-term future but it also had a profound effect on the rest of my life.

CHAPTER 28
HEADING HOME

MY TRANSFER FROM the searing desert heat of the Middle East, often described as seasonless, to the contrasting coolness of England, experiencing not uncommon early autumn single digit temperatures, was an awakening I had not contemplated. I didn't mind. It was part of coming home if you were English.

Thrilled to be back on home soil, if not my home in Berkshire, I was ambulanced to the advanced DMS Hospital in Birmingham. I was checked in by a very caring and attentive nurse, Corporal Susan Hennessey, and then settled into my new hospital bed, a far cry from whence I had just come.

From the moment Corporal Hennessey attended my admittance, she would always find time during her lunch break, or before she left to go home, to come to my bedside and chat a while and check on my progress. As a result, I had no difficulty in arranging to make phone calls, the first of which was to phone home. I called and nonchalantly asked my mum if she could come to Birmingham in the next few days to pick me up, as I was coming home.

"Oh God, Sunbeam," my mother answered. "You are back in England! Of course I will." Then after a moment's thought she added, "But I have one question. Is it for good?"

I didn't immediately answer, but I was nodding my head in the affirmative. Realising what I was doing, I finally said a simple, "Yes."

In that moment, I had made a final decision about my RAF career and in the process, defined a large part of my future, a difficult decision, given how much I loved the Air Force.

The next day, I called Gigi to let her and Charlotte know I was in hospital in Birmingham and that, in the next few days, I would be going home to Rockwell Manor. They immediately made plans to come and visit me, which I thoroughly appreciated. I had not known what to expect of seeing Charlotte again after such a long absence. It would be so easy and comfortable for me to just rekindle our old relationship, but deep down, I knew a lot would have changed during the time we had been apart. Added to that was Gigi's hesitation around Charlotte. And once again I was not sure what lay ahead of me, given my decision to move forward in a new direction in my life.

All these thoughts and reservations flew out of the window as I watched Charlotte, followed by Gigi, bounding towards me in Ward D of the Birmingham hospital.

"Babe. Oh, Charles, just look at you! You haven't changed a bit," Charlotte announced as she flung her arms around me.

Once Charlotte had finished her affectionate greeting, Gigi came to my bedside and kissed me around four or five times on the cheeks.

"Thank God you're home, darling. I'm so pleased you are home," she said with grave sincerity.

We spent a good hour together catching up on the news, which didn't take much catching up at all. During the course of the conversation, the one topic we did not touch on was what had happened in Charlotte's love life. The only clue I got was when I did venture, "and in other personal news, is there anything happening there?" as if directing the question to both of them. Charlotte's response of "let's not go there," spoke volumes.

My father had often said to me that, in life, there are typically just two types of decisions: easy ones and correct ones. Too often, he warned, we make the easy decisions because that's what they are, easy. It is the correct decisions that are the toughest.

With that sage advice in the back of my mind, I took the decision not to wonder and waiver about a relationship between Charlotte and me. Right then, I made my own decision not to look back, notwithstanding the tremendous feelings I still had for Charlotte.

It seemed that the Queen Elizabeth Military Hospital in Birmingham was a good place for decision-making.

The next day, my mum arrived unannounced. "Sunbeam, Sunbeam, my darling Sunbeam, am I happy to see you?" she exclaimed, leaning over my bed and embracing me, not bothering to hide her emotions even though we were in public.

"Oh, Mum, I am so happy to *see you*," was all I could say. "But you are a few days early," I finished off.

"No. Seeing my son can never happen *too early*. I will simply find a local boutique hotel and stay nearby so I can visit you until such time as they discharge you."

There was no point in arguing as the deed had already been done. Deep down I knew that nothing would have kept my mother from coming to me the moment she was able to.

After I counted down the days of my recovery, my hospital discharge finally arrived.

I'd told my mum I would be cleared at around two o'clock. There was still forty minutes to go, enough time for me to do the last bits of paperwork. I arrived at Corporal Susan Hennessey's desk to the warmest welcome.

"So, Lieutenant, you're leaving me today—*us* today—but we'll see each other again in two weeks. If you need anything before then, just give us a call.

It was so nice of her to be so caring.

She started filling out the forms and made a little light conversation. "So, who is picking you up today? A brother or sister, your mum, or *that girl?*"

I couldn't help smiling to myself that Corporal Hennessy had noticed Charlotte having visited me. "No, my mum will come and get me," I replied.

"Good," was all she said.

It was not lost on me that she thought this was a good outcome.

"Now don't forget, Lieutenant, if you need anything, and I mean *anything*, give me a call. In case you have difficulty with the hospital switchboard system, here are my direct numbers." She handed me a little note with two numbers - (W) and (H), her name, and curiously, a heart scribbled in the corner. I couldn't help wondering if I would have been given the note if *that girl* was the one who would be picking me up. Given that a future with Charlotte and me was off the table, I took some care in placing the note in my wallet.

I was finally discharged from the Queen Elizabeth Hospital, officially for six weeks R&R leave before returning to RAF Shawbury. I knew that was not going to happen and once I was back at Rockwell Manor, I would begin the process of terminating my permanent service contract with the RAF in favour of reserve service.

Still on crutches for support, we went outside to the car park and the warmest welcome from Hamilton.

"So good to see you, sir. Welcome back," he said, extending his hand to shake mine.

We set off for Berkshire, my mum and I in the back of the Bentley, with me feeling an unusual calm with the decisions I had made. The first part of the journey was unusually quiet, perhaps as a result of something my mother had brought up.

"Sunbeam, when you're ready, we must speak about what happened to you, William, and Jamie. All in your own time, but we must speak about it."

The instant shake of my head made it clear this was not the time.

My mother's hand on my shoulder told me she understood.

I was so caught up in my thoughts that it surprised me when the GPS said, "You are now halfway. You have ninety-two miles to go."

That had seemed quick. I was on the downhill leg now, heading home to my future.

I had missed those old, familiar surroundings, not having seen them for several months now. I couldn't help feeling a glowing warmth towards my mother. Her reassuring voice over the phone earlier had made me feel better. Rockwell Manor was indeed my *rock,* not least because of my ever-dependable parents.

My thoughts around the RAF were quite straightforward. I had made the decision to leave. My mother would be thrilled once she had seen the confirmation of it, but I knew she would not be too quick to show it.

Jamie was due back at RAF Shawbury from the Middle East any day now. I would find out when he got there and then invite him for the weekend. Between his mother and me, there would be no difficulty in convincing him to do what I had already decided for my RAF career, which was to convert the remainder of his service to a reservist role.

There was a lot I should have been looking forward to. Going into business had been top of my agenda. Technology was what I had studied, along with economics, and that was what I had wanted to do.

Let me focus on that, I thought.

I still had to concentrate to not let my mind drift back to Charlotte.

As I shifted my thoughts to the future, I thought about other things that should also have really excited me. Developing Rockwell Manor Polo Team was one. Getting in some good shooting was another. Would I get another dog? Would I dare to think about building a heliport at Rockwell Manor and, in time, buying my own helicopter as had been suggested?

There was something that didn't feel right, and right then I didn't know what it was.

I turned on my Walkman connected to my car's stereo and solemnly listened to a recently added song. It had a special significance now.

"Here I Go Again" – Whitesnake

YouTube　　　　Spotify　　　　Apple

The very first line of the song said it all, because right then, I did not know where I was going, but I sure knew where I'd been.

Getting on with it was how I'd managed being without Charlotte before. With little choice, I'd made up my mind and couldn't waste any more time. I would do that again.

Will it be that easy?

As the words played out, they resonated more and more with me.

Here I was again. Would I keep searching for an answer, and would I find what I was looking for?

Ooh, Lord, I pray you give me strength to carry on.

CHAPTER 29
THE REALITIES OF LIFE

A S I DROVE into rockwell manor, I couldn't help noticing the trees had shed their autumn leaves. *Depressing!* Not a thought I'd ever had about my home. None of the elation I normally felt. Not surprising, given all I had gone through, I surmised, trying to rationalise my feelings. The warm greeting from my father made me feel a little better, even though even he was somewhat subdued.

As is often the case, things did not play out as anticipated. I had hoped to invite Jamie back to Rockwell Manor, at least to speak about his RAF future, but as it turned out, we discussed all that we needed to over the phone. With my decision to leave the Air Force and the ending of my relationship with Charlotte, he had already started making his own plans for his future.

When I quipped that I liked his independence, he replied, "When you left, I knew you wouldn't be coming back. There was no point in me hanging around, and I wasn't going to stay here without you."

I got two things out of that: Jamie was not *that* independent when it came to the RAF, and he probably knew me better than I knew myself.

Our circumstances had made it impossible for our relationship to endure and as a result I had lost a very special friend in Jamie. I would miss him terribly, and already I was feeling the loss of not having him and his roguish sense of humour around me. It seemed strange that he, Gigi, and Charlotte would likely never come back to Rockwell Manor.

With no Jamie to entertain, the first few days after arriving back at Rockwell Manor were strange. Not being much of a sleeper, I would get up at dawn without being sure what I should do next. It was a little like an

My Rude Awakening

Olympic athlete looking for his kit, then realising he didn't even know what event he was competing in.

There should have been so much to look forward to now that I was back home. Shooting still had a few weeks left of the season. Polo would be starting soon, and arranging a mini tournament for the kick-off on our home field should have really excited me, but I barely gave it a thought. Going into business should've been top of my agenda. Technology was what I had studied, along with economics, and that was what I should do.

Let me focus on those things! I thought, but it made no difference. I couldn't.

This carried on for over two months. Something that could only be described as a "lethargic approach to life." Something that was totally out of character for me—the person who could not walk up stairs but had to bound up them four or five steps at a time.

What is wrong with me?

The stables were empty with the horses having been turned out after the season, so there was no reason to go over there. Guy wasn't around either, still being away on his offseason break. No doubt he would be somewhere in the Southern Hemisphere. Argentina was my guess, where he not only had the summer but also some good polo. It was also my guess that Grace would be with him. I found myself feeling envious of them.

Leafless trees and animals in hibernation. Nature shrinking away from the onset of a cold, depressing winter. Had winter taken me down with her?

Christmas at Rockwell Manor was always a highlight, and this year was no different. Lots of guests, dinners, which now I mostly missed, preferring to just be in my own space in my North Wing suite. Fabrizio was also trying to play his part in lifting me out of my doldrums with food. Not even that was working.

The one thing that did get me out of my room was the rowdy kitchen pizza evenings. I had a feeling my dad had arranged them with that purpose in mind. It worked to an extent but nothing like the old days. Even so, I mostly kept to myself, lost in thoughts of the past, like my handprints on Charlotte's top or her little dance on the centre of the field as we made our way over to the stables. That's when I would take myself up to my room.

It struck me that there was no small talk about the RAF or what had happened there. Had everyone been briefed about steering clear of that topic? It suited me.

In the grip of a cold, gloomy winter, looking out of my bedroom window, staring at Osric's memorial, wondering why there wasn't one for Granddad, I was feeling decidedly miserable.

It was all getting too much. Then one evening in the family dining room while we were having dinner, I decided to speak to my parents. After explaining to them what I was feeling, my dad let my mother do the talking. It would have surprised me if he hadn't.

"Sunbeam, you have Yuppie Flu."

"What?" I replied, and then a little bit disrespectfully, "I don't have flu! I don't think I have ever had flu."

"No, Yuppie Flu is not flu," was my mother's curt response. "Its formal name is chronic fatigue syndrome."

Once we had got past that little hurdle, we carried on chatting quietly about my condition and how it was quite normal for returning servicemen. Uncle Alexander had also given my parents some insight. After all, he was an ex-RAF airman. He had explained to them that almost every serviceman, after several years in the armed forces, invariably struggled with this.

"Fran, just remember, for the last six or seven years, Charles has been in a system where every minute of every day, every activity, even meals, has been set out for him. Then suddenly he comes back into civilian life. How could he not be anything but affected?" he had told them.

Then, as if it were a delicate subject, my mother voiced my parents' belief that I was also suffering with the early onset of PTSD.

"You should see someone, a doctor," my mother suggested in her most appealing voice.

"I don't need a doctor," again my reply too abrupt and impolite. "Sorry, Mum, I know you are just trying to help, but I really don't need to see a shrink."

All my father could do was look on helplessly.

"Think about it, Sunbeam. It makes perfect sense after all you have been through," my mother impressed reassuringly, holding my hand.

We had carried on speaking for a good while thereafter, enjoying an after-dinner port together. As we all began to relax more, I thought about all I had heard, and it began to make more sense to me.

What wasn't mentioned during the conversation was my relationship with Charlotte, but there was no question my mum was acutely aware that this was a big factor as well. Her remark at the end of the evening confirmed it.

"It's time to get out there, Sunbeam. Just don't go breaking too many hearts."

I guessed every mother thought this of their sons.

Five months since I'd left the Middle East and subsequently the Royal Air Force, I was slowly getting on top of my chronic fatigue syndrome. I had gingerly begun with aspects of my new life but was still beset with slow starts and unrelenting lethargy.
Then late one Friday afternoon, I received a letter from Eleanor Granger, CPG William Granger's mother.

I had occasionally called Will to find out how he was getting on and how he was coping with his paraplegia. Whenever we spoke, he sounded upbeat and positive. On more than one occasion though, I put the phone down wondering if that was really the case. He was English, after all, and being honest about his feelings was more than likely something he'd never be too comfortable with. I was regularly plagued by the nagging concerns I had about him.

Dear Charles,

I hope this finds you well.

I am writing to you in confidence and to ask if you could make your way to Norfolk to see William sometime soon.

You're probably unaware, but from the outset he has been struggling with pressure sores that he got shortly after his accident, brought about because of his immobility and not being able to feel anything below his midriff.

It seemed so innocuous at first, but without getting into the details, it led to him getting septicaemia. This in turn very nearly brought an end to his life in a most devastating way, as, in the final throes, the major organs begin shutting down. Let me hasten to say that thankfully he is finally over it. However, it has left him very weak both physically and emotionally, which is why I am contacting you.

I am hoping a visit from you will improve his spirits.

He used to love telling stories of what an incredible pilot you were and how you saved his and your own life, something that I will always be grateful for. Unfortunately, that spark is absent now.

Please let me know when it'll be convenient for you.

William Sr. sends his best wishes.

My very fond regards,

Eleanor

Feeling sick with guilt that I had had no idea what my friend was going through, I immediately rang Eleanor and arranged to visit the following day. It was around a three- to three-and-a-half-hour drive to Norwich, and I said I would be there before lunch, which Eleanor said they would have at around one o'clock.
I ended the phone call with, "Let Will know I'm coming. Before noon."
"I will, Charles."
The next morning at 8:23, I was driving out of Rockwell Manor gates, my navigation system telling me I would arrive at 11:41 a.m. I would have plenty of time with Will before lunch. In fairness, I didn't know how I felt about this trip except that I didn't want to delay seeing him for another moment.
It also had me pondering some of the questions that had been playing over and over in my mind for many months. I just knew that losing the use of his legs didn't tell half the story. What Will had gone through in the past five months was a case in point. When they referred to "life-changing

injuries," were they even remotely aware of just how much of an understatement that was?

According to my GPS, I arrived thirty-seven minutes ahead of time, a testament to my speeding. This time, I didn't give it a second thought.

I didn't need to knock as William Sr. opened the door, having heard me arrive. I walked into the warm and sunny conservatory and gave two quick kisses on Eleanor's cheeks, paving the way for my more protracted greeting with Will. I bent down and hugged my friend, feeling my throat closing as a lump formed and tears welled in my eyes. I simultaneously drew up a stool so I could be at the same level he was in his wheelchair. Almost immediately, his parents left the room so we could be alone.

Will had suffered pressure sores almost immediately after arriving at the rudimentary One ME Hospital. In the rush to get him back to England, infection of this serious injury was unnoticed. Within days, he'd contracted septicaemia, which he eventually overcame by being bedridden for a prolonged period. As a result, muscular atrophy had quickly depleted his statuesque body of around 60 percent of his muscle tissue. It was still in this state that I found my dear friend.

I was shocked at his condition, seeing firsthand how muscular atrophy had ravaged his once powerful, athletic legs. His belly distended into pot-like disfigurement, replacing the corrugations of what used to be "the best six-pack in the squadron," and his once broad, open shoulders were slumped into surrendered submission. As alarming as this was, it did not compare to where he showed the consequences of his injury the most. The wounded expression on his sullen face and the vacant look in his eyes told of the excruciating suffering of these past five months.

We chatted for a long time, so long that Eleanor moved what was meant to be an early lunch out to a late lunch.

Given that my parents felt I may have suffered PTSD, then Will certainly would have. By now I knew enough about post-traumatic stress disorder to know the best thing for Will to do was to speak about the circumstances, which are referred to as a PTSD event.

Eventually, we got onto speaking about what he had lost. This was, after all, the crux of the matter. Had Will *only* lost the use of his legs, it might have been tolerable. I knew he had lost so much more—his pride, his confidence, his self-esteem, and his stature in every sense of the word. Once his mind told him he was less, he was less.

We spoke about these losses, and he said they weren't his biggest loss.

Holding his hand, I pressed him. "What, Will? What is the biggest thing you've lost?"

"I've lost the chance of having children," was his terse reply.

"Doesn't it work?" I asked, alarmed.

"It works, not that I could be bothered," was his solemn reply.

I didn't want to push him further, but I needed to hear the rest and felt he needed to get it out. As I took his hands in mine, he continued speaking.

"If I am able to get a wife in my state, I could never offer her a family. I could never bring a son into this world and not be able to kick a ball with him. Or a daughter, and never swing her around or help her practise ballet dance steps."

The tears welled up in my eyes again. I had just heard Will, who had been thought of as the squadron catch, a man who "could get any girl," questioning, *Can I get any girl?* And was he going to miss out on one of the greatest gifts of all, having children?

I didn't care that his parents saw me holding his hands. I didn't care that we were two grown men sitting there with tears streaming down our faces.

When we had consoled ourselves, we went through and had our very late lunch. The conversation was light—just small talk, like the health of my parents, the weather.

"And you play polo, don't you? How is that going?" William Sr. questioned.

Anything outside of the pleasantries, I understood, not wanting Will to feel as if he was missing out on anything. How tired he must have been of these types of conversations with people trying to protect his feelings around all the things he couldn't do. *But what else could one do?*

It was after five o'clock and already dark outside when we got up from the dining-room table. Correction: William Sr., Eleanor, and I got up from the dining-room table. Will wheeled himself away, and all of us wished there was some way we could help him so he didn't have to do that.

"Thank you for the visit, Charlie." I didn't mind what he called me then. "You don't know what this means to me. You are still the best combat helicopter pilot I have ever known." But he stopped short of thanking me for saving his life.

"Great to see you, Will. I won't leave it so long till next time."

Whatever time I had saved driving from Rockwell Manor up to Norwich, I gave back with interest as I slowly went back home. No rush. No radio. Just my own solitude as I absorbed the six-odd hours I'd just spent with my old friend and CPG.

Unbeknownst to anyone, after having seen me, he had given himself a very specific amount of time to see if things would change or if he could find the will.

Very sadly, things didn't change during that time, neither could he find the will.

We lost William Granger on his own terms, exactly forty days after I had seen him in Norwich.

My conundrum of whether I had helped or harmed Will when I had saved our lives was answered in the most upsetting way imaginable.

I was aware that forty days had biblical relevance, so I went to the study and did a little research.

Matthew 4:1-11 portrays Jesus being tempted by the devil after fasting for forty days and forty nights.

Acts chapter 1 talks about there having been forty days between Jesus's resurrection and ascension to Heaven.

Lent (Ash Wednesday until Easter) is a forty-day period of reflection, repentance, and spiritual growth observed by Christians as a solemn reminder of human mortality and the need for reconciliation with God.

And I didn't even know he was religious.

The obvious emotional response, *if only we had known*, was almost certainly the most overused sentiment in circumstances like this.

His mother had reached out to me, hoping I could help her son. She knew he needed saving. Had our accident given him the most painfully slow death?

My melancholy turned to anger. Anger directed at myself for not having realised. Not having paid attention. Not being there when my friend needed me the most. I dwelt further on these thoughts before slowly bringing myself back to equilibrium.

I managed to get my hands on a single blade from an Apache helicopter tail rotor and had the connection point fixed onto a base. A four-foot-tall metallic tombstone. I placed it a short distance from where Osric was buried, under his brace of flushed pheasant.

I then said goodbye to my dearest friend, my golfing partner, my combat flying partner, my CPG. My loss was nothing compared to what his family had lost that day. More than they could ever possibly list. I shuddered.

I went up to my room and looked down from my north-wing bedroom window at these two unusual memorials now standing in our garden. This was the second very special person I had lost in my life, Granddad and now Will. And I had no Osric to comfort me. And as before, the tears rolled down my cheeks and I made no effort to dry them. But as before, I eventually did.

In Memoriam

Osric
Twelve years of childhood bliss.

William
A CPG like no other.

My mother's words echoed in my head, *"Chin up, Sunbeam. Chin up."*

I later learnt more about the place Will had found himself in. Those men and women who "put themselves out there" and suffered a spinal cord injury are sometimes referred to as the "hero to zero" spinal cord injury group.

Will was the first of my friends to become a victim of a Hero to Zero spinal cord injury. Once all powerful, more than just capable, at the top of his game, until in the blink of an eye, he found himself fighting death… and winning, only to be rewarded with a life sentence of dependency on others, in a prison of immobility.

Veteran or other, statistically there is a high probability that a person in this group is an alpha male with around a 90/10 male to female split, I am told. An obvious reason for this is that alpha males show a propensity for joining the military, playing physical sports, or generally engaging themselves in more risky behaviour compared to their female counterparts. You may know, or at least understand, that the highest incidence of suicides is in this group.

To all those veterans and others who have suffered a hero to zero spinal cord or neurological injury resulting in them becoming imprisoned by their immobility and risen above it, I salute you.

For those who are understandably still under the debilitating psychological oppression of it, find something you can succeed in, no matter how small, and build on it.

My grandfather was right. Success, no matter how small, is the foundation for more success.

CHAPTER 30
A NEW LIFE

I NEVER FULLY UNDERSTOOD what Yuppie Flu was, but if I needed a catalyst to free me from the restraints of chronic fatigue syndrome, then what happened to Will was it.

After having visited him in Norwich, and perhaps because of the guilt I felt for having been so lucky, I went through a period of mourning, then soul-searching and introspection. As a result, my situation began to improve. But it was his death and then pallbearing at his funeral opposite his father as we led the way that ratcheted up my determination.

How dare I be so lethargic, I berated myself.

After several days of trying to come to terms with what had happened to my dear friend, my approach to life changed dramatically.

I had everything, and I wasn't speaking about Rockwell Manor and its trappings. I was speaking about my health, my vitality, and a myriad of other things that should have fuelled my enthusiasm for life in no uncertain manner. *How dare I waste that?* was my brutally honest condemnation of myself.

And then, as if it were unusual, winter was drawing to a close. A sure telltale sign were the polo horses having come in to begin their preparation for the season that lay ahead. I loved the muffled sound of their hooves on the silica sand track. The slower tempo signalled a gentle introduction to their training program.

It was Monday morning, the first days of spring, clear and crisp, and with my mind in overdrive, I sprang out of bed. *I remember that feeling.* And it was good.

As I arrived at the breakfast table, my seat between my parents having mostly been vacant these past six months, I blurted, "Right, Dad, time to get my head around my future. What are your thoughts?"

My parents had already seen that I had been moving in the right direction as far as getting on with my new life was concerned, but neither of them commented on this obvious new clarity and determination. Perhaps they feared jinxing it.

My father had plenty of suggestions. "Give Hugh Mackintosh a call," he said without hesitation.

Hugh was an old school friend of mine who had ended up studying economics and business science at university, not unlike my majors.

"And let me set up for you to meet one of the partners at Deloitte's, our auditors, to see what business-acquisition possibilities are out there. There are often good businesses that are just short of working capital that we could potentially buy," he continued.

As I shifted my thoughts to the future, for the first time in months I felt a twinge of excitement welling up inside me. Apart from business, playing polo and shooting, there were other things that excited me. Developing Rockwell Manor Polo Team was one. Would I get another dog? Yes, there was a lot to be excited about. And what about building a heliport at Rockwell Manor and, in time, buying my own helicopter?

Whilst I had been mulling over the prospect of going into business, I knew my approach would be different. This was something I wanted to do myself, not an endeavour that would be thanks to my family.

I did not have much time to think about it as my dad then caught me off guard when he announced to his audience of two, "It's time for you to take over Rockwell Manor Polo Team, son." His tone made it clear it was not up for debate. "I have spoken to Guy, and he is ready to discuss any management ideas you may have."

There was no surprise in this decision. I had just not expected it quite so soon. I finished my breakfast in high spirits, my parents noticeably more relaxed than I'd seen for a while.

"Excuse me, Mum, Dad, I think I will go for a stick and ball."

Smiles lit up their faces.

As I walked across to the stables, I smiled to myself. Yes, they were feeling better about me. Ordinarily, telling them I was going to ride a horse would not have earned a smile.

It was the perfect day to start the new chapter of my polo career. Guy was not around, which suited me fine, and I had one of the grooms prepare a horse for me for my quiet stick and ball session.

I was particularly enjoying cantering around our beautifully manicured polo field that morning, watching how my polo ball left long, straight lines on the dewy emerald-green surface. I was so absorbed in what I was doing that I only noticed Guy when he cantered up alongside me a short while later.

"Good morning, Patrón," he said, chuckling, knowing full well that I disliked that title.

"Piss off, Watkins," I replied with an element of seriousness.

"No, seriously, it is wonderful that your dad has handed over the reins to you. It's the right time," Guy said with sincerity. "What are your thoughts for *your* team now?" he said as we began a gentle canter up and down the field, passing the ball between each other.

"Well, we can't be too far off from being able to field a Queen's Cup team," I replied, knowing the Rockwell Manor horses and players had become a very competitive unit.

"Yes, I quite like that plan," Guy responded a little unconvincingly.

"You have a different idea?" I challenged.

"I like the thought of the Argentine Gold Cup. It's at the same level as the Queen's Cup and our own Cowdray Gold Cup, but a far more difficult competition for an English team to win. It would present a whole new dimension to a world we are so familiar with."

I kept a deadpan face as the thought caused an excitement in my belly that threatened to tangle my intestines. Guy had made a suggestion I hadn't previously considered, but no sooner had the words left his lips than they resonated with me.

I could not help remembering a recent comical incident though and decided to tease him, thereby disguising my enthusiasm. As nonchalantly as possible, I asked, "Guy, is this all because of that lost-in-translation incident with those visiting Argentinian polo groupies?" My smiling eyes betrayed my efforts to keep a straight face.

My Rude Awakening

Guy's spontaneous laughter meant he knew exactly what I was speaking about.

We had just finished playing a match at Guards Polo Club when three attractive, slender, brown-eyed, olive-skinned, Argentinian girls came over to us. Two of them looked to be in their early twenties and seemingly quite shy, while the third was a lot more confident and probably a few years older. Finding courage in their numbers, backing each other up, they'd attempted to strike up a conversation.

"¿Quieres un beso de victoria?" said the eldest and naughtiest of the trio, biting her bottom lip.

Guy and I looked at each other blankly as the cute, younger ones giggled mischievously. "*No entiendo española*," Guy volunteered, shrugging his shoulders.

All three of them now giggling happily, it was the eldest one who attempted to say something in English. "Vee vant ta geev you kees… youra, how you say, beso de victoria," blurted the one who had seemed the quietest. She clearly had the most urgent intent.

The romance was certainly lost in translation, especially when I still had to spell it out to Guy that what they wanted was to give us a victory kiss.

Playing in the Argentine Gold Cup would need serious planning. No time for any romantic or other thoughts.

Over the next months, I began reviewing and sifting through different business opportunities as Guy and I secretly worked towards taking Rockwell Manor Polo to the next level, which primarily involved replacing the bottom end of our string with horses that would come in at the very top. At £40,000 to £80,000 a horse (some people even paid over £100,000 for true champions) they were not cheap. We had a few of those. I had to remind myself I should be grateful that I didn't have to worry too much about the budget. Even as a twenty-six-year-old, whilst I understood economics, I had very little direct awareness of the cost or value of things. This may seem surprising. Consider for a moment that up until the age of eighteen, I was just a scholar. Then I went to the Air Force. No chance of learning about the value of things there, when you routinely jump into a £50 million helicopter. And that was just the beginning. The cost per hour to operate this rotorcraft—over £4,000. Then throw in a few missiles—a Brimstone fire-and-forget—£160,000. A Stinger Missile—£30,000, and that's each, of course. I have used present-day cost estimates, because back then this was the furthest thing from our minds. Had they told us, assuming they knew themselves, it would have drawn nothing but blank looks. It just wasn't relevant.

I soon had a busy schedule researching different business opportunities and advancing my polo aspirations, yet I still couldn't put Charlotte behind me. Was that about to change?

Guy and I had been having a polo meeting and had just finished having lunch on the downstairs patio with my dad when Hamilton arrived, portable phone in hand. Turning to me, he disdainfully looked down his nose and announced, "Miss Sandra Rawling on the line for you, *sir*."

I couldn't help noticing the wry tone of his voice. Was he trying to remind me how I should behave? I had a sense that Miss Rawling's reputation was not lost on our butler.

As if subconsciously giving myself space for some privacy, and more than just a quick conversation, I took the handset from Hamilton and made my way through to the north wing and my bedroom.

As I lay down on my bed, taking the phone off mute, I greeted my caller. "Hello, Sandra."

"Hello, Charles," Sandra's sultry voice sounded down the phone line.

"To what do I owe this pleasure?" I asked, in a flirtatious tone.

"Ooh, well, that depends on what *pleasure* tickles your fancy," she said provocatively.

I smiled, knowing the game was on, and I was feeling more than willing to play along.

"Sandra, you called me, don't forget." I teasingly reminded her.

Her little giggle was a sure sign she was enjoying herself.

"Well, before we get into what pleasures you, I was just wondering if you were ready to come out of your shell and play a bit?" she said with more than just a little suggestive mischievousness.

"What do you have in mind?" I asked as coolly as I could, doing my best to hide my sudden excitement.

"Well, *to start with,* there's a dinner dance at Royal Berks on Saturday night, and I have two tickets," she said, referring to the Royal Berkshire Polo Club.

I smiled again. This had been well planned. "Oh, okay," I said without even giving it much thought.

"I could come to you early evening, and since I know what a gentleman you are, we could then go together from there."

I smiled again and said nothing, even though I liked her plan. Definitely no spontaneity here.

No longer smiling, my heart skipping a beat I replied with a simple, "See you Saturday evening, Sandy." I was not sure where the more affectionate "Sandy" had come from, nor why I had butterflies in my stomach.

I couldn't help contemplating what Saturday night would bring. The last time I had been out with a girl, Charlotte, had clearly been a lot longer than I realised.

I knew I had to move on. Would Sandra be the one to put me on that road? Was this the first step in moving on with this part of my new life too?

INTERLUDE

I NEVER SAW ANY of the Blackwoods again. Under normal circumstances that would not have been altogether unusual. Many, if not most servicemen try and put their military careers behind them once they go back into civilian life, especially if they have been beset by traumatic events. Added to that, as much as I liked Jamie, him being with his sister's ex-boyfriend would be awkward for everyone.

There is nothing unique in that I, like everyone else, am the product of my background, upbringing, and experiences. There is also nothing unique in that it was the first quarter century of my life that moulded me the most. Some of what shaped me remains a mystery, even though I have delved so deeply into my past. What is unique for all of us though, is that background, upbringing, and our experiences. I realise mine were more privileged than most, which included more opportunities for a wider range of experiences. I now appreciate those differences and have done my best in my life to make the most of it. I am also acutely aware that what happened to Will and the circumstances of his death, are what helped me recognise other aspects of my good fortune.

The sequel will shed light on the man I became as a result of my first quarter century. And was it a blessing or a curse that my life continued to be filled with many triumphs and tragedies? You can be the judge.

TO BE CONTINUED…

ABOUT THE AUTHOR

Edward Charles Featherstone is a pseudonym for a hugely successful international entrepreneur. Having grown up amongst immense privilege in the bucolic English countryside, he went on to enjoy an unrivalled education, both academically and socially. The lessons he learnt from these teachers would guide him throughout the rest of his life as he triumphed on the polo field, as a combat helicopter pilot, and in business, with interesting romantic liaisons along the way. He lives between London and Berkshire, still enjoys polo, and is occasionally a guest in the Royal Box at Guards Polo Club. Most of all he loves being in the English countryside shooting clay pigeons, but also game birds in the shooting season. There is a difference now though. He gets immense pleasure enjoying these traditional English pastimes with his young son, who is already one of the leading young Colt clay-pigeon marksmen in the United Kingdom.

Visit the website:
www.anenglishmansjourney.com

Connect on social media:
Instagram – @ecfeatherstone_author
Facebook – ecfeatherstone
X – @ECFeatherstone
YouTube – @ecfeatherstone